THE I CHING ON BUSINESS
AND DECISION-MAKING

RIDER

THE *I CHING* ON BUSINESS AND DECISION MAKING

A Corporate, Economic and Political Policy-Making Manual

Guy Damian-Knight

RIDER
London Melbourne Auckland Johannesburg

For
Thomas Edward Knight
and the noble hearted

Copyright © Guy Damian-Knight

All rights reserved

First published in 1986 by Rider & Co. Ltd,
an imprint of Century Hutchinson Ltd, Brookmount House,
62–65 Chandos Place,
Covent Garden, London WC2N 4NW

Century Hutchinson Publishing Group (Australia) Pty Ltd
16–22 Church Street, Hawthorn, Melbourne, Victoria 3122

Century Hutchinson Group (NZ) Ltd
32–34 View Road, PO Box 40–086, Glenfield, Auckland 10

Century Hutchinson Group (SA) Pty Ltd
PO Box 337, Bergvlei 2012, South Africa

Phototypeset by Wyvern Typesetting Ltd, Bristol

Printed and bound in Great Britain by
Anchor Brendon Ltd, Tiptree, Essex

British Library Cataloguing in Publication Data
Damian-Knight, Guy
The I Ching on business and decision-
making: successful management strategy
based on the ancient oracle of China.
1. I Ching   2. Problem solving
I. Title
133.3'3   BF441
ISBN 0–7126–1263–7

Contents

Acknowledgements

I would especially like to thank Ludwig, David Perkins, Oliver Caldecott, Deb, David and Richard Torrington for all their kindness and support during the preparation of this book.

Moreover I must express my deep indebtedness to the great sages Lao Tzu and Confucius.

The whole is greater than the sum of its parts

Truth does not depart from human nature. If what is
regarded as truth departs from human nature, it may not be
regarded as truth.

Confucius

Do not find fault and disorder outside, find it within.
To bring peace to the world first bring peace to yourself.
From this peace will come universal prosperity.

Author's note

It is the fundamental assumption of *The I Ching on Business and Decision Making* that the business man and business woman seek good fortune. Everything in this work is arrived at describing the means to achieve and define good fortune for practice in commercial life. The book is organized therefore as a working tool.

I don't think it would be going too far to say that this reinterpretation of the *I Ching* represents a new concept in business and decision making. It is something of a paradox that this 'new' concept has been around for thousands of years. As one of the first works of philosophy to be written, the *I Ching* represents the beginnings of civilized understanding. Its fascinating construction is not a blind artifice of Chinese thought, but a precise formulation from which many secrets of nature have yet to be unearthed. What remains truly astonishing is that the structure and the ideas which comprise what we today understand as *The Book of Changes* are still in many respects far ahead of the systems in use today.

It will be patently obvious to users of this book that, so far as political and economic thought is concerned, we are only at the beginnings of understanding how to construct a world economy which is tuned to provide for more than the most fundamental needs of people – without harming the eco-system and without bloodshed.

Guy Damian-Knight, 1986

Preface

The principal aim of this interpretive work is to unfold a Tao of economics; it has always seemed to me appropriate to establish and re-establish a truer alignment of political and economic forces with natural processes and, through the ancient Chinese *I Ching*, such an endeavour is possible. On the basis of an understanding of natural dynamics *and their relationships to each other*, it is possible to divine a way to restructure economic and political policies so that they work together harmoniously. It is the revelation of the possible integration of structural ideas in the political and economic sphere which itself provides the possibility of developing a more solid and dependable science of organization.

But, beyond that, I want *The* I Ching *on Business and Decision Making* to be, above all, useful and applicable in the daily business of decision making, to be used in the commercial world as a means of gaining an objective additional opinion on the considerations of any individual case.

The basic structure of the book is designed as an oracle to be consulted. You may find some value in reading it through from cover to cover; this gives an immediate view of all the key ideas which fit together in a certain ordered way. The depths of meaning of each of the sixty-four hexagrams (see below) cannot, however, be derived completely via a straightforward reading. Your specific mental perspective is a vital part of the interpretation of each hexagram at each consultation. But before I go on to explore the method of consulting this book, I will describe its structure.

The *I Ching* is organized into sixty-four sections, called 'hexagrams' – sixty-four codings. Each hexagram has six 'lines' which I also call 'changes' or 'future-links'. These lines describe six variations of circumstance which are themselves derived from the main dynamic described in the hexagram. I have tried to clarify these dynamics by breaking down each hexagram into sections so that the elements may more easily be identified. Traditionally, the *I Ching* is divided into:

1. Judgement

2.   Explanation of the Judgement
3.   The Image
4.   Explanation of the Image
5.   The six Lines.

Each hexagram describes a specific natural dynamic. The lines add a more detailed focus and also provide a future-link or change from the present into the future.

In the case of *The* I Ching *on Business and Decision Making*, however, it has been necessary to develop the basic structure of the hexagrams in order to enhance clarity and poignancy. I have therefore adopted the following interpretive model for each hexagram, with slight variations when necessary:

1.   *Judgement*
This gives a brief view of the import of the hexagram and whether or not the position is favourable, and why. The expressions 'misfortune', 'success', 'good fortune', 'great good fortune' and 'supreme good fortune' indicate the level or special quality of auspiciousness.

2.   *Specific Modality*
This refers to what is generally required *in practice*: a summary of what you should do, or watch for, or especially consider, in each case. This helps to focus the mind on the scope or field of action.

3.   *Ambience*
This describes the climate, or tone, of the hexagram and assists understanding of the colour or feeling of the situation, for example: 'bright', 'tense', 'amiable', 'quiet', and so on.

There follows a short description under the heading '*Concept Model*'. There are key words in each concept model which will touch off associations and contribute towards the richness of the mental dialogue which takes place in each consultation.

The *Decision-Base Assumptions* follow. In this section a range of sub-headings provide commentaries which may form the basis of considerations upon which a decision can be made. Some or all of the following appear in each hexagram, where relevant: Management, Planning, Growth and Productivity, Feedback, Advertising, Marketing, Risks, Product Choice, Service, Start-up, Backing, Creative Judgement, Intuition, Investment and Finance, Contracts and Agreements, Timing, Creative Input, Communications, Adequacy of Resources, International Trade, Research and Development, Sources of Misfortune, Sources of Good Fortune.

Each of the Decision-Base Assumptions describes the position in the 'here and now'. How you understand the meanings given depends to some extent on the question you ask. It is for this reason that the range of interpretations is as comprehensive as possible.

——————— ASKING QUESTIONS ———————

In order to consult this book, you must have a question in mind. This is the immediate reference point, or overall concept, which makes sense of the specific answers given. The application of the interpretations provided is part of the dialogue which takes place between the reader and the book in each consultation. It is the dialogue itself which is important. This is the process by which a deeper understanding can be reached. You may be an entrepreneur who wishes to consult the book about a new venture. Such a question will involve investment, start-up, risk and then expand into other considerations which may involve international trade, management, marketing and planning, and so on. Some of the points raised in the hexagram will be important and others will not. What factors come into play are a matter for your creative judgement and general interpretation. The process of consultation will itself enhance these abilities. Continued use of this book develops general understanding and familiarity with the natural dynamics of change.

Each hexagram, therefore, may be regarded as a sort of blueprint of change. If, for example, your question concerns investment of time, energy and money (resources and management) in the development of a new computer system, and you receive, 'in reply', Hexagram 50: The Cauldron, the text will indicate that your ideas are very auspicious because they involve cultural matters which, when applied, may be generally beneficial. Beyond that you will also be able to evaluate your position in the light of many criteria. Your understanding will therefore be more complete.

The experience of using this book will develop refinements of understanding which are impossible to detail. But asking or framing questions (itself a clarifying process) is an exercise which you will have to practise and improve if the value of the book is to be enhanced. The less clear the question at the outset, the more nebulous the answer will appear. It is very difficult, however, to maintain a position of confusion when using the *I Ching*. In this sense, the *I Ching* is a tool which enhances mental clarity.

Further to that, clarity of understanding is the making of the right decisions at the right time. *The* I Ching *on Business and Decision Making* can help you to make the right decisions because it is based upon nature's dynamic of change. As for timing, this is largely a matter of intuition and use of the book. If you are at a critical stage of negotiations, for example, and you are not sure whether to withdraw or to go forward, consulting the *I Ching* can provide an objective second opinion.

The human mind is itself an ingenious and deceptive tool. It is often instructive to watch one's own self-deception; discovering that this is what you are doing is possibly the most valuable discovery you could make. The applications for this book can be as ingenious as you are – it is no more than a tool, another dimension on the present to be used or not according to your disposition. The final responsibility for action and decision is always your own.

It is my hope that this book will help you make the correct decision at the right time so that you can fulfil your potential, creative, commercial and spiritual, and embrace good fortune and, as far as possible, avoid making mistakes.

PROCEDURE TO FOLLOW IN CONSULTING THE *I CHING* ON BUSINESS AND ───────── DECISION MAKING ─────────

Drawing your hexagram

There are a variety of ways of creating a hexagram. The ancient, meditative system uses fifty yarrow stalks, and is the one preferred by traditionalists who recognize the *I Ching* as an intuitive tool. The relatively lengthy process employed in moving yarrow stalks from one hand to the other in the creation of each line is an aid to concentration and meditation.

The most widely used system involves throwing three coins six times. The values of the combinations of heads and tails are given in Figure 1. This is quicker but far less elegant. There are other ways of generating the individual lines which are even faster and perhaps more elegant; they also follow the procedure below for the coin system.

9	────0────	3 HEADS	= 9	
8	──── ────	2 HEADS	+ 1 TAIL	= 8
7	────────	2 TAILS	+ 1 HEAD	= 7
6	────X────	3 TAILS	= 6	

Figure 1

1. Take three coins (any three – preferably of the same denomination) and throw them on the table.
2. Using Figure 1, add up the values. In each case, they will always be 6, 7, 8 or 9. (Heads has a value of 3, tails a value of 2.)
3. Starting from the bottom, draw the line which corresponds with the total addition. For example: you throw 2 heads and 1 tail. Look up 7 in the table and draw ——————, i.e., a straight line. See figure 2.
4. Repeat this procedure another five times in succession, drawing one line on top of the other, starting from the bottom. Make certain that you draw the line exactly as it is shown on the table. For example: you next throw a six, ——X——. You draw it on top of the other line. Notice that it has a cross in the middle. This means that the line will 'change' into its opposite, i.e., the ——X—— will change into a ——————, and this new line will appear in and modify the new hexagram (the future).

   In the example (Figure 2), the next line thrown was a seven ——————, followed by another seven, ——————, followed by a nine, ——O——. Notice that the nine has a circle in the middle. This means that it will change from ——O—— to —— —— in the new hexagram. The last (top) line is another seven, ——————.

   If you have followed this procedure correctly, you will have drawn a hexagram which looks like this:

Hexagram 13

6th	——————	
5th	——O——	This line changes to this
4th	——————	
3rd	——————	
2nd	——X——	This line changes to this
1st	——————	

THE PRESENT

Figure 2

Hexagram 14

6th	——————
5th	—— ——
4th	——————
3rd	——————
2nd	——————
1st	——————

⟶ THE FUTURE

Figure 3

Figure 2 is a hexagram, a six-line picture of the present situation ('present' means at the time of throwing the coins and making the hexagram). Figure 3 is the second hexagram which has been derived by transferring the *moving* or *changing lines* to their new values. In this case, the second and fifth lines have changed and now appear in the second hexagram as their opposites. Notice, though, that the order of the lines has been preserved from the first to the sixth, and that lines 1, 3, 4 and 6 are unchanged. If there are no moving lines there is only one hexagram to study.

At the back of this book, a chart gives the names and numbers of hexagrams. Look up the bottom three lines (in Figure 2,

```
————————
————  ———— ) in the left-hand column, and the top three lines (in
————————
```

```
          ————————
Figure 2, ———————————— ) in the top column. Now cross-reference
          ————————
```

the two columns to find the number of the hexagram. Figure 2 is Hexagram 13: Fellowship With Men. If you have drawn a second hexagram as here, repeat the procedure. Figure 3 is Hexagram 14: Possession in Great Measure/Wealth.

Look up your hexagram in the text and read the Judgement, Specific Modality, Ambience and the Concept Model. Then read through the list of comments given under the head, Decision-Base Assumptions. It may be that your question was so specific that only one head in this section satisfies your present need – Management, for example. Read the parts most relevant and helpful to you. One particular word might leap out at you, and that might be all you need. It all depends on your state of mind.

When you read the hexagram, you will be reading it through the mental frame of your question, a curious mental process which takes place all the time. Your question is your 'present reality' and the answer will conform to the terms of reference you have constructed. It all depends on your state of mind. Two people could receive the same 'answer' to two different questions, but it would mean different things to each of them. Even if their questions were the same, the significance of the answer would differ according to state of mind and circumstances.

The important thing is that you are placed in a position to examine an objective reflection, cast in certain business terms, of your own state of mind. What you read may even disagree with your state of mind as you understand it. *The Book of Changes* is no sycophant.

———————————— *The Moving Lines* ————————————

Having read your hexagram, next read the lines. In the example just given, Hexagram 13 had two Moving Lines or Changes. These are the specific situations of the moment which link with your *future* situation. In the example, the first moving line is the second, written in the book as 'Six in the Second Place'. Line five is also moving, written in the book as 'Nine in the Fifth Place'.

The *I Ching* represents bridges (moving lines) to a future situation, characterized by the next hexagram. In the example, the second hexagram was Hexagram 14: Possession in Great Measure. Digest the meaning of the first hexagram, then read the second. Make a note of the changes. With practice you can become adept at the process.

It is possible that you will have no moving Lines, or all the lines may be moving (a very dynamic state of affairs), or any number from one to six, but, as long as you follow the procedure, you will always draw the hexagram correctly. To summarize: always draw the hexagrams as shown in the example, from the bottom upwards. Always transpose the lines into their opposites, making a second hexagram, if the values on the coins add up to six or nine. Always read the moving lines in the first of the hexagrams; these will be the bridge to the second meaning. Do not read the lines in the second hexagram as they are not relevant at this time. In this way you can gain access to the *I Ching*, and so receive a 'newsflash' on the present at any time.

Introduction

In ancient China the *I Ching* (or *Book of Changes*) was the book of kings and statesmen. Now anybody who can read and count to ten can gain access to a system of guidance which has existed in the world for well over 3000 years. The form of the book remains essentially the same, but its style of presentation has varied. The present volume is one such modern rendering.

The basic structure of the *I Ching* has been preserved, but its application to the demands of the modern world necessitates an update. *The* I Ching *on Business and Decision Making* refines the *Book of Changes* in so far as it focuses upon a wide range of salient and important considerations which will be of particular interest to people engaged in commercial practice. Of course, the present work can be generally useful in the management of any life situation as the basic dynamics of the hexagrams do not change. They embody the principle dynamics of nature, the basis of life.

The value of reinterpretation is simply to ease understanding and make available the transposition of fundamental concepts into modern parlance – key words, key concepts. It involves the recognition of natural dynamics as they might be viewed in the context of commercial values.

─────────── MORE INTERRELATIONSHIPS ───────────

The I Ching *on Business and Decision Making* can highlight factors which may not have been foreseen. There may be (there usually are) elements of a situation which lie outside the individual's perceptual range. He may not have all the facts at his hand; unseen elements may make the position insecure. But because everything is symbiotically connected – every cause has an effect, whether perceived or not – there is a connection between present thoughts, present business, present considerations and present decisions and actions.

The natural idea of interconnection, though often invisible, is tangible and real. We are each transmitting and receiving waves all the time. They are manifested in what we say, do, think, feel, communicate, plan, want, touch. If, then, by acting according to a wider natural scheme, you act in tune with that wider scheme, will this not bring good fortune? It is my belief that there is a natural order and that it can be expressed through economic and political policies – right up to the behaviour of a global cash-flow situation. The problem is, how can the businessman keep in tune with the wider natural scheme, avoid misfortune and realize good fortune? How can he account for factors which he is unable to see (beyond his situation) but which affect him just the same? Is it possible to articulate that process and make use of it, assuming that such a macro-dynamic of nature knows what *it* is doing? This is essentially what the *I Ching* was designed to do.

When you consult the *I Ching* you are receiving a kind of abstract photograph of your relative position in the cosmos of events. You can see in that instant (or will see with practice) the resonances and events which are affecting you and your situation. In this sense, the *I Ching* functions in two ways: 1. as a catalyst, and 2. as an amplifier. Through the consultation, you receive a message which is amplified, relevant to your situation (you caused the reflection to occur by looking into the 'mirror') and brought into the scope of consciousness. You are made aware of something which is germane to your situation, even though it may be, for example, happening in the street outside or in the boardroom of a company on the other side of the world. Making these relational links is a matter both of logic and intuition. But now, because you have been addressed by more data, you know more and your decision is going to be that much better.

The lines are the future links. There are six situations in each hexagram which represent smaller dynamics within the larger dynamic described by the Concept Frame. Like the Concept Frame, the lines represent blueprints of specific matters associated with your question. Those associations become increasingly conscious with practice. The process of using the *I Ching* enhances the power of intuition and gradually fine-tunes the nervous system to pick up resonances. With this book in his hands, a stockbroker with a finely tuned nervous system can come to astounding conclusions which may seem at first to have no rational explanation but which nevertheless represent a true insight: 'The price of gold is going to go up next week rather unexpectedly'; 'This company, contrary to all reports and expectations is going to fail.'

The patterns and interrelations of events have an order, a cause and effect. There is no mystery, merely a pragmatic assumption that if you have a dynamic map of those 'capabilities' and the patience to develop your intuitive powers it is possible to make the right decision more often. If an individual can tune in with the natural order of events, his success is assured. If all systems interface with each other naturally, overall success would become reality. The index of failure on a global scale is the amount of starvation, war and poverty. These are not merely matters of sentiment, but are the by-products of incompetent systems based on the wrong assumptions, wrong world view, ignorance of the truth, ignorance of the relationships between things.

The predictive system works in the same way as that which makes weather forecasts possible. You can see which way the wind is blowing if you can get a bigger picture. Magic is only magic when you can't see the bigger picture. There was a time when, for man, even the wind itself was magic!

THE
HEXAGRAMS

HEXAGRAM 1

The Creative

The future is seeded in the actions of today.

JUDGEMENT

Great good fortune. The beginnings. The world of ideas. The creative impetus underlies all form, action, perception. The position is highly auspicious and will lead to a gradual flowering. Inspiration and the force of the new.

SPECIFIC MODALITY

Impulse to action, energy regeneration, untiring perseverance. The drive towards the perfection of ideas. The power to work comes from a primal source. The energy is great and powerful. Although effort is required, achievements are made easy by this placement. Auspicious.

AMBIENCE

Ideals, formulating plans, aspiration, upward striving, beginnings of growth, originality, creative energy. Organization of concepts. Patterns.

CONCEPT MODEL

All action begins with the formation of ideas. Action is an idea made manifest. The creative principle is the originator of ideas. Through the Creative, everything becomes possible. Receiving this hexagram points to a time of great creative activity. Much can be achieved with relative ease.

DECISION-BASE ASSUMPTIONS
the Future-Links

The following values are given subject to the information given in the Changes. Remember, the Changes take precedence.

Management
You have the creative energy of the leader and organizer of people and resources. Take the initiative in the work of making what is potential, actual, and, provided you are consistent, eventual success is assured, despite difficulties.

Planning
You may proceed with optimism. All the decision-base assumptions contain no ambiguity and are completely positive. Act with confidence.

Communications
There is no judgement as to whether this is a good time to communicate your ideas to other people. You must therefore judge for yourself or consult this book again with that specific question in mind. With regard to the expression of ideas in general, the time is highly propitious.

Growth and Productivity
An excellent time, excellent prospects.

Risks
There is no such thing as risk in the Tao, but if you conceive of your situation as a risk, you can rely on your judgement.

Investment and Finance
Excellent prospects.

Timing
This is the time for action.

Adequacy of Resources
Abundant.

Start-Up
The prospects are especially auspicious.

Feedback
Completely positive. Be supportive.

Information Availability
You have all the necessary information, or it is easily available to you.

Product Choice
Your judgement is sound.

Creative Judgement
High and fertile.

Intuition
Sound.

Advertising
Auspicious.

Marketing
Exploit potential to the full.

Backing
Auspicious.

Contracts and Agreements
Satisfactory.

Research and Development
The project will bear fruit when it is developed. Auspicious. This is certainly a time of invention and discovery. Good fortune.

International Trade
Auspicious in the long term.

Sources of Misfortune
Inaction.

Sources of Good Fortune
Immediate creative action.

—————— THE LINES (CHANGES) ——————

Nine at the beginning
This is not the time to act. This is the time to store energy in preparation for future action. You have to be self-contained and learn to be patient. This does not mean compromise. There is no need to fear that you are missing out or forestalling a golden opportunity. If you were to act now your strength would not last. Therefore your wisdom lies in knowing when the right time to act has come. While you are waiting, cultivate yourself, review your situation, go over all your plans, spend time in contemplation, centre yourself. The businessman who does not learn to store energy cannot give his actions any potency when the time comes.

Nine in the second place
You are equal to the task which lies before you. Do not be distracted by vain glory. Your motives are improper if you act solely with a view to winning the approval of others, gaining personal recognition or obtaining personal wealth. This line signifies that success can be attained through cultivating a wide vision.

But your time has come to enter the field of action. In addition to your talents there are two qualities which recommend you to the person with whom you will work: your dedication and reliability. The time is right to join with the head of an enterprise (he may be your new employer) who recognizes in you great potential. Mutual respect is in evidence. The project will be successful.

Nine in the third place
The project begins to gain ground. Unlooked-for influence becomes manifest. People beyond your field of activity recognize and approve of your work. This means greater influence, greater success and, most important of all, the opportunity to expand your field of action. This you may do with great confidence as the momentum of your past work has enabled you to develop the strength to meet the demands of the increased challenge.

It will not serve your interests in the long run to worry and fret. It is important to balance your day with relaxation. The secret of this line, in the light of the above good fortune, is in the art of self-renewal. This idea extends deeper than mere physical relaxation or the replenishment of physical energy and encompasses a daily renewal of perspective. This is the secret of perseverance. A warning is added: do not allow yourself to be carried away or obsessed with the *idea* of great plans and schemes. Though the ideas may in themselves be great and hold great promise, your personal attitude is all the more critical. In times of great transition an incorrect attitude to good fortune can ruin your integrity. If you are going to make a mistake, it will be now. The mistake is conceit – no room for it here.

Nine in the fourth place
A measure of independence of choice is now yours. You can choose how you will develop yourself and in what mode of activity you will express your energy. This choice is depicted as follows: 1. you can throw yourself into working with other people and become involved in the hurly-burly of daily business life, or 2. you can work alone and develop your creativity. The choice is yours and you must decide now. Whatever decision you make will be the correct one providing you follow your heart.

Nine in the fifth place
You have attained 'greatness'. This means visibility. You can be seen through your work by people the world over. The word 'greatness' is not understood in terms of the shallow ideal of simple fame. There is a spiritual quality implied. You are able to resonate with the highest ideals to which mankind as a whole strives. Therefore those who identify with those ideals recognize your part in the great work and you in your turn recognize their part. This means supreme good fortune which lasts.

Nine in the last place
This is the line of the person who has had the opportunity to achieve great things but now falls into the temptation of becoming an arrogant bigot. The misfortune of this predicament is that you become separated in your mind from your view of yourself as an individual and your view of yourself as a

creative participant in great work. No greatness can come out of an attitude of this kind which, if persisted in, will lead to a decline in influence, a fall from grace. But it is, at this stage, only a warning. There is time to review your position and to change it radically.

When all the lines align (change at the same time)
When all the lines align and are changing at the same time, the condition described by Hexagram 2, The Receptive, comes into balance. When creative power is perfectly balanced with the gentle disposition of one who is able to cultivate his energy, there will be great good fortune. The power of decision and the power of action are united in harmony. The result is clarity of vision, energy economically used to great effect. Cooperation from others is a concomitant of this state of affairs. Power therefore expresses itself gracefully and no mistakes are made. (See Hexagrams 14: Possession in Great Measure and 22: Grace.)

HEXAGRAM 2

THE RECEPTIVE (CARE)

'Through selfless action, he attains self-fulfilment.'
Lao Tsu, *Tao Te Ching*

JUDGEMENT

Supreme good fortune. Ideas take form. The blueprint is turned into a tangible, physical product. The Receptive follows the Creative. Openness. The manifestation of nature. The coding unfolds. Manifestation.

SPECIFIC MODALITY

To implement plans and apply concepts. Following the creative impetus. Making things grow.

AMBIENCE

To be receptive to ideas, to listen, to care and to nurture. Mildness.

CONCEPT MODEL

Since the essence of the Receptive is fertility, you draw upon your natural, intuitive understanding of how things grow, of the relationship between the concept and its manifestation. You have the propensity to give quality and beauty to form. How something appears is also your responsibility.

In the light of the foregoing, it will be clear that all your energies are devoted to the fulfilment of the original idea, not to challenging it. You enter the sphere of action only after the idea has been agreed.

DECISION-BASE ASSUMPTIONS

The following values are given subject to the information given in the Changes. Remember, the Changes take precedence.

Planning
Long term only. Take the wider view. Auspicious.

Communications
Promote integration of resources. Mostly internal. A highly propitious time to make contact with people who will help develop ideas.

Growth and Productivity
If the original idea is sound, you can make it grow.

Risks
You will not be concerned with risk taking.

Investment and Finance
Use only what is necessary in the realization of clearly defined goals. Excellent prospects.

Adequacy of Resources
Abundant.

Start-Up
The prospects are excellent so long as you are not the prime mover. Work with innovators and follow their lead. Auspicious.

Feedback
Completely positive. Be supportive and receptive to direction.

Information Availability
You have all the necessary information or it is easily available to you.

Product Choice
Your judgement is sound. But take a second opinion from outside.

Creative Judgement
Excellent. Make full use of ideas. The results will be noteworthy. Auspicious.

Advertising
Premature to consider at this time, unless at the planning stage. The possibilities are positive. Auspicious.

Backing
The support is available. Your support is also appreciated, even vital to the project.

Contracts and Agreements
Fair. The requirements are fulfilled. Think it through alone.

Research and Development
Concentrate efforts. Highly auspicious.

Marketing
Consideration of market appropriate. Marketing premature. Auspicious. Best to respond to the initiative of others.

International Trade
Auspicious. Best to respond to the initiative of others.

Getting the Best out of People
Listen to their ideas. Warm cooperation.

Sources of Misfortune
Aggressive attitudes. Seizing the initiative. Questioning the original concepts.

Sources of Good Fortune
Following the lead. Helping to integrate resources.

—————————— **THE LINES (CHANGES)** ——————————
the Future-Links

Six at the beginning
All businesses go through periods of prosperity and decline. These seasonal variations are inevitable. In the coming months, the business will experience a decline. Take appropriate measures. Conserve resources; confine expenditure to keeping the business running, but make no attempt to expand. Although you may not be able to see the signs at this moment, they will soon become noticeable. Use past good fortune as a foundation for taking advantage of the period of growth which will follow the decline.

Now is the time to weed out any bad practices within the company as the conditions are right for corrupting elements to flourish. Nip them in the bud.

Six in the second place
This is the time to let achievements stand modestly upon their own merits. Thus do not waste money on advertising. If the product or service provided is excellent, it will be recognized as such and good fortune will result.

Six in the third place
Good fortune will result if you do not claim the special attentions of others. If your work has been sound and of good quality it will be recognized.

As you are still developing your abilities, you should stay out of the limelight until you are ready for it.

Six in the fourth place
Danger. Keep your achievements to yourself, as there are people near you who are disposed to be envious and antagonistic. You should not challenge them. If you invite any kind of public attention at this time, the work will be

seriously impeded, if not stopped, by people who have an interest in seeing it *not* completed.

Six in the fifth place
Your influence within the company arises from the excellence of your work and from a quiet, unassuming disposition. Because you do not flaunt yourself, you are all the more appreciated and are able to communicate subtleties. Supreme good fortune.

Six in the last place
Here the Receptive tries to overthrow the Creative. But because the Creative and the Receptive are primal powers, and therefore of comparable strength, such an attempt throws the relationship into chaos. Therefore both primal powers are injured.

Many companies collapse due to this state of affairs. It has nothing to do with a misjudgement of the market, for example, but has come about because of a serious internal conflict in management.

When all the lines align (change at the same time)
This is a state of dynamic equilibrium. The company has not expanded or contracted, but functions within clearly defined boundaries. It stays buoyant and holds its position in the market-place by vigorously treading water. (See Hexagram 12: Stagnation.)

HEXAGRAM 3

Difficult Beginnings

JUDGEMENT

Supreme success. Sustain or enhance self-confidence. Work to a routine. Be consistent. The position is undeveloped, but the evolutionary prospects are auspicious. You need the cooperation of others.

SPECIFIC MODALITY

Getting a grip on the situation. Finding one's feet. Generate working terms of reference and stick within them until confidence comes. Perseverance is the secret of success. You can make progress. Do not try to go it alone.

AMBIENCE

A flurry of activity. Some confusion and uncertainty. This can be turned to advantage if you work at ordering affairs. Organize yourself. Effort is required over a three-month period. Everything is acquiring a definite form.

CONCEPT MODEL

The beginning of a project requires greater organizational clarity than at the later stage. The matter requires sustained energy and perseverance to ensure success. The aim is to achieve a stable unification of forces, often working (apparently) against each other.

The evolution of a company has its own momentum. The experience is intense at the beginning.

DECISION-BASE ASSUMPTIONS

The following values are given subject to the information given in the Changes. Remember, the Changes take precedence.

Management
You cannot work alone at this time. Share all decisions. Cooperate.
(See Hexagram 45: Gathering Together, for further consider-
ations.)

Planning
A plan is fast emerging. Do not decide finally upon any one scenario
at present. See what happens. Be prepared to be flexible and
adaptable. Key directions have not been fixed. Plans must be
considered to be short term for the time being.

Growth and Productivity
Premature. Wait and see how the plan evolves. Long- and middle-
term prospects may be excellent.

Investment and Finance
Details to be determined at a later date.

Time
This is the birth of a new enterprise.

Start-Up
Excellent. Persistent effort will show results.

Feedback
Positive.

Priority
To establish foundations solidly.

Product Choice
To be finally decided and determined at a later date.

Services
Scale and ambit of activity to be determined at a later date.

Creative Judgement
Improving. But consult with others. Be wary of making and acting
upon judgements arrived at on your own.

Advertising and Marketing
You do not know the potential reach or extent of the project. Make
no firm commitments on expenditure at present. Be cautious. Err on
the side of restraint.

Backing
Seek it. Auspicious.

Contracts and Agreements
No firm commitments should be entered into at this stage. The position is not sufficiently clear.

Expenditure
Only short-term expenditure is required. In all other considerations, hold back.

Input
Maximum and diverse in character and quality.

Output
In the initial stages keep commitments and communications to the absolute minimum.

Decisions
It needs to be emphasized that this is not the time to make any important planning or management decisions, though temporary decisions will have to be made to be ratified or discarded later.

Sources of Misfortune
Trying to go it alone. Over-reacting to opportunities. Jumping the gun.

Sources of Good Fortune
Let the stability come ·before any decisions are taken. All the key elements must find their place before they can function properly. Restraint is needed. This process cannot be artificially hurried.

───────────── THE LINES (CHANGES) ─────────────
the Future-Links

Nine at the beginning
Only if your business intentions are clearly defined before you enter into active organization of resources can you attract suitably qualified and experienced assistance. As this is a learning situation, preserve an open mind. It takes time to gauge the scale of commitments. This is what is meant by stability.

Six in the second place
The new enterprise is under incredible pressure and begins to fall apart. You are offered help by an experienced person coming from outside whose intentions you mistrust unjustifiably. You are tempted to accept the help that this person offers but, in *this* case, you must decline. In a few years you will be able to work together on a new project – but not this one. Thus even under extreme difficulty you must learn to refuse help.

Six in the third place
You are encountering challenging situations and opportunities for the very first time. You have no idea how to conduct or orchestrate the complexities and therefore you must actively seek a qualified marketing manager.

Six in the fourth place
You begin to realize the enormity and complexity of what you have taken on and, despite the fact that you are bringing all your energy and resources to bear, you are not making any real progress. You therefore need another shoulder to the wheel to help get things moving. This may not be a permanent appointment, but it is certainly a necessary one. With the right help it is still possible to make a success of the situation.

Nine in the fifth place
The general objects and aims of the enterprise have been established but there are disagreements in management as to the procedure to follow. Most of the arguments being put forward by the opposition are facile and absurd and implementing an important strategy or project is impossible without the confidence of the whole management team. Each member of the decision-making body should go away and work through the proposals individually to produce an analysis of each of the steps, giving full reasons. Then clear lines of agreement will become apparent and the strategy will emerge.

Six in the last place
Difficulties are piled upon difficulties. You have become swamped by them to the extent that you begin to feel there is no point in going on. You are utterly convinced that success cannot be achieved and so you may abandon the project in a state of despair. If you have the nerve to stay with it, the way to progress, however unusual, may present itself. On the other hand, it may be right that the enterprise stops here. This outcome was probably brought about by conditions over which you had no control. The failure of businesses is very often a judgement on the lack of supportiveness of business systems and government policies, rather than on the quality of personal effort. The decision is still yours. (See Hexagrams 16: Enthusiasm and 62: The Preponderance of the Small.)

HEXAGRAM 4

The Inexperience of the Young –
(The Student)

'It is not easy for a man to study for three years without thinking about earning a salary.'

The Analects of Confucius, Book Eight

------------------------------ JUDGEMENT ------------------------------

Providing you learn from your mistakes, success.

------------------------------ SPECIFIC MODALITY ------------------------------

Learning situation. This is a matter of accepting tuition, instruction, training. Apprenticeships, courses, updates, information gathering. The acquisition of experience. The testing of competence and the development of character.

------------------------------ AMBIENCE ------------------------------

Danger through not taking things seriously. The consequences of immaturity can be avoided through a reappraisal of attitude and a willingness to be receptive. (See Hexagram 2: The Receptive, for a more balanced image to which to aspire.)

------------------------------ CONCEPT MODEL ------------------------------
The Teacher/Student Relationship

Inexperience is usually associated with youth, but this is not always the case. More accurately, what is presented here is a new enterprise, and so it is the unfamiliarity of the work to which the word 'inexperience' refers. Therefore this hexagram deals with the predicament of the 'new boy'.

Being new to a situation implies the need for, and reliance upon, wise counsel, teachers and experienced advice. The idea of the wise teacher figures strongly in relation to the inexperienced person, but the teacher can take many forms 'He' is the voice of experience in a new situation, so he may be an old book of wisdom, an experienced friend, a manager, the person to whom your training has been entrusted, a business consultant, anyone to whom you may turn for advice.

It is the responsibility of the inexperienced businessman to find himself the right teacher to whom he can put his questions. The student should approach the teacher, and not the other way around, so that he will be receptive to advice and it will be valued.

Once the student has approached the teacher for counsel, it is only respectful that he should listen to the advice given and act upon his strictures. If the student persists in his questions in an immodest and unreceptive manner, the teacher will lose confidence in him and refuse to help any further. This is what is meant when we say that learning can only take place when the heart is humble.

It is the teacher's job clearly and patiently to provide the student or trainee with the material he needs to resolve a problem, or the information he requires in order to come to a decision.

—————— DECISION-BASE ASSUMPTIONS ——————

The following values are given subject to the information given in the Changes. Remember, the Changes take precedence.

Management
Focus on trainees' education. Review the training course. For the acquisition of skills, more than broad experience is required; formal rules must also be learned. If the rules are learned correctly, then experience can deepen understanding. In every learning situation there must be a combination of formal instruction (theory) and practical experience. There are no short cuts.

Trainee
Spend time in assimilating instruction and experience. Take it more seriously.

Planning
There is need for more foresight. This is a key problem. You should spend time examining the relationships, causes and effects between ideas. See Hexagram 20: Contemplation, for a broader exposition of the requirements here.

Communications
The potential is excellent for maximum communication.

Growth and Productivity
Clarity of understanding should be your aim. Practise consistently.
Auspicious, as much can be achieved.

Risks
Take no unwarranted chances. You will fall foul of them.

Investment and Finance
Invest in education and training materials. Give time.

Best Use of Time
Thinking, studying.

Adequacy of Resources
Insufficient quality.

Feedback
Positive feedback for both teacher and student is absolutely essential
in every learning situation. The absence of it destroys enthusiasm for
the work and erodes self-confidence.

Creative Judgement
Needs to be developed.

Advertising
Explore further before committing ideas or resources. Examine
options. Consult.

Marketing
You require more up-to-date and wider-ranging information.

Contracts and Agreements
Take qualified advice *before* entering into binding commitments.
The position is more complicated than you imagine.

International Trade
There may be problems of diplomacy. Clarify and agree some basic
working assumptions first.

Objectives
The efficient application of principles. Usefulness in practical
situations. Competence.

Getting the Best out of People
Show interest, even in difficult times. Be willing to talk.

Input
Increase your stock of ideas by discussion and reading. Investigate.

Output

The proof of the pudding is in the eating: the quality of your understanding will be put to the test.

Sources of Misfortune

Insincerity, laziness, lack of comprehension.

Sources of Good Fortune

Consistent hard work, self-discipline, receptivity to good advice.

─────────── THE LINES (CHANGES) ───────────
the Future-Links

Six at the beginning

Too much self-discipline creates a narrow mind. Too much discipline imposed from outside destroys initiative and breaks the spirit. No self-discipline makes any kind of achievement impossible. Some self-discipline reasonably reinforced by a teacher creates just the right atmosphere for learning. (See Hexagram 60: Limitation.)

Nine in the second place

The teacher must be tolerant and not inconsiderate if students find the work difficult. Here, the teacher is considerate, even when students may not appear to deserve it. (See also Hexagram 58: The Joyous, Lake for an exposition on generating the most auspicious learning environment.)

Six in the third place

The trainee should be objective about his relationship with the teacher and resist the temptation to be a sycophant or to curry favour. The teacher should not favour trainees whose work is not truly meritorious as the dignity of the relationship would break down. Credit should be given where credit is due, however, and the student should demand a fair appraisal of his work.

Six in the fourth place

The student is allowing his mind to wander aimlessly. The teacher, however, knows that the student will eventually come back to his senses, without being told to do so.

Six in the fifth place

The sincere student comes to his work with an open mind. Teachers find this attitude meritorious and are willing to help him. (See Hexagrams 19: Approach and 35: Progress.)

Nine in the last place

The sole aim of punishment is not to humiliate, but to bring unruly and disruptive behaviour under control. Punishment is only justifiable where reasonable and respectful warnings have had no effect and are unlikely to have any effect. In employment terms, this kind of behaviour usually invites demotion or dismissal.

HEXAGRAM 5

Patience

'In business, be competent. In action,
watch the timing.'

Lao Tsu, *Tao Te Ching*

JUDGEMENT

Good fortune. The situation is already set and the wheels are in
motion. Objectives may disappear from view. This creates anxiety.
Precipitate action should be avoided at all costs. Let developments
take their own course.

SPECIFIC MODALITY

Waiting for a propitious time to act. You cannot make your situation,
in real terms, any more fortunate than it already is. The seed has
already been planted. (See Hexagram 25: Innocence, for a picture of
another, more appropriate, attitude.)

AMBIENCE

An impatient attitude can be supplanted successfully by purposeful
and constructive use of time. Solid preparatory work.

CONCEPT MODEL

We picture here an essentially successful enterprise and a well-
integrated management team. What is required is:
1. Patience
2. The adoption of a suitable pace of work
3. The avoidance of erratic decision-making
4. Knowing when not to push forward
5. More economical use of resources and personal energy.

There are no problems of motivation, there is evidence of a good
sense of direction. Morale can be maintained by being more

observant of prevailing conditions. Point 4 is the most important at present.

──────── DECISION-BASE ASSUMPTIONS ────────

The following values are given subject to the information given in the Changes. Remember, the Changes take precedence.

Planning
It is likely that you have your future strategy well schemed out. Impatience, however, will produce further planning sessions and many changes of plan and much confusion.

Growth and Productivity
Your past work will take you far. A period of rapid growth to come.

Risks
This is not the time to take risks.

Investment and Finance
This is not the time to ask for investment or to decide on how future expenditure will be deployed.

Sense of Timing
This must be developed. Relax.

Adequacy of Resources
You have enough to get by reasonably comfortably, but you are probably impatient for more.

Feedback
Make the effort to be more positive. Take a wider view.

Best Use of Time
Diversify your interests. The bigot rarely succeeds for long. (See Hexagram 17).

Product Choice
Consider each decision carefully. You are likely to be highly volatile unless you have a well worked-out scheme or speciality.

Creative Judgement
Consider your conclusions carefully over a period of time before acting.

Advertising
If you have invested in promotions, wait for results. This is certainly not the time to invest further.

Getting the Best out of People
Give them space to relax when their efforts are not needed, and do not push too hard for too long. Respect their individual needs and, when you can, provide for them.

Objectives
They will be achieved, but not yet.

Personal Attitude
This is the time to relax, socialize, take the evening off. Companies of any scale should provide the time and/or the facilities for congenial relaxation, so that constructive use can be made of time while the company is treading water. Management should not keep staff under working pressure when conditions do not warrant it. It is important to conserve the strength of the team as well as that of management.

Sources of Misfortune
Wasting or misdirecting resources.

Sources of Good Fortune
A more persevering attitude. Trust yourself.

─────────── **THE LINES (CHANGES)** ───────────
the Future-Links

Nine at the beginning
A sense of expectancy pervades the air. What is on the horizon cannot be determined. Be watchful, therefore, and conserve energy. Don't change your routine because you sense a change is on its way.

Nine in the second place
Do not be made uneasy by inaccurate or unfair reports. Certainly do not reply. The calmest in the ranks will win the day.

Nine in the third place
You have jumped the gun in an already tight situation. That makes you vulnerable. Competitors can take advantage of you, so minimize the harm that could result.

Six in the fourth place
The situation is critical. Serious loss could result. You must not unbalance the situation. Compose yourself, even brace yourself. There might still be a way out.

Nine in the fifth place
The struggle is not over, but you are in the eye of the storm. You have to do two things at the same time: relax and store energy, and keep your eye on

your objectives. The art of success is to make progress every time an opportunity presents itself and, whenever progress is halted, to replenish yourself. If you and your company can adjust to this strange rhythm in the topsy-turvy world of business you can be extremely effective and highly resilient in the face of obstacles. These qualities, properly developed, can mean the difference between sinking or swimming.

Six in the last place
Amazingly enough, the situation is destined to have a successful outcome but, to all appearances, this definitely looks like the end of the road. Fate plays you the unexpected card of good fortune but, even as it is being turned over, you think it is the Ace of Spades. Although all your feelings make you want to leave the game, don't leave before the turn of the card. You are still in the game.

HEXAGRAM 6

Deadlock (Conflict)

---------------------- JUDGEMENT ----------------------

Good fortune if you compromise, misfortune if you do not. It
may be necessary to defer to an arbitrator. (See Hexagrams 40:
Deliverance, and 49: Revolution, in order to balance present perspectives.)

---------------------- SPECIFIC MODALITY ----------------------

Confrontation; negotiation; antagonism; dispute. This is not a
productive situation.

---------------------- AMBIENCE ----------------------

Tension, discomfort. Uncomfortable disagreement.

---------------------- CONCEPT MODEL ----------------------

The theme of this model is conflict, but conflict need not be
expressed between parties in an openly antagonistic way, whatever
their true feelings. The two opposing camps, or the two opposing
individuals, both feel themselves to be justified but their rightness or
wrongness is not being judged. It is the fact of conflict which is
unsatisfactory. If one party forces his view, the other may appear to
retreat, but he is in fact driven to adopt underhand means of getting
his own way.

Both parties have this propensity, which is why no agreement can
be struck. The only way forward is compromise. This requires a
profound adjustment of attitude which, though difficult to achieve, is
the implicit test of the situation.

There is also a warning. The conflict was partly brought about by
the will to take on an important challenge, which would advance your
position. A living opponent (as opposed to an intangible obstacle)
stands between you and your objective – an agreement on your own
terms. You should abandon the near-term objective completely and

rethink your position. (See Hexagrams 38: Opposition, and 33: Retreat/Strategic Withdrawal.)

The challenge is a fair one. There is the possibility of serious loss, and therefore the wise thing to do is not to place yourself deliberately in a position of vulnerability. Avoid steering your ship into a collision.

—————— DECISION-BASE ASSUMPTIONS ——————

The following values are given subject to the information given in the Changes. Remember, the Changes take precedence.

Management
Primary or principal objectives need serious modification. Avoid open confrontation with competitors on secondary objectives.

Planning
All plans are comprised of clearly articulated objectives and strategies. Rethink your position in respect of both. Consider the option of sharing or complete change of plan as both you and the opposition could lose by dint of mutual destruction.

Communications
Be receptive. Listen as well as speak. Check facts. Do not accept hearsay. This must include your own assertions.

Growth and Productivity
Temporarily impaired. Degree of impairment is a matter for personal judgement.

Risks
Avoid all risks. You are not in a position to shoulder responsibility.

Investment and Finance
Commit no funds. They will be wasted.

Timing
Wait. Further negotiation is required and critically important. Do not act presumptuously.

Adequacy of Resources
A potential loss-making situation.

Start-Up
Negative; inauspicious.

Feedback
Desired feedback is conciliatory. Actual feedback is negative. You are also responsible.

Creative Judgement
Frustrated and unreliable. Do not act upon it.

Backing
Do not seek it. Inauspicious. It is ill-advised to involve outsiders, unless they are part of a conciliation team.

Contracts and Agreements
Study conditions and warranties in detail. Do not sign anything. Seek independent counsel. This is no time to make decisions upon which the future of the company may depend.

National or International Trade or Agreements
Abide by the rulings of an independent and mutually agreed body of arbitration. This may be the only way to avoid damaging resources and relations.

Sources of Misfortune
Persistent aggression. Egotistical perspective. Factionalism. Insistence on your point of view can be divisive.

Sources of Good Fortune
Avoid aggravating the conflict. Conciliation.

─────────── THE LINES (CHANGES) ───────────
the Future-Links

Six at the beginning
The sensible thing is not to push disagreements so far that relations are broken off in a spirit of ill-will. Let it go.

Nine in the second place
Your adversary is stronger. There is no point in picking up the gauntlet when the outcome of a fight is a foregone conclusion. You lose no face in declining this challenge, particularly as the consequences of losing would affect others (perhaps even a whole community).

Six in the third place
You are the victim of a breach of copyright agreement or patent ownership. The *I Ching* teaches in this situation that, in a very real sense, such a breach has only a superficial significance in so far as anyone claiming title to work you have done *knows* that he is lying. The real work will always be yours. The *I Ching* counsels you not to contest such a despicable breach, and especially not on the grounds of preserving prestige.

   In the modern world, however, the concepts of copyright and patent are needed to protect an individual's work from just such an abuse and, where there is a breach, a legal remedy is available.

What is of lasting significance is that the work is done and is available to others.

Nine in the fourth place
You can take advantage of your opponent's vulnerability but, because you know that his moral position is superior to your own, you refrain from profiting from the situation. The result is good fortune and peace of mind.

Nine in the fifth place
This line refers to a settlement of the dispute. Even if the matter is settled out of court, it is still mediated by an impartial arbiter or system of justice by whose judgement both parties are willing to abide.

Nine in the last place
There are two ways of viewing this situation. The first is when a victory has been won by relentless pursuit of the opponent (the victory is worthless because it is unjust). The second view concerns entering into winning/losing situations for the sake of the conflict. The gratification of the winner is always shortlived, so why bother? The spirit behind the line is to isolate the 'bloody-minded attitude' which causes interminable disputes.

HEXAGRAM 7

The Army
(Challenge/Concentrating Resources)

───────────── JUDGEMENT ─────────────

Good fortune if fair play is observed in all particulars. The correct treatment of staff, workforce and management. Loyalties can only be relied upon if the position has been equitable in the past. Motivation by fear is not appropriate. Pecuniary incentives are partially acceptable. Real solidarity is the force behind successful achievement here.

───────────── SPECIFIC MODALITY ─────────────

The work of the sales force. The organization of the sales director and/or the marketing director. The proportionate deployment of resources within the company and in the field of action. Marshalling, concentrating and focusing of personal and management resources. Everything must work in a tightly coordinated way. Tighten up distribution.

───────────── AMBIENCE ─────────────

A major challenge, to which the whole company is committed. Tight organization, clearly defined objectives, clearly defined strategy.

───────────── CONCEPT MODEL ─────────────

The germane idea is the maximum and most efficient utilization of the company's resources, with specific emphasis on the role of those individuals who come into direct contact with public and customers. These people are responsible for the orders which are the basis of any company's prosperity. The concept embraces both service and sales-based industries and companies.

   To be truly effective, the energy of the sales force must be carefully and strategically deployed, and therefore the overall company plan must be agreed by the management team, as only a concerted effort will suffice in a major challenge for growth or consolidation.

An energetic and loyal working force is priceless. Managements may resort to incentive schemes as a surrogate for a really compelling, unifying idea. But the motivation arising from a higher idea is the real generator of commitment and quality.

It is important to emphasize this idea in its wider social context. In Western economies a minimum standard of commitment has become acceptable at a level which demeans human dignity. When people are cheated of a full and integrated life, one cannot expect a wholehearted commitment to causes or ideas.

The *I Ching* sets off these standards of human dignity against the background of a people required by their leader to become part of the military force defending their country and culture. They must believe in the cause they are asked to defend. If a people are exploited at home, how can they be asked to die in defence of it?

───────── DECISION-BASE ASSUMPTIONS ─────────

The following values are given subject to the information given in the Changes. Remember, the Changes take precedence.

Management

If the policy of management is to rule with an iron rod, the company is likely to have a rapid turnover of staff, weak commitment and, despite apparently attractive pecuniary incentives, sporadic quality and dedication. When consistency is the secret of success, the manner of management is as important as its strategy. Loyalty and competence are the two qualities which unite any company and, since work claims the most energetic hours of the day, a system which consistently cheats its workforce of self-fulfilment, eventually cheats itself of prosperity.

An enlightened management, even though functioning on a tight budget, can cultivate enthusiasm by displaying a genuinely caring attitude. This enables people to act on initiative beyond the call of duty, and releases creativity. It reduces the need for excessive discipline.

Thus, management must achieve a just *modus operandus* in the company's interests – which are to *transcend* the point at which survival is the key imperative.

Communications

There must be a free flow of up-to-date information at all levels, and this information must be integrated and fed back into the overall design and strategy in order to monitor the impetus and effectiveness of the work done. The sales force and the workforce are thus symbiotically integrated.

Risks
Since the whole company is committed, every decision must be unanimously agreed by management and each move strategically planned.

Product Choice
Use the best materials. Highest quality brings best results.

Objectives
To earn more prominence and standing in the market place.

Information Intelligence/Availability
Make sure that your strategy is based on all the available facts.

Creative Judgement
If the support given to the sales or marketing director (the person responsible for coordinating resources in the field) is sincere, then his creative judgement is sound. If not, he must review it.

Advertising
Some provision must be made.

Marketing
Concentrate on the organizational aspects. Identify targets with care.

Getting the Best out of People
Explain the strategy and tactics to the whole company. There must be no secrets. Confidence is based on suitable training, reinforced by encouragement in the field.

Attitude
If the people in the field are motivated by enthusiasm for the company and the product, they will tend to attract positive situations. This sets up a chain reaction because the profile of the company is enhanced. In such a manner a company achieves a reputation for positive energy. (See Hexagram 16: Enthusiasm.)

Sources of Misfortune
Lack of belief in the product or service by the whole or part of the company. Inept strategy. Poor coordination. Poor quality.

Sources of Good Fortune
The efficient and economic deployment of resources undertaken in an atmosphere of confidence.

─────────────── THE LINES (CHANGES) ───────────────
the Future-Links

Six at the beginning
All the members of the team must be relied upon for competence. Their respective roles must be carefully integrated into one clearly defined objective. Tactics must lead to the goal.

Nine in the second place
Good fortune if the sales or marketing director stays in close touch with his staff in the field. He must have the support of the whole company.

Six in the third place
When there is confusion among staff as to the strategy, they must know who in management is responsible for their orders. If different managers give different orders to the same people, staff will end up doing what they think is best. If this happens, strategy and coordination break down and there is no possibility of good timing.

Six in the fourth place
If it becomes apparent that the market is not being influenced by the activities of the sales and marketing force, then expenditure must be quickly curtailed and forces withdrawn from the field before they drain the resources of the company.

Six in the fifth place
A good market is available and is richer than expected. Because there is little competition you are able to saturate the market, but is this a good thing to do? If you do not act with some measure of prudence, there might be an unwholesome reaction in the long term. Room must be left to consider alternatives, even after victory. Do not cultivate all the land, particularly with only one crop.

Six in the last place
Pecuniary awards are appropriate to people who have acquitted themselves well in the field but management should not promote people regardless. As a general rule, decisions about promotion should never be made in the afterglow of success, but only when normal conditions have been reinstated. Promotion in an expanding enterprise should always be based on evidence of wider ability, independent decision-making and established character.

HEXAGRAM 8

Holding Together
(Unity through Leadership)

────────── JUDGEMENT ──────────

If you are the right leader, good fortune. You must coordinate people around a common objective, be the catalyst and impetus behind action and be sure of yourself as well as committed.

────────── SPECIFIC MODALITY ──────────

Forming a company. Consult this book again to establish your ability and commitment to the project. If the answer is in the affirmative, you need partners who are specialists.

────────── AMBIENCE ──────────

Attracting the right people is a natural process. These are matters of charisma, resonance, personal magnetism. One cannot 'plot' for people's cooperation. (See Hexagram 25: Innocence.)

────────── CONCEPT MODEL ──────────

An individual who wishes to start a company must be sure that he has the necessary strength not only to attract the right people but also to form ideas which are sound enough to warrant the formation of a company to develop them. Forming a company is not a long-drawn-out affair. Once the goals have been set, and the decision to go ahead has been made, there has to be a fixed time limit for advertising for personnel. The leader must have a clear idea of who he wants. Thus, people who want to join the enterprise must make their intentions known to the leader as promptly as possible, lest they lose the opportunity altogether. The implication here is that those who are truly motivated by the work offered, eventually do join. The image is one of people rallying round an individual who is the exponent of a good idea.

If the individual who receives this hexagram perceives himself as the prime mover in this enterprise but is, nevertheless, not sure whether or not he is up to the job, he should consult this book once again, asking himself the specific question: 'Do I have the necessary perseverance and resilience to launch this company?'

—————— DECISION-BASE ASSUMPTIONS ——————

The following values are given subject to the information given in the Changes. Remember, the Changes take precedence.

Management
First, it should be comprised of independent specialists. Second, success will come only if the right people are attracted for the right reasons, i.e., if they agree with the principal objectives. Sometimes qualifications and experience are of less importance than a vocational commitment to the ideas.

Planning
Auspicious, but full consultation with qualified colleagues is required.

Communications
Positive, but only objective considerations are of any value. Subjective attitudes might lead to decisions based upon sentimentality.

Growth and Productivity
The prospects are positive, but you have many ifs and buts to overcome. Most of these arise from an attitude of personal uncertainty. (See Hexagram 34: The Power of the Great.)

Risks
The right leader surrounded by the right people can make the project work.

Investent and Finance
Consult this book once again.

Integration
First establish the team, but consider personality factors.

Symbiosis
There must be an open communication system through all levels of decision-making. Maximum consultation is essential at the beginning of an enterprise.

Start-Up
Everything depends on the quality of the management team. This is

the principal focus. You must be confident of your own competence and that of colleagues and partners.

Feedback
Positive. (See Hexagram 16: Enthusiasm.)

Personnel
A sense of vocation – a genuine feeling for the work – is a central consideration. Do not rely on paper qualifications. Use your intuition.

Advertising
Generally auspicious. (See Hexagrams 35: Progress, and 53: Development, for a sense of scale.)

Marketing
Test the ground. Further cooperation is required. Be assured of commitments before parting with money or signing agreements.

Backing
Seek it, but do not force issues. This might be a way of testing your credibility.

Contracts and Agreements
It will be better if they are made in writing and conditions imposed, as the situation is still experimental. Those conditions must give rise to equitable responsibilities of the parties. Unfair advantage should not be claimed as this might well precipitate a drastic failure of confidence later, and this will be costly.

International Trade
Are the options sufficiently clear? If there are no agreements to honour, wait.

Sources of Misfortune
Creative misjudgement, lack of perseverance.

Sources of Good Fortune
The principal idea must be sound and the leader must be the right leader. He must feel a strong sense of vocation which others will see and trust.

——————— THE LINES (CHANGES) ———————
the Future-Links

Six at the beginning
In an interview, the interviewer should listen for sincerity, rather than what is being said, as this is the real content of an individual's worth and suitability. Good fortune if you do this.

Six in the second place
Do the work consistently and well, but don't do everything with an eye on promotion. Let your work be judged for itself.

Six in the third place
No, these are not your people. If the job is offered, do not accept it. Keep yourself available for the right opportunity.

Six in the fourth place
Here the attraction is felt to be correct, but do not be afraid to show your loyalty consistently.

Nine in the fifth place
The perspective of the leader is indicated here. If you are truly the right leader in this enterprise, you will naturally attract the right people. They will come to you – you won't have to search them out. The beauty of the situation is that, if the enterprise begins like this, then the relationships will work out properly. This is a prerequisite for the free flow of information among management personnel. The odd man out is the one who tries to cultivate secret allegiances.

Six in the last place
Seize the opportunity now. Do not procrastinate any longer.

HEXAGRAM 9

Limited Influence

'He who does not trust enough will not be trusted.'
Lao Tsu, *Tao Te Ching*

―――――――――――― JUDGEMENT ―――――――――――――

Success if you do not try to seize the initiative. Let others suggest a course of action. You may 'suggest' that *they* suggest a course of action, but choose your moment well. (See Hexagram 2: The Receptive.)

―――――――――――― SPECIFIC MODALITY ―――――――――――

The act of persuasion. You can be more effective than you would have yourself believe, but it is a friendly and conciliatory tone which wins the day. Brusque behaviour will invite people to withdraw support or even retaliate. Be on your guard.

―――――――――――――― AMBIENCE ―――――――――――――

A relatively weak force is able to influence a much greater force by means of subtle and diplomatic suggestions. 'It is rare, indeed, for a man with cunning words and an ingratiating face to be benevolent.' *Analects of Confucius*, Book One.

―――――――――――――― CONCEPT MODEL ―――――――――――

The hexagram pictures an inequality of bargaining power. You are in the weaker position. You can influence the situation to your advantage if you recognize the relative power the other party possesses. Distinguish the nature of your influence from that described in Hexagrams 10: Conduct, and 26: The Taming Power of the Great.

―――――――――― DECISION-BASE ASSUMPTIONS ―――――――――

The following values are given subject to the information given in the Changes. Remember, the Changes take precedence.

General Note
See Hexagram 61: Inner Truth, for an exposition of the power of
influence at its best. Hexagram 26: The Taming Power of the Great,
represents the opposite dynamic, when an unruly force is well and
truly controlled by a superior setting.

Objective
To retain your individual status and independence of mind; to
protect both freedom of choice and freedom to accept or reject offers
definitely, but unobtrusively, upon terms you find truly satisfactory.

Getting the Best out of People
Do not *tell* them anything outright. If you have anything to say, imply
it, suggest it, hint. But do not act upon any insights.

Communications
Be skilful, diplomatic. Ruffle no feathers, arouse no resentments.
Good fortune. Other people have the upper hand. They cannot be
trusted to behave honourably by you.

Growth and Productivity
Expect very limited achievements in the short term. Do not plan on
great gains.

Risks
Never defer to a tyrant's form of persuasion (see Hexagram 33).

Investment and Finance
Do not act.

Best use of time
During a time of unavoidable waiting, do not attempt major projects
or discuss matters of great importance. Concentrate on improving or
practising a talent or ability.

Adequacy of Resources
You have unmet needs, but they will be provided for.

Start-Up
Inauspicious.

Feedback
Possibly negative. If unacceptable, consider withdrawing altogether.
Neutrality is a preferred option, as good fortune is in the wings.

Intuition
You can trust it. If the circumstances are very important to your long-
term aims, record your intuitions so that you can use them later,

especially with regard to people where their cooperation is of primary importance.

Advertising
Inauspicious. Do not commit funds. You have to think in the medium to long term.

Marketing
Inauspicious. Be prudent with all resources. Expenditures which have no guaranteed return should be avoided. This does not include charity.

Backing
Make no demands, but asking cannot harm. Inauspicious.

Contracts and Agreements
They are best put into abeyance until a more propitious time. You could be unfairly exploited if you are not careful.

Sources of Misfortune
Brusqueness; an over-challenging style; threatening postures. But even these will not preclude success, as the atmosphere is right.

Sources of Good Fortune
Waiting. Keep yourself occupied in positive and personally enjoyable activities. Don't waste yourself on people who require too much effort at this time.

-------------------- **THE LINES (CHANGES)** --------------------
the Future-Links

Nine at the beginning
Good fortune if you recognize that the difficulties you have been encountering are a signal that you are trying to achieve the wrong things; you should adjust course accordingly.

Nine in the second place
As a member of a team driving towards a common objective, you see, as do the others in the team, that you are up against a brick wall. Without having to have the matter spelt out to you, you take the hint that there has been a change of plan and follow the others in backing out. Good fortune.

Nine in the third place
An embarrassing situation has arisen because an intimation that you were on the wrong path was ignored. You therefore committed the team's resources in a gross error of judgement and, worse, you overestimated your own capacity to act alone. Your failure to recognize the importance of cooperation in the venture has given others the opportunity of exploiting the

vulnerability either of yourself or of the whole team. The actual effect of all this, however, is not catastrophic, but rather a breakdown in communications. No one should rely on their own judgement at present, as all the elements for decision-making are not in the right perspective.

Six in the fourth place
Your job is to advise on important matters. Decisions will be made on the basis of what you say. You have to be especially careful as people may be physically harmed. Good fortune, however, is indicated if you do not become enmeshed in details. Providing the truth only is served, nobody need worry about anything.

Nine in the fifth place
Real loyalty between people expresses itself as a natural and unselfish sharing of resources, both material and personal. Among friends, there is no greater joy than to share what you have with them.

Nine in the last place
The most vulnerable moment is just before the goal is reached. Much has been accomplished, but the effect of the achievement is tied up in the act of completion. Concentrate on the final job. Do not adopt a presumptious attitude towards your achievement; rather, preserve your opportunities for future achievement. The best attitude is to act as if you have achieved nothing so that you try as hard as you did at the beginning. It is difficult for others to take advantage of those who feel like this.

HEXAGRAM 10

Sincerity (Conduct)

———————— JUDGEMENT ————————

Success. Your actions speak louder than words. Your influence works by being seen to embody certain principles. Your personality is your advantage. (See also Hexagram 61: Inner Truth.)

———————— SPECIFIC MODALITY ————————

The relationship between the weak and the strong. The good conduct of the weak. (See Hexagram 9: The Taming Power of the Small, concerning inequality of rank, bargaining power, position.) Here, however, you do not have to be on your guard. You can swing the situation around by being charming.

———————— AMBIENCE ————————

The good humour of the strong in relation to the weak. A friendly and tolerant exchange.

———————— CONCEPT MODEL ————————

It is intrinsic to the processes of nature that all things cannot be equal. There always exists an inequality of strengths between people, organizations and powers. But there has to be a balanced interplay between creative states and receptive states, yin and yang. What is important in this balance, however, is that the strong forces and the weak forces are in their proper place in relation to each other.

In rare circumstances a weak force is able to undermine the status quo and bring about imbalance; this invariably causes harm to both the weak and the strong. The usual state of affairs is that the weak does not even attempt to threaten the position of the strong; it does not necessarily follow that the strong does not take advantage of the weak in an improper way. Indeed, it is assumed that it does.

———————— DECISION-BASE ASSUMPTIONS ————————

The following values are given subject to the information given in the Changes. Remember, the Changes take precedence.

Management
Raw ability is not a sufficiently adequate criterion for management. Criteria for management selection must be based upon a balance between raw ability and service towards the weak if peaceful relations are to be maintained in carrying out the company's objectives.

Objective for the Weak Side
To win the attention of the strong without bringing harm to itself. (See Judgement.)

Risks
Do not move without strong support.

Investment and Finance
Hopeful, but be wary. Check the facts and be certain of cooperation before commitments are made.

Opportunities
Be quietly optimistic.

Feedback
Unexpectedly and unusually positive. Good fortune.

Creative Judgement
Either excellent or exceedingly poor. There is no middle ground here. If in doubt, remain silent.

Contracts and Agreements
There is nothing to preclude success and, if success comes, this could be a breakthrough.

Personal Attitude and Conduct
The strong should always be well disposed towards the weak and should not take advantage of its weakness. The weak should respect the strong and display an attitude of courtesy, even if the strong is belligerent. Otherwise the position would be dangerous for the weak. (See also Hexagrams 41: Decrease, and 42: Increase, for the wider implications of organization.)

Interviews
Presumptuousness is tolerated.

Sources of Misfortune
Where confident honesty degenerates into obsequiousness or sycophancy.

Sources of Good Fortune
If you have got this far, don't push your luck. Be on your best behaviour but do not compromise your principles.

―――――――――――― THE LINES (CHANGES) ――――――――――――
the Future-Links

Nine at the beginning
This line refers to someone who wishes to make a rapid advance through the promotion ranks. This makes it hard for him to settle down to his work. The ill effects of his attitude are that he does not advance his cause at all. The only thing he can do is to settle to the work in hand otherwise the position will become unbearably complicated.

Nine in the second place
A wise and able person deserves promotion but is nevertheless ignored. Because he is wise, however, he is not concerned and makes no protest. He is therefore more effective in his work and is able to retain his freedom of choice. If he decides that he does not want to stay any longer, he can leave, and the loss will be his employer's.

Six in the third place
When a man takes on a challenge which is really beyond his strength, he is deliberately placing himself in a position of vulnerability, where his efforts are likely to end in failure. Thus his actions are ill advised, unless he represents a noble cause which he feels must be defended whatever the cost.

Nine in the fourth place
You have the strength to carry off a great victory, but you hesitate because you are not sure of yourself. Go ahead.

Nine in the fifth place.
It is indeed a sterling quality to be determined in one's actions, but keep your eyes open and be aware that others might wish to oppose your plans. That is no reason to stop, however. Just be aware of it.

Nine in the last place
You want to know whether or not the work you have done will be successful now that it is completed. It is very difficult to be objective about your own achievements but, nevertheless, the intimation of this line is that you have succeeded and that you can expect supreme good fortune.

HEXAGRAM 11

Peace

JUDGEMENT

Good fortune and success. There will be, in the mid-term, a great expansion of possibilities. The field of action is gradually opening up even now. Your alignment with certain values is the reason for such auspicious developments in your personal circumstances. You win the support of others.

SPECIFIC MODALITY

The work comes to fruition. It is well received and appropriate recognition is already in the wings. Auspicious and very promising.

AMBIENCE

A pleasant harmony.

CONCEPT MODEL

The situation is very favourable. Because all the right preparations have been made at the right time, the fruit of your labour will yield a good harvest. When a business enterprise prospers, an atmosphere of peace and harmony exists between management and staff and everybody shares the good fortune. This is what happens when companies observe and act upon the natural seasonal changes.

The company that has the wisdom to tune its activities according to the cycles of nature, i.e., the natural cycle reflected in the growth cycles of plants, must seasonally experience perfect equilibrium and prosperity. This idea is developed in the sequential considerations of the hexagrams taken as a whole. The whole philosophy of the *I Ching* is caught in the flavour of this hexagram.

DECISION-BASE ASSUMPTIONS

The following values are given subject to the information given in the Changes. Remember, the Changes take precedence.

Management
Now is the time to give salary increments, bonuses and presents.

Planning
Revise short- and medium-term plans in a more optimistic light.

Growth and Productivity
There will be substantial growth, but do not expect this to be dramatic.

Investment and Finance
Past difficulties will be eradicated. Expect greater cooperation in the future. You will be able to invest in, and expand, your operation.

Adequacy of Resources
Whatever the past situation, you will have more scope in the future to expand your possibilities.

Start-Up
Auspicious.

Feedback
Management and staff rapport excellent. This should be reinforced by common social activities.

Creative Judgement
The evidence will show that this has been spot on.

Advertising
You will earn your investment back with ease.

Marketing
You will find a strong demand.

Contracts and Agreements
You can afford to be fair, even generous, though this should be a matter of principle.

Sources of Misfortune
In times of prosperity it is important to show a spirit of kindness and generosity to everybody who has been instrumental in working towards a common goal. Therefore any misfortune will arise from a mean spirit. This, of course, applies to staff as well as management.

Sources of Good Fortune
Observe the cycles of nature and follow them closely. By doing this, you will experience what you might like to call 'luck', but really luck has nothing to do with it. Luck is the manifestation of higher forces at

work which, of course, can be attracted or repelled. The spirit of gratitude is implied.

THE LINES (CHANGES)
the Future-Links

Nine at the beginning
Like-minded people are always irresistibly attracted to good and positive influences. Make plans in relation to developing the work along these lines.

Nine in the second place
You can afford to be magnanimous and pass over the faults of others. A truly resourceful man wastes nothing. Pay attention to detail but fit in with a larger scheme. There is always a tendency to overlook important things when there is no pressure. Use the freedom from pressure to perfect work.

Nine in the third place
It is well known that periods of good fortune do not last forever in the affairs of individuals or companies, but there is continuing good fortune in being aware of this and not placing too great an emphasis on material good fortune, as real good fortune is a state of mind. Once this is grasped, you can work without anxiety.

Six in the fourth place
When there is a good atmosphere between people, regardless of standing or wealth, wealth is shared readily and in an open spirit – that is, without the taint of condescension.

Six in the fifth place
A union of the great and small takes place regardless of exterior rank or wealth. This is a joyful occasion and brings good fortune in its train.

Six in the last place
Here misfortune has come in external matters, not by virtue of mistakes but as an inevitable product of the cycle of good fortune. Since there is nothing you can do to prevent general misfortune, the wisest course of action is to protect others from its effects. To openly and defiantly oppose it would be a waste of energy.

HEXAGRAM 12

Stagnation (Standstill)

----------------- JUDGEMENT -----------------

Misfortune if you cooperate with people with poor intentions. You are required to keep yourself active, your intentions well focused, even when events make real progress hard to achieve.

----------------- SPECIFIC MODALITY -----------------

Actions are not coordinated. Take time to plan. (See Hexagrams 61: Inner Truth and 20: Contemplation.) Your current position is not reliable. Caution. Suspicious practices at work.

----------------- AMBIENCE -----------------

Dishonesty, disharmony, discordance. Faulty perspective: things are not what they seem.

----------------- CONCEPT MODEL -----------------

Only a superficial impression can be made, with the best will in the world. The beneficial influence of 'good intentions' has deserted the scene. As a result, people who bear the organization no good will make offers with hidden strings attached. The situation is not to be trusted. Covert activities, division of interests, selfishness and secret designs rule the day. Do not get involved and do not make yourself a target.

   This is not a time to be thinking of progress, nor a time to follow up creative ideas. It is difficult to get things done. Do not desert your principles. The temptation will be offered. Decline it, firmly, but without making a big production out of the predicament.

----------------- DECISION-BASE ASSUMPTIONS -----------------

The following values are given subject to the information given in the Changes. Remember, the Changes take precedence.

Management
Look at all the facts and decisions personally. Do not defer on any issue to the advice or recommendation of anyone else. Lamentably, you must assume either incompetence or malpractice as the cause of any mistakes which arise at this time in the company's dealings. Avoid confrontations, however.

Planning
This is not the time to make any new plans or to communicate them. This may be a time to abandon plans altogether.

Objectives
This is a time of decline and standstill. Put a hold on plans. In a hostile and untrusting atmosphere it is better to keep quiet about any short-term or long-term objectives until you know where you stand with everybody.

Growth
It has been arrested. Do not seek growth at this time.

Timing
Put everything on 'Hold' until your position clarifies and your reason, supported by intuition, justifies a more relaxed attitude.

Resources
Be careful with them. Make them last. They may be under threat.

Feedback
Negative. Any positive feedback must be treated with strict reservations.

Best Use of Time
Secure your own situation as best you can and work on projects which require information-gathering rather than synthesis.

Decisions
Avoid making really important decisions, except negative decisions requiring 'No', or 'Give me time to think this through' answers.

Intuition
Sharpen your intuition so that you can make objective assessments of character, as this will help you to distinguish the genuine from the bogus.

Personal Projection
Be inscrutable.

Perspective

If you retain a clear position on personally held values, nothing can harm you and you have nothing to worry about. Misfortune can be turned into good fortune when the right time comes.

Advertising

Advertising, where possible, glamourizes products or companies. This is not a time to take notice of a calculated, distorted self-image in so far as it may affect the decision-making of your company. It may well be a lie.

Sources of Misfortune

Yielding to temptations which may seem attractive but which involve hidden elements. Do not allow others to entice you with justifications of their ruthlessness (greediness). It is a favourite ploy which masquerades as 'good judgement' and goes by many other names such as 'self-interest', 'every man for himself', 'realism'.

Sources of Good Fortune

Avoid making mistakes you can identify. Show strength of character even when placed under pressure. Do not compromise principles or values which have stood you in good stead in the past – those which have brought real happiness to you and to others.

--------------- **THE LINES (CHANGES)** ---------------
the Future-Links

Six at the beginning

It may be that a change of fortunes compels a man to retire from a career in business because, to have continued, would have meant a compromise of principles, but remember – good fortune can come in spheres beyond business for those who preserve their integrity.

Six in the second place

A man of principle is prepared if necessary to make personal sacrifices rather than see his principles violated by untrustworthy types. In this way he attains success, but people obsequiously try to cling to him, possibly through bribery and flattery, so as to avoid making decisions for themselves. He is not tempted, however, even though in a material sense the overtures may have been attractive.

Six in the third place

Sometimes people whose practices are highly questionable, even though they may achieve riches and power through them, realize they cannot cope with finding themselves in a position of power. They do not have decision-making calibre and find themselves overwhelmed by an organizational infrastructure. Such an experience is humbling and is the first step to a change of heart.

Nine in the fourth place
Energy is being restored to the situation and the forces of opposition now begin to give way so that progress is once again made possible. But the process has only just begun. In order to complete the process, an individual of strong character and clear priorities is needed, as the job of restoring order is by no means an easy one. If the right person is chosen, he will get all the help he needs and good fortune will be the result.

Nine in the fifth place
Following on from the last line, the appropriate individual takes control of the situation and begins the work of restoring order. The line concerns his attitude. He should at all times in the course of the work be conscious of the fragility of the situation and avoid being duped by any false sense of security. He should proceed as if success is not a forgone conclusion. He must make every move count. In this situation he must think like a chess player.

Nine in the last place
If nothing is done, the situation will deteriorate and move through a process of standstill to stagnation and finally fall to pieces. This process can be arrested through the regenerative energy of a creative and dynamic individual. Only through such a catalyst can a condition of prosperity be realized out of stagnation. The situation bodes well.

HEXAGRAM 13

Fellowship with Men
(Cooperation)

JUDGEMENT

Success if you work with others. This hexagram emphasizes cooperation, joint ventures, partnerships, international agreements, mergers, and the successful and generally beneficial expansion of the field of action. The spirit of cooperation brings good fortune and is auspicious if you are consistent.

SPECIFIC MODALITY

Joining with others sharing lofty aims. There is a general condition attached to good fortune here: the effect of cooperation must lead to a general benefit.

AMBIENCE

Mutual confidence. A solid basis for agreement, but the organizational framework must be appropriate to its aims. A national to global perspective is favoured.

CONCEPT MODEL

The grander the scheme, the greater its potential gift to others, the more likely it is to get off the ground. This is an unusual state of affairs, as people are accustomed to the idea that one must keep one's plans cautious and small. There are many cases in this book where precisely that state of affairs is an imperative for success. But here people come together around compelling humanitarian aims of immense value to others. This is why joining with others with noble ideas is described as 'fortunate'.

There are no problems of motivation, as everybody involved understands these high values. They know, in general terms, what needs to be achieved. Ideas need to be refined and developed consistently and in a spirit of optimism.

This is a period when enlightening ideas bubble to the surface. Motivation is directed along inspired and clearly defined ideas. It would be well to keep a notebook at hand day and night, as this is a time when new ideas, answers to problems, resolutions of difficulties are likely to occur. It is all too easy to let these ideas get lost in a plethora of other thoughts. Be careful about passing over ideas which may conceal in another form brilliant insights.

―――――――― DECISION-BASE ASSUMPTIONS ――――――――

The following values are given subject to the information given in the Changes. Remember, the Changes take precedence.

Management
The more open and trusting management are with each other the greater the field of available ideas. Nothing is to be feared in this. The pleasant and unexpected (luck?) tends to occur to people and organizations which are open and receptive. People feel happiest in a working environment in which they feel they belong. The position is strong and positive. Omens are good.

Planning
With vision so clear at present, this is an auspicious time to lay out long-term objectives. Follow with short-term objectives. It is a good idea to draw the plan diagramatically so that the principal aims show clearly in a time sequence, and place the diagram in a very prominent place so that it is seen frequently by everybody involved in its development.

Growth and Productivity
Excellent prospects. A coming together of talents. Nurture them.

Risks
There are no risks involved. There is an implicit logic in the developing ideas, and this must become conscious.

Adequacy of Resources
Good. If insufficient for the short term, the proper presentation of your ideas to people or companies will attract a serious response. Take care to seek funding, especially if this is a start-up situation, by people who *understand* the nature of the project, either in detail or intuitively. It is no good taking the unpatented blueprints of a new circuit diagram for a new computer to your bank manager, for example. He is not paid to understand start-up investment requirements, however good your idea. Seek investors with a more personal and caring attitude.

Start-Up
Propitious. Once the team is established, there will be rapid clarification of aims. Patience is necessary, however, when the new project takes shape.

Product Choice
Many ideas will suggest themselves. Note them all and consider each according to its various merits: application, originality, state of the art, presentation, cost, *et al.* Don't throw any new ideas out at this time – make this a policy. But make no hard and fast decisions or final proclamations, especially of a negative nature.

Creative Judgement
You can trust it. Develop ideas in order to realize their potential. Focus on expanding perceptions in every suggested direction. Explore, as opportunities are still to be discovered. Involve others.

Contracts and Agreements
The atmosphere is favourable, the time propitious.

Competition
This is likely to turn to cooperation. Do not be paranoid about secrecy as it is inappropriate to your objectives.

Sources of Misfortune
Failure to organize ideas and record them.

Sources of Good Fortune
To set up an organized structure so that people can maximize their creative ability and output. Organize objectives, work programmes, systems. Generate a clearly defined free and open context for the realization and dissemination of ideas. Make this an objective primary goal.

THE LINES (CHANGES)
the Future-Links

Nine at the beginning
There is a need for an open declaration of commitment before the job of planning the work is seriously entered into. Everybody must be warm and frank with each other and no secret liaisons are to be entertained.

Six in the second place
The work is spoiled because the team has divided itself into selfishly motivated interest groups. Selfish interests cannot prevail if a common higher goal is to be realized.

Nine in the third place
The company is divided in two and mutual mistrust rules the day. Both sides scheme and plot for advantage. Nothing can be achieved in this situation. It is a waste of time and money and only causes further estrangement. Someone has got to come out into the open and make a declaration of trust.

Nine in the fourth place
The way to resolve a stalemate is to clear the board and start again, but avoiding confrontation. When you realize that both sides can't win, work together for a common good.

Nine in the fifth place
When people who belong together are kept apart by temporarily insurmountable hardships which are beyond their respective control, both are unhappy. However, as long as they want to get back together, nothing will keep them apart for long. Their eventual reunion will be a wonderful event.

Nine in the last place
We feel a powerful resonance with people who believe as we do and it is a natural impulsion to want to join them in action. It is inevitable that, as long as we keep this feeling strong, we will eventually succeed without fear of self-recriminations. Keep your objectives clear. Believe in your intuitions of affinity and empathy.

HEXAGRAM 14

Possession in Great Measure

'The good man remembers what is right at the sight of profit.'
The Analects of Confucius

JUDGEMENT

Great good fortune – material good fortune. Personal circumstances make the judgement positive, but this is relative. An enhancement of possibilities, an expansion of choices and options, but there is a corresponding increase in personal responsibility and accountability.

SPECIFIC MODALITY

The graceful exercise of power and the administration of wealth. Progress comes easily. The work goes well. There is sufficient energy to achieve desirable results. The personal sense of wellbeing enhances the will to efficiency.

AMBIENCE

Confident and knowledgeable action. Competence.

CONCEPT MODEL

Great wealth is accompanied by a strong commitment. Without clarity of direction and consistent application of energy, wealth dissipates, resources are squandered, and no benefit accrues to others who might make good use of it. Therefore, there is an attendant responsibility on those who possess material wealth (or control wealth) to see that wealth is used to serve only the very best aims.

The *I Ching* says that those to whom wealth, or possession in great measure, is entrusted, possess it as a matter of fate, as destiny.

This is a highly productive time during which you could achieve a good deal. All the necessary energy is available and there are no blocks to progress. Take advantage of the propitiousness of the time. The rewards will be substantial, providing that what you are doing is intended to increase benefit to others.

—————— DECISION-BASE ASSUMPTIONS ——————

The following values are given subject to the information given in the Changes. Remember, the Changes take precedence.

Management
There are no obstacles to cooperation. Be the guiding light. Do not ignore new departures of personal interest and specialization as you will be able to expand your field of activity significantly. Choose managers who have great mental scope and friendly disposition, as they will be receptive to the needs of the environment and are much more likely to understand your motivations.

Planning
Do not be afraid to make bold long-term plans. People will fall into line with them without too much prompting.

Attitude
With everything going well people respond to your thoughtfulness and kindness. This is a time when any acts of consideration will have a great impact and will not be forgotten.

Communications
Easy. Understanding comes naturally.

Risks
Do what you know to be *right* and you will not fail.

Investment and Finance
Auspicious.

Adequacy of Resources
Material resources are available. In any event, the meaning which always applies is the abundance of energetic resource. Immense capacity for getting things done, and successfully.

Start-Up
Very auspicious. Be absolutely committed and the enterprise will succeed. People rally round if you need them.

Feedback
Maximum and cooperative. Unless conditioned by a changing hexagram to the contrary, nothing is standing in the way.

Product Choice
You can make these judgements with confidence. Evaluate the considerations of others without too much effort and no anxiety.

Creative Judgement
Natural and perfectly balanced. Don't waste time procrastinating over creative decisions, the correct decisions are those that come most naturally.

Intuition
Be guided by it and make a note of your keenest insights; following hunches could release forces which bring immense good fortune, providing what you do has an objective benefit to others.

Inspiration
Ideas will flow easily and with clarity. What you achieve will not usually be achievable at another time. There is a capacity for synthesizing innumerable impressions and creative expression. But it is not enough merely to see with great clarity; one must also be able to act upon one's perceptions with objectivity. The power to do just that is inherent in this situation.

Marketing
If the work is *right* it will reach people without undue expenditure. Real promotion is more a matter of *empathic resonance*: ideas connect those who have a natural resonance with them. This is as it should be. Vast resources spent upon advertising are not a guarantee of commercial success, though ideas must be presented before the public in an unpretentious way.

Contracts and Agreements
There will be no problem in bringing these to fruition. People are responding to you keenly. Be open and responsive.

Competition
The situation lends you cooperation. There is no fear of being thwarted by competition. The negative actions of others will have no retarding effect upon your work now.

Concentration
Steady and prolonged.

Sources of Misfortune
Application of time, energy and wealth to projects which abuse an advantageous position and bring harm to others. These will always fail in the end.

Sources of Good Fortune
Simply to make productive use of the time.

──────────── THE LINES (CHANGES) ────────────
the Future-Links

Nine at the beginning
You do not have the wealth yet but it is on its way. This is no time to relax.
Keep your concentration, stay humble and work hard.

Nine in the second place
Wealth does not only mean piles of money but also *resources*, the *use* and
availability of facilities; the individual who has great possessions has one
very valuable and indispensable quality: the cooperation of others without
which nothing is possible. The key to all this is making good and economical
use of everything, so that people are able to fulfill the potential of money,
goods and services.

The people involved in your enterprise know their jobs and can work
without supervision. Projects which have to be impeccably organized and
carried through to completion must have in attendance completely trustworthy and competent people. This is wealth.

Nine in the third place
Great possession is not appropriate to the greedy and selfish. Such people
do not realize that one cannot, in reality, own anything. In the broadest
sense, everything is entrusted to us for a short time, the duration, if we are
fortunate, of our lives. Thus, wealth must be shared and benefit must be felt
among those who do not have wealth in such measure. Great wealth must be
accompanied by great-heartedness. If the two do not go together great
misfortune arises.

Nine in the fourth place
Do not complicate your state of mind by coveting the material and social
possessions of those who live and work around you. Such a state of mind
communicates a very unpleasant image which reflects back upon you.
Change it.

Six in the fifth place
In your giving avoid outright profligacy as people will take you for a fool (that
is *their* lack of generosity). Giving only has the right effect if it comes from
the heart. Integrity radiates.

Nine in the last place
When a person of great wealth places it at the disposal of people who are
good, wise and well intentioned they honour their wealth and position.
Through helping people of quality many others are helped forward through
them, and a good chain is set up. It is, therefore, a highly significant action
and is attended by great good fortune which is called, in the *I Ching*,
Supreme Success.

HEXAGRAM 15

Modesty

--- JUDGEMENT ---

Consistent effort brings success. Personal and company profiles invite cooperation. There is great aptitude and potential, but it must be realized over time. Monitor progress over a period of a year.

--- SPECIFIC MODALITY ---

The power to change weak to strong, poverty to wealth. Opportunities for recognition and promotion follow closely upon tangible achievements.

--- AMBIENCE ---

The effect of a modest attitude is to change the *status quo*. In this atmosphere, the arrogant fall and the modestly diligent assume prominence.

> 'How does one recognize men of talent to promote?' asked Tzu-lu of the Master.
>
> 'Promote those you do recognize. Do you suppose others will allow those you fail to recognize to be passed over?'
>
> *The Analects of Confucius*, Book 13

--- CONCEPT MODEL ---

You will be promoted. The company will be promoted. A modest person may have been working conscientiously for a long time without proper help, support or recognition from his peers but, nevertheless, he perseveres. A long accumulation of effort which has been consistently applied in a specific field of activity eventually becomes visible to others. This is the effect of sustained and modest work.

———————— DECISION-BASE ASSUMPTIONS ————————

The following values are given subject to the information given in the Changes. Remember, the Changes take precedence.

Management

Be objective about the abilities of people. What do their achievements indicate about their capabilities? Nobody in a company should be above this kind of scrutiny. Act accordingly. It is a rare person who volunteers to leave room for a promotion because his own work is, on his own objective assessment, not up to scratch. Such an individual should be allowed to step down for a short while only, as the ability to be *that* objective is the mark of a leader. The people who have proved incompetent and yet cling to their positions should either shape up or ship out, as the nautical expression has it.

Planning

Review key objectives and make changes of emphasis. This might mean bringing forward ideas into the priority file and throwing out outworn priorities which are just dead weight.

Growth

It is in the preparatory stages. Changes must be made laterally so that growth is possible later. Certain features in the organization's personal landscape will become visible after being long in obscurity. Do they bear a common quality? What quality?

Investment

Be careful. There is a reversal indicated here. If you have enjoyed prosperous times they can only be maintained now if the situation in the company is correspondingly reversed, in keeping with the overall change. If within does not change in tune with without you could lose out.

Start-Up

There is a reversal taking place. This could be your chance to make your presentation. Take care not to overstate your case, but state it. Some people cannot read minds.

Feedback

Do not deliberately seek it. If you have been overlooked in the past, the position is about to be reversed in your favour. This is auspicious. But do not try to do more than you are able. Do what you have practised and perfected.

Creative Judgement

If success has made you complacent, you are about to make a really expensive decision. If you are on your toes, you could make the prime judgement which transforms your future prosperity.

Objectivity
All-important at present.

Promotion
For the unnoticed 'backbone' your time has come. Can you rise to the challenge?

How to Get the Best out of People
Reward people who do the work, even though they might not expect it.

Advertising
Present ideas and products. Expenditure used to 'push' the product or idea beyond a simple presentation will have the opposite effect to that desired. People will be repelled rather than attracted. The wastage of resources is often the downfall of companies who have over-advertised. Over-exposure tends to blind people to quality. When this happens it is the beginning of the end.

Sources of Misfortune
The most important thing to guard against in a promotion situation is a conceited attitude now that one's possibilities have been expanded. Remember, promotion gives credit for work done in the past, as a result of past efforts. (See Hexagram 60: Limitation.)

Sources of Good Fortune
It is simply a matter of consistent effort and resilience to outside negative forces. Do the *right thing* which may not be following policy – which may be wrong.

————————— THE LINES (CHANGES) —————————
the Future-Links

Six at the beginning
Avoid making a big production out of the simplest issues. Even relatively difficult jobs can be done competently if you don't allow yourself to be blocked by thinking too much about the awesomeness of a project.

Six in the second place
A truly modest person radiates this quality in everything he does. Obstacles are easily overcome. People either cooperate or they stand aside.

Nine in the third place
There is nothing quite so harmful as stopping halfway through good work in

order to get praise. Finish the work. People naturally admire those who get the job done without taking bows.

Six in the fourth place
Here's the catch: you have to be modest about being modest. Reactivate interest in your work; it is the only place that modesty feels at home.

Six in the fifth place
Modesty is a tricky concept to grasp. It controls the ego. Modesty should not consist in self-effacement or lack of action. The key is to be modest in an *objective* way.

Six in the last place
Modesty sets a high goal of personal excellence. If a modest person fails to live up to his own expectations he does not give up or sink into a mire of self-pity. He gets a grip on himself and reorganizes himself to put it right. He treats others with whom he has close dealings in the same way, so that a real improvement can be made.

HEXAGRAM 16

Enthusiasm (Positive Energy)

----------- JUDGEMENT -----------

Success if you are positive. The power of communication and natural empathy is strong. This is a good time to meet people. (See also Hexagram 58: The Joyous, Lake.)

----------- SPECIFIC MODALITY -----------

Getting things moving. Energizing others to achieve. Following the line of least resistance. Regenerating and raising people's spirits. Raising the tone and quality of response.

----------- AMBIENCE -----------

Bright. Music at the place of work. Refreshing, reinvigorating climate. Progress is considerably eased in this atmosphere.

----------- CONCEPT MODEL -----------

The key idea is to give the people what they need or want. This is not intended to cover every situation but to pinpoint the fact that people respond to ideas with which they feel comfortable and at ease. The products and services which are the most sought after, and therefore the most successful, are those which people most like or need. Filling a gap in the market place can, all other things being equal, bring companies from obscurity to prominence.

The lesson to be drawn is that enthusiasm is a real force in society and particularly in business. Enthusiasm is a vital element in every situation, not only in management attitude but also in work, products, services, and the manner in which staff conduct themselves. (But see Hexagram 62: The Preponderance of the Small, which deals with over-enthusiasm.)

———————— DECISION-BASE ASSUMPTIONS ————————

The following values are given subject to the information given in the Changes. Remember, the Changes take precedence.

Management

Be adaptable. Do not force staff to adapt to you. Make an effort to fulfil *their* requirements of leadership and working environment. If you are uncertain what these are, ask them personally (though not by means of questionnaires). Accept the responsibility personally.

It is important never to forget that each person is giving the best hours of his life to the work every day, and money is not the only valuable part of the equation which should be offered in return. A sense of belonging, dignity and personal appreciation form part of the same equation. It is not right to expect less, and it is not right to expect to offer less.

Take advantage of a time of enthusiasm. It is a time for action, a time to expand the company's field of activity and to explore new avenues for self-expression.

Objectives

Expand the terms of reference of the enterprise but without breaking down the sense of unity between staff or management.

Getting the Best out of People

No secrets. Management and staff work as one force. Be enthusiastic. If you feel it, express it.

Communications

Smooth. Make it personal, if possible. Avoid letters.

Growth and Productivity

Unfettered. Enthusiasm plus quality of work generate energy – and profits.

Investment and Finance

You could be in for a pleasant surprise. Invite investors to get the feel of the business personally. This deserves serious attention.

Start-Up

Auspicious. First impressions count for a lot. Let your true colours show. Be enthusiastic – the effects can be magical.

Feedback

Super-positive.

Inspiration

Enthusiasm and creativity go together naturally. The controlled release of tension in creative activity can bring forth new flowers. There is more than an element of magic to times like these.

Advertising
Be adventurous. Think in terms of music and harmony.

Marketing
Highly auspicious. Sales could be brilliant.

Contracts and Agreements
Favourable, but always get a second opinion. This is always advisable because mistakes are very costly and litigation is still barbarously inefficient and primitive. There is no reason to go in fear, however, that understandings have not been reached.

Attitude
This is not the time to hide one's light. Ideas will be well received both outside and within the company. Do not be frivolous, however, but do not be restricted as described in Hexagram 60: Limitation.

Sources of Misfortune
Even the most well-organized and well-structured company cannot achieve optimum productivity from workforce and management if there is no uplifting force. If voluntary initiatives are damped down and if feedback between workforce and management is cold, regimented and generally negative, the organization will fail to realize its full potential. This can mean outright failure. This is very much a 'people first' situation.

Sources of Good Fortune
Productivity in the workplace is always greatly enhanced by the creation of a salubrious and enthusiastic environment. This is the hidden influence in any management set-up which cannot be 'bought' and yet is the key to getting the most out of resources. Fostering an open exchange of ideas and making a policy of positive feedback between workforce and management can, and here does, make the difference between success and failure.

─────────── **THE LINES (CHANGES)** ───────────
the Future-Links

Six at the beginning
Enthusiastically 'name-dropping' entirely misses the point and doesn't impress. The idea is to bring people together.

Six in the second place
You see through events with clarity, read the signs of the times and know

how to interpret them. When you can do this, without boasting or obsequiousness, you have *timing*. So long as you keep your eyes open you won't fall foul of other people's errors of judgement.

Six in the third place
Watch carefully for the right time to make your move. Do *not* rely upon a cue from anybody else. They might be wrong or, worse, they might be watching for the same things. Act on your own. Think for yourself.

Nine in the fourth place
The qualities which come to expression here are brilliant: self-belief without arrogance; sincerity without an eye to profit; clear vision to act at the right time; generosity in your willingness to help others achieve their aims. You can achieve anything. You have friends.

Six in the fifth place
You may be upset that your freedom to express your enthusiasm has been curtailed. In hindsight you will realize it was a waste of energy anyway.

Six in the last place
Don't get carried away. Nothing is spoiled if you check yourself.

HEXAGRAM 17

Following (Adaptation to the Times)

JUDGEMENT

Being without secrets and adaptable, keeping up with the demands of the time, brings supreme success. Use resources to maximum effect. Show discrimination.

SPECIFIC MODALITY

Public acclaim through hard work. Perceiving new possibilities; working towards new applications of established ideas and technologies; developing new technologies. Supreme success.

AMBIENCE

Strong creative energy without cold expediency. You must not seek personal advantage at any cost. *The end does not justify the means.* Supreme success can turn to abject misfortune without proper discrimination as to means of action.

CONCEPT MODEL

A great deal can be achieved if people work to a time schedule and stick to it. Self-disciplined and organized activity points to a consistency of production. Providing this can be achieved without compromise of principles, it will lead to a very substantial success. Any kind of factional thinking is divisive and in error. It spoils productivity and breaks the flow of creative energy.

Loyalty and allegiance should only be shown to people who demonstrate a willingness to be guided by higher principles. These are the limits of the work ethic. Leaders and followers, management, staff and workforce must agree as to the quality of what is being done, and the way in which the work is done. Inferior quality cannot be passed over without an awareness that there will be consequences.

——————— DECISION-BASE ASSUMPTIONS ———————

The following values are given subject to the information given in the Changes. Remember, the Changes take precedence.

Management
Material benefits can be achieved successfully, but you should always ask 'At what cost?'

Planning
Although the principle objectives are clear, keep certain options open.

Communications
Useful and effective.

Growth and Productivity
The prospects are increasingly improving. Auspicious.

Investment and Finance
There are valuable ideas in the air – don't be too quick to pass them up. Do not waste time, however, and avoid being restrictive through inappropriate caution.

Start-Up
Very auspicious.

Feedback
Be flexible and friendly. Watch for prejudiced attitudes.

Information Intelligence/Availability
Be thorough in your research; read widely, keep an open mind.

Product Choice
You could be on to something profitable. Pursue it. Be adaptable. The secret of adaptability is knowing what is appropriate to the time.

Creative Judgement
Generally sound, but don't make snap decisions – consult with others. The situation is highly auspicious.

Self-Image
Confident, but see that this isn't at the expense of other people's failings.

How to Get the Best out of People
Avoid casting aspersions on the characters of others, especially those from whom you expect cooperation.

Advertising and Marketing
Make the product and/or service known in the trade, but don't overdo your claims.

Backing
Yes, if you can convince backers of your integrity, and for some this may mean a change of heart. Auspicious.

Contracts and Agreements
If you conduct your affairs in an open way, these could be favourable. The offers will come to you if you put yourself in the market.

Profits
A vertical rise. Very auspicious.

Research and Development
Ideas are of great value. Pursue them.

International Trade
The right atmosphere for general success, but see Hexagram 56: The Traveller.

Sources of Misfortune
Manipulating people.

Sources of Good Fortune
Manipulating ideas.

---------------- **THE LINES (CHANGES)** ----------------
the Future-Links

Nine at the beginning
Take the widest possible view of any issue. Actively broaden your creative input. You need more information, especially when its source is unfamiliar to you. Avoid looking exclusively for the reflection or support of your own viewpoint. Make a note of the differences between your thinking on a particular subject and the thinking of others. The disparities could lead you into interesting waters.

Six in the second place
The opportunity comes to forego the little fish to catch the big one. If all your resources are taken up with objectives which do no justice to the opportunity you will lose it. Move on.

Six in the third place
Sad though you may feel, it's time to move on. If you are offered a new job, a promotion, take it. The time for you to stay has passed and it would be wrong to pass up this opportunity for sentimental reasons.

Nine in the fourth place
To give and accept praise, you require a certain amount of inner stability, otherwise it is all too easy to be manipulated by others. Be objective, especially with new people who show an over-zealous interest in you. If you bring your own ego under control, what foothold is there for the wrong kind of person? The right person seeks no personal advantage at your expense. (See Hexagram 16: Enthusiasm.)

Nine in the fifth place
What idea is it that you seek to live up to? Who is it, for you, who embodies your highest ideals? Cultivate the image of your guiding light and follow it.

Six in the last place
Your close friend or teacher decides that he will respond to your need for guidance and help even though, to all intents and purposes, he has retired. There is a very powerful bond between you and much good will come of this.

HEXAGRAM 18

Work on What has been Spoiled

'For happiness is only a bye product of function, as light is a
bye product of the electric current running through the
wires. If the current does not run efficiently, the light does
not come. That is why nobody finds happiness who seeks it
on its own account. But man must seek to be . . . like the
unimpeded run of electricity. . . . So the light shines. That is
happiness: working well.'

T. H. White, *The Book of Merlyn*

------------------------------ JUDGEMENT ------------------------------

Supreme success if you are not lazy. (See Hexagram 34: The Power
of the Great.)

------------------------------ SPECIFIC MODALITY ------------------------------

Preparing your ground for sustained hard work. Reorganization.
There is a need for a work schedule.

------------------------------ AMBIENCE ------------------------------

Regaining control of yourself.

------------------------------ CONCEPT MODEL ------------------------------

The momentum of events has fallen off. The object of the exercise is
to get back into the work. Start slowly and then pick up speed until
you reach a pace of work which can be sustained. This should take
about three days of preparation and a further three days to establish
the momentum. After that time, you will have shaken away the
complacency and started to get sharp again.

You must make a conscious effort and a firm decision, as the
beginning is always the hardest. There is much to do, but you have to
start somewhere, so stop procrastinating.

Once the wheels are in motion, energy starts to generate and other people are inspired by your example. The important things now are to establish your objectives and a working pace as quickly as possible, both with the minimum of fuss and bother. Overcome an attitude of indifference.

─────────── DECISION-BASE ASSUMPTIONS ───────────

The following values are given subject to the information given in the Changes. Remember, the Changes take precedence.

Management
Kindness will pay dividends. Make it a consistent policy. *Indifference is deadly.*

Planning
Review plans thoroughly, as changes are in order.

Investment and Finance
The market could appear volatile very shortly. You will need inside information before committing yourself, but the position looks promising in the medium term.

Start-Up
Don't attempt anything too ambitious just yet. Start slowly, clarify your objectives and work hard.

Rhythm, Routine, Pace
Establish them and don't lose ground, once having begun. Make it a point to sustain the pattern when everything is running.

Feedback
A marked improvement is called for.

Creativity
Immense potential.

Personal Attitude
Be willing

Self-Image
Sharpen up.

Organization
Make sure *you* understand it. Clarify it to yourself.

Advertising
Look at the ideas again. They could be improved.

Marketing
Energy is being wasted. Go through the strategy again and tighten it up.

Backing
Do not ask for financial support just yet.

Sources of Misfortune
Laziness.

Sources of Good Fortune
Energy.

───────────────── THE LINES (CHANGES) ─────────────────
the Future-Links

Six at the beginning
Past mistakes press upon you, probably not of your own making. Do what you can to put them right but, although it is important, don't become obsessive.

Nine in the second place.
The difficulty may have been caused through the insensitivity of a woman, just as line one originated with a man. You can show consideration by letting it pass.

Nine in the third place
You are right to care about the mistakes of others deeply enough to want to do something about it. But your actions could be counterproductive if you display too much obvious keenness. People are always touchy about their mistakes.

Six in the fourth place
If you can see that it is wrong you have to show courage and correct it. Don't let it get worse, do something about it while the option is still available.

Six in the fifth place
Every genuine attempt to eradicate faults attracts favour. If, in your efforts, you need help, ask for it – people help more easily when they can see that you, yourself, are trying. Good fortune.

Nine in the last place
You may not choose the path which takes you into the world of helping others improve their lives. That is fair enough, you don't have to. The work of self-development never stops, however. Whether you work on yourself *through* working for others or work on yourself alone is always a matter of personal choice, but those are the choices. The option to sit back idly and dish out negative criticism is, of course, a trap.

HEXAGRAM 19

Advance/Approach
(A Clear Road Ahead)

———————————— JUDGEMENT ————————————

Supreme good fortune if you drive forward. (See also Hexagram 35: Progress.) People are approachable and receptive to your favourite projects and ideas.

———————————— SPECIFIC MODALITY ————————————

Teaching, training others, connecting and comprehending ideas. This is an aid to even greater effectiveness. Meetings are favoured. Communication is beneficial. New possibilities emerge. Opportunities for collaboration.

———————————— AMBIENCE ————————————

The door to progress is wide open.

———————————— CONCEPT MODEL ————————————

The time is perfect for growth and expansion. Energy to increase your ambit of work is forthcoming, an upswing of creative work characterized by the coming of spring. The force of growth can overcome any obstacles. It is implicit in the cycle that there will be a period of decline also, but this will not be until the year is drawing to a close. What remains of importance is that an investment of energy will pay dividends and, that done, you can provide for periods of decline if you show foresight.

People in positions of strength and understanding feel motivated to give their time and attention to others who would benefit from nurturing. This is the time to bring on the young and inexperienced in the world. A teacher can illuminate ideas with great effect at such times.

—————————— DECISION-BASE ASSUMPTIONS ——————————

The following values are given subject to the information given in the
Changes. Remember, the Changes take precedence.

Objectives for Management
Teach and train.

Objectives for Students
Learn all you can. Favourable.

Planning
Expand, develop, activate ideas, move.

Communications
Well starred. People are receptive.

Growth and Productivity
Vertical and rapid, sudden. Auspicious.

Risks
The time is right to put forward ideas and make moves. Success.

Investment and Finance
Favourable if you act quickly. Short-term gains are highlighted.

Start-Up
Highly auspicious. Be prepared - you can make things happen.

Feedback
Positive. Promote interactive systems.

Creative Judgement
Excellent. Supreme good fortune.

Creative Input
Increase. Watch the media.

Creative Output.
Great potential. New ideas are favourably received.

Advertising
Successful. Follow up.

Marketing
Extra work brings more success. Auspicious.

Backing
Highly auspicious. Approach the right people.

Contracts and Agreements
Highly auspicious. Terms are mutually favourable and fair.

International Trade
Be adventurous. Auspicious.

Sources of Misfortune
It is difficult *not* to achieve when the forces of the time are impelling you forward. Over-caution, fear, general negativity, can distort an otherwise positive process. Do not allow this to happen.

Sources of Good Fortune
Forward motion. Be active. Communicate, attend meetings. Work hard.

―――――――――― **THE LINES (CHANGES)** ――――――――――
the Future-Links

Nine at the beginning
Inspiration and vision begin to make themselves felt in the corridors of power; great and positive changes will follow in their train. Don't be distracted from your course. This is the right direction to take. An auspicious time.

Nine in the second place
People in positions of responsibility and power invite you to contribute. The future is roses. Don't worry about the rises and falls of fortune. Just focus on what is at hand and let the future take care of itself.

Six in the third place
Live up to your responsibilities. The power to make decisions on behalf of others is an act of service, not a testament to sovereignty. The *I Ching* always warns, even in wonderfully auspicious times, against the abuse of power which causes hardship and disturbs the flow of energy. That flow can only be maintained and contained if people in important positions show honesty, strength and energy. Good fortune if you do well what you are employed to do.

Six in the fourth place
Here an individual of great power and influence steps outside his own circle and offers another a position of influence. This is an auspicious act.

Six in the fifth place
A head of a company has to be, among other things, an excellent judge of ability. When recruiting management he must recognize those who are competent and can act without supervision. No company can thrive without people of initiative and self-motivation.

Six in the last place
An individual of proven worth and high reputation may often be invited out of retirement to help in the running of a company or in the reorganization of resources. His experience is so highly valued that he is honoured with special facilities and freedom of action. The company has done well to appoint such a person and should learn carefully from everything he does.

HEXAGRAM 20

A Panoramic View
(Planning/Projecting)

─────────── JUDGEMENT ───────────

Careful and serious contemplation brings great good fortune.

─────────── SPECIFIC MODALITY ───────────

Taking in the whole picture, understanding. Clarifying key
reference points. Making short-, medium- and long-term plans.
Thinking through and coordinating ideas. Comprehending relationships and forces. Getting one's bearings. Simplification is the
test of comprehension.

─────────── AMBIENCE ───────────

Quietness.

─────────── CONCEPT MODEL ───────────

Use your present point of elevation to note patterns, tendencies and
trends in the market place. This is a time to take stock of the
surrounding view. Assimilate the meaning of what you see, then take
practical action. The hexagram underlines the importance of contemplation in quietness – concentration, in other words. The
purpose of the exercise is to plan your strategy at all levels – short,
medium and long term, personal and business. Dovetail the latter
two in order to fulfil the needs of both you and the company. The act
should be one of imagination and projection. Avoid pressing concerns and any distraction, perhaps go away for a while to help
objectivity.

    The time for planning is always a crucial one, as events take form
and shape. Choose perspectives and courses of action, evaluate
objectives, prevailing forces and conditions with care and precision.
The decision, so long as the questions asked in reaching it are

framed with precision, should be obvious – a matter of crystal-clear logic.

This is what is meant in the *I Ching* by the often-reiterated statement that, if the beginnings are correct, all that follows should also be correct. Thus we should not underestimate the importance of planning in fine detail.

People with an aptitude for understanding spatial reality are best qualified as planners because they see things in more than three dimensions, produce an act of synthesis and bring a team of specialists together. A planner must have a marked creative ability – all creativity requires a synthesis of impressions, abstract ideas, and expression in form – application. This practice of synthesis cannot be taught, but it can be learned.

────────── DECISION-BASE ASSUMPTIONS ──────────

The following values are given subject to the information given in the Changes. Remember, the Changes take precedence.

Getting the Best out of People
Consult them in detail. Do not implement any ideas until you have done so.

Belief
You have to understand your actions but you also need to believe in them. This is not doubted, however.

Communications
The plan itself must be representative of exemplary values.

Growth and Productivity
Mid- and long-term prospects are excellent.

Risks
Where is the risk? No action at this time. Evaluate options and make plans.

Investment
Definitely.

Start-Up
Consider all the foregoing. Auspicious beginning indeed. Conserve your energies. The next 6 months will test you.

Feedback
This is the second imperative of planning but prepare well before involving colleagues.

Information Intelligence/Availability
Comprehensive and complete.

Creative Judgement
Excellent but compare notes with colleagues.

Intuition
Excellent but confine yourself to planning only at this stage.

Inspiration
Others can be guided by it. Write it all down.

Advertising
It will pay off if you persist and carry through the project.

Marketing
You understand it well. Auspicious.

Backing
Seek it.

Contracts and Agreements
Your own appraisal is sound enough to act upon.

International Trade
Very auspicious. (See also Hexagrams 40: Deliverance, 60: Limitation and 56: The Traveller.)

Sources of Misfortune
Failure to recognize a pattern in the scheme of things. Ignoring navigational landmarks. Forgetfulness. Lack of attention to detail. Procrastination. Failure to follow-through.

Sources of Good Fortune
This is an auspicious time to make a careful note of long-term trends. Make your plans accordingly though, of course, they will need to be flexible.

─────────── THE LINES (CHANGES) ───────────
the Future-Links

Six at the beginning
Your understanding does not go deep enough. You must not act upon superficial assumptions. Think about it again. Take the whole scenario first, then the meaning of particular instances can be grasped more fully.

So long as those in responsibility understand the situation, there is no failure. Therefore, you must take better advantage of the available aids to understanding.

Six in the second place
You are not being sufficiently *objective*. Your view is egocentric and personal. Adopt an objective stance and take a broader view.

Six in the third place
Be self-aware. Consider your actions to establish whether what you have done is useful and effective or merely egocentric. Be objective about this by evaluating the benefit or lack of benefit commensurate with resources and action. Is there an equation?

Six in the fourth place
The man who knows what to do to make events prosper and work, has arrived. Such people are rare. This is how he should be treated: he must be given the full support of the organization and freedom and resources to act, not as an employee but as a friend of the enterprise. His independence should be preserved at all costs so that he can do what is necessary where most needed. The result will be a flowering for all concerned.

Nine in the fifth place
Only you can know whether you have really done the right thing or not. It is imperative that you act correctly if others depend on you, in these circumstances, to act with their interests at heart. Understanding requires a rigorous act of self-scrutiny.

Nine in the last place
You already know from your state of inner freedom that everything is exactly as it should be.

HEXAGRAM 21

Being Decisive

─────────── JUDGEMENT ───────────

Legal action. Favourable, but establish the relevant facts and act quickly.

─────────── SPECIFIC MODALITY ───────────

Criminal offences. One must act to overcome impediments to justice. If people are in the wrong, do not let the matter pass without action. Keep careful records. Make the truth public.

─────────── AMBIENCE ───────────

Tension. Avoid negative influences and conflict.

─────────── CONCEPT MODEL ───────────

Although the hexagram concerns itself with a situation in which a particular criminal offence may have been committed, it also provides a framework for an attitude, i.e., that in important matters such as a criminal offence, redress does not come about of its own accord. Definite and strategic plans must be made to bring the matter to a state of clarity. If the case is closed, the position is favourable.

─────────── DECISION-BASE ASSUMPTIONS ───────────

The following values are given subject to the information given in the Changes. Remember, the Changes take precedence.

Objectives
To establish the facts even in the face of deliberate concealment and to bring the matter before the appropriate authorities to be decided immediately. Action and perseverance is required.

Communications
Treat them with a healthy scepticism. Question everything which

is not self-evidently true. Trust your intuition as well as your reason.

Risks
Ill-advised. Clarify procedures. Do they help to establish the truth of the matter?

Timing
Act now.

Feedback
Reply to all communications promptly, but keep records. Instigate communication and feedback if none is forthcoming voluntarily. Be deliberately active in this regard. Keep an independent mind.

Information Intelligence/Availability
Collate all information on the matter in hand and put it into a clear order so that it can be understood.

Intuition
False rumours are obscuring the facts. People are telling deliberate and possibly calculated lies in order to engender a state of confusion. The appropriate response is to be increasingly clear about your own position – repetitively, if necessary. This is crucial.

Attitude
Be firm and decisive. A wishy-washy attitude will cause delays which will work against you.

Contracts and Agreements
Ill-advised. Treat legal matters with care while keeping to the spirit of agreements.

Sources of Misfortune
Allowing matters to get out of hand through delays in communication and inaccurate paperwork. Not probing deeply enough.

Sources of Good Fortune
Having matters quickly adjudicated by the proper authorities. Full cooperation with the proper authorities who must serve the truth and provide accurate, up to date information.

─────────────── **THE LINES (CHANGES)** ───────────────
the Future-Links

Nine at the beginning
A first offence should have an immediate but lenient punishment.

Six in the second place
Punishment, though deserved by an individual who repeatedly derides a just law, should never be administered in anger or in revenge.

Six in the third place
Deep feelings of antagonism are directed at an individual who is considered by the offender to lack the required authority to administer a punishment upon him. This may be true. But what can be done about it?

Nine in the fourth place
A difficult judgement is, in the end, made successfully.

Six in the fifth place
It is always preferable to be lenient in making judgements which carry penalties which bring hardship to the offender (*punishment is not, and must never be, allowed to deteriorate into revenge* or the effect is that, in their hearts, people lose faith and respect in the judicial process). The punishment, however, if it is deemed necessary, must at least have the merit of being effective so that the offender understands the implications of his action and will not repeat it in the future.

Nine in the last place
Some offenders have no intention whatsoever of changing their ways in the face of *just* laws; such offenders bring disgrace upon themselves and threaten to bring the law into contempt. Such people require special reform and instruction. Provision should be made to deal positively with people of stubborn and monumental ignorance.

HEXAGRAM 22

Grace

———————— JUDGEMENT ————————

Supreme success. Creative judgement, artistic expression. The position is auspicious. (See also Hexagram 50: The Cauldron.)

———————— SPECIFIC MODALITY ————————

Illustrating ideas; illuminating thoughts; explaining things and rendering them into shape and form. Dealings with cultural artefacts and culturally-oriented services. Auspicious.

———————— AMBIENCE ————————

Pleasant and very bright. Highly auspicious.

———————— CONCEPT MODEL ————————

We are concerned here with art, symmetry, outward manifestation of inner realities, the creation of 'the beautiful', the truthful marriage of idea and form. See the Concept Model of Hexagram 2: The Receptive, for an explanation of the relationship of the Creative and the Receptive in the scheme of things.

———————— DECISION-BASE ASSUMPTIONS ————————

The following values are given subject to the information given in the Changes. Remember, the Changes take precedence.

Management
Concentrate on making the working environment more pleasant and harmonious. Products and services maintain high standard of quality and originality.

Planning
Present ideas, but make no important decisions on the basis of communication.

Communications
You can illuminate and illustrate ideas so that they are comprehensive to others. If this furthers clarity of understanding in a *descriptive* way, it will be valuable. Only quality is remembered and revered.

Investment and Finance
Cultural products and services favoured. Very auspicious for work of high quality.

Impetus
Direct your energy into developing ideas a step closer to completion. Make and create objects or plans. It matters not what level of creation your work has reached. The impetus is to continue the process and have something tangible to show. Make your ideas communicable to others.

Since it is the value of the *process* which is being emphasized here, you do not have to produce a masterpiece or conceive of a *magnum opus*.

Start-Up
The position is not yet strong enough. More groundwork is required.

Product Choice
Some good ideas will be presented. Note them carefully as they may well start something. If Hexagram 17 figures in your considerations with regard to product choice, you could be on to something highly profitable.

Creative Judgement
Very strong. Very auspicious. Supreme good fortune.

Advertising
Good ideas. Choose the unusual and original.

Marketing
Lead with the presentation of the products themselves, not descriptions of them.

Backing
Do not expect agreements at this stage but they will come.

Sources of Misfortune
Presenting ideas which confuse rather than illuminate.

Sources of Good Fortune
The more beautiful, the more colourful, the more eye-catching your ideas, the more successful they will be.

THE LINES (CHANGES)
the Future-Links

Nine at the beginning
Decline offers which give a false impression of your work. Be self-reliant and avoid pretentiousness in all its guises.

Six in the second place
What is a book if it has no words? What is a form if it has no content? What is appearance if it has no reality? It is vanity.

Nine in the third place
If a human being is constantly preoccupied with trivial pursuits his life loses form and purpose, momentum and meaning. Certain ideas can hold an individual together and these must not be degraded at the expense of a bubbly exterior.

Six in the fourth place
'The winged horse is the symbol of the thoughts which transcend all limits of space and time.' This is the great visitor who comes to choose between reality and illusion. Your real friend is waiting in the wings.

Six in the fifth place
The truly wise are never far away. When we have become satiated with the trivial we seek them in sincerity. People *need* to know that the deeper side of life is real, especially when they feel a certain regret about the way they have been living.

Nine in the last place
When inner equals outer, beauty and meaning are attained. The outer form of something *illustrates* what is within. This is the very best art.

HEXAGRAM 23

Separation

—————————— JUDGEMENT ——————————

If you suffer in silence, good fortune. If not, misfortune. (See also
Hexagram 49: Revolution.)

—————————— SPECIFIC MODALITY ——————————

Those in positions of strength and wealth must give to the poor and
weak or everything will become top-heavy and crumble, taking them
down with the house. (See also Hexagrams 41: Decrease and 42:
Increase.)

—————————— AMBIENCE ——————————

Shadow undermines light.

—————————— CONCEPT MODEL ——————————

An imbalance. A top-heavy situation. Although it is passing it is
difficult to retain *personal* calm at such times. A conscious effort has
to be made to control outbursts. Relations between management and
staff could be strained. There might be reshuffles, leave-takings.
Resources must be relocated and redirected. The current situation
cannot be sustained – something will cave in.

—————————— DECISION-BASE ASSUMPTIONS ——————————

The following values are given subject to the information given in the
Changes. Remember, the Changes take precedence.

Management and Leadership
Severe breakdown and misfortune if resources are not spread evenly
throughout the whole structure of the enterprise.

Planning
All *fundamental* assumptions need to be reviewed immediately.

Communications
Poor, must be improved. What are the real issues? Where is the common ground of concern?

Growth and Productivity
Zero, unless conditional on decision-base assumptions.

Risks
Can you afford *not* to take a risk?

Investors
There will be a return on an investment if the object is a going concern; this is not determinable exclusively by track record.

Banks
Misfortune if adequate resources are not brought to bear immediately. Companies going under at this time do so not as the result of mismanagement but because of a natural period of decline. They must be kept afloat or the loss will affect your fortunes directly, perhaps critically. This applies across the board.

Loss
Potentially critical.

Gain
If you act now, medium and long-term prospects can be excellent. Take the long view and have faith in it.

Feedback
Must be substantially improved.

Information Intelligence/Availability
Needs to be brought into a condition of comprehensibility. More information is a necessary precondition to long-term plans and solutions.

Attitude
Use no force. You cannot *oppose* a natural force but you can ameliorate its potentially disastrous effects. Take note of all the advice given in this hexagram.

Input
Vital.

Symbiosis
Critically poor.

Cooperation
Critically poor. See *Communication*.

Sources of Good Fortune and Misfortune
These can be readily inferred from the above, but to summarize: you need more up-to-date conceptual tools. You need to refine your terms of reference.

THE LINES (CHANGES)
the Future-Links

Six at the beginning
The position is being *deliberately* undermined by individuals whose intentions are far from good. Loyalties are wrongly questioned. Intrigue is at work in unseen places.

Six in the second place
Malevolent forces are close by. Use your intuition to detect their presence. Avoid them. Be careful with whom you communicate. If in doubt don't communicate at all.

Six in the third place
Remain loyal to the individual who you know to be in the right. In so doing, you too become prey to the malevolent force. But the decision is right.

Six in the fourth place
The malevolent force has broken through. The effect cannot be any longer avoided. Even caution may not help here.

Six in the fifth place
When a malevolent force grows close to its opposite its nature is modified, mollified, even transformed. By its willing submission to a 'force of light' the position becomes more favourable, less dangerous.

Nine in the last place
A period of misfortune cannot continue indefinitely. It must eventually run out of steam. When this happens a general transition occurs and events begin to show an upswing. Part of the natural cycle of change ensures, however, that individuals (as described in the first line) have placed themselves, through their actions, in a position of great vulnerability. Those who take advantage of the shadows in order to cause chaos are now exposed in the light as the ascending force of light is restored. This is why the hexagram speaks not of using force but of waiting.

HEXAGRAM 24

The Return
(The Turning Point or Transition)

——————————— JUDGEMENT ———————————

Success through being carried forward by the time. Natural transition of dark to light. Gradual easing of tensions. Definite progress. The beginning of a new cycle or phase of work. Good fortune.

——————————— SPECIFIC MODALITY ———————————

Carrying on with business in the normal way. Patience. Force no changes. Renewal.

——————————— AMBIENCE ———————————

No extra effort required. A sense of ease and relief.

——————————— CONCEPT MODEL ———————————

The natural cycle has its own momentum. Even after a period of uncertainty characterized by toughness, slow progress and lack of cooperation, there is a change of atmosphere. Matters will improve of their own accord, without any special effort on your part. (There are other hexagrams which deal with situations in which a special effort has to be made in order to take advantage of the time, such as Hexagram 11: Peace.) This means that you will achieve more mileage than before by doing a normal day's work. A natural momentum takes over. Simple routine activity will enable you to achieve success. People will be more responsive to communications, more willing to cooperate. Tensions will ease and the atmosphere will grow lighter.

It is important, therefore, not to interfere with this process by trying to anticipate the trend, even though being mentally prepared for new opportunities can do no harm. Business and social life can blend well during these times.

—————————— DECISION-BASE ASSUMPTIONS ——————————

The following values are given subject to the information given in the Changes. Remember, the Changes take precedence.

Management
It is not wise, after a period of slowness or difficulty or new situation, to rush ahead and compel people to pull out all the stops. Treat the situation like a new car that needs several miles on the clock before you can put it through its paces without ruining the pistons and blowing the gaskets.

Planning
The plan will unfold. Avoid the temptation to extrapolate too much.

Investment and Finance
The indications are good. You can act with some caution for a medium-term return. Wild speculation is not recommended.

Feedback
Positive, but subtle. Diplomacy of the megaphone variety is not called for. It should be personal, well-mannered, socially relaxed and civilized.

Information Intelligence/Availability
Be especially receptive. Read around the subject. Use the time to get to know the lie of the land and the nature of the business.

Creative Ideas
Let the newly installed ideas find their range before throwing your weight into them.

Advertising
Employ only very moderate expenditure.

Marketing
Avoid being too exploratory. Wait until the road opens out a little.

Symbiosis
Go through the tuning routine, testing that all the connections are working.

Sources of Misfortune
Violent use of the accelerator before the machine is balanced.

Sources of Good Fortune
Gentleness. There is no rush.

THE LINES (CHANGES)
the Future-Links

Nine at the beginning
No right turn. No left turn. Some curiosity can be tolerated but the course lies straight ahead.

Six in the second place
First you have to make a conscious decision that you want matters to improve. Old habits die hard but, with a little help from your friends, you can do it.

Six in the third place
You know the difference between the right and the wrong path. While travelling along the right path you forget yourself and stray onto the wrong path. The problem is not serious or out of control, however, and it is still possible to make your decisions stick or, rather, make yourself stick to them.

Six in the fourth place
You are travelling down the wrong road with the wrong people. You overcome their alluring influence and depart to where your friend, who is travelling on the right road, is calling. But it is a choice you have to make and act upon.

Six in the fifth place
You change course with a powerful resolve. This is excellent and is well met.

Six in the last place
Misfortune due to clinging to false ideas. If you do not grasp the opportunity for self-correction or self-realignment the implicit logic of a faulty perception shows itself in everything you do and you find yourself hitting obstacle after obstacle (See Hexagrams 7, 13, 14, 18 and 22.)

HEXAGRAM 25

Innocence (The Unexpected)

JUDGEMENT

Acting naturally (in an unpremeditated way) brings supreme success. Misfortune if you entertain doubts, plot or calculate effects. Spontaneous progress. Natural ability is at work here.

SPECIFIC MODALITY

Any action with others. High culture. A naturally caring attitude, of wide benefit to others. The individual is sincere and without guile. Supreme success.

AMBIENCE

The mind is true, the communication innocent and trustworthy. Trust is right.

CONCEPT MODEL

The hexagram is called 'Innocence' because natural, spontaneous action which is not tainted by material designs brings good fortune and communicates to others who can trust it. Acting from any other source brings misfortune. This is emphasized here because it is important to establish the sources of motivation in others of whom you might be suspicious, in order to decide whether to do business with them.

The lines will give particulars if they are germane to your question, but the sources of untainted intentions – innocence – are in the roots of man's view of himself in the world – and they can no longer be ignored. The resolution of these issues will redefine business and the conduct required of it, either as an out-and-out free for all or as something about which individuals require a more connected and responsible view. (See Hexagram 23: Separation.)

Innocence which comes from a lifetime of experience, as distinct from the untarnished innocence of a newborn baby, manifests as wisdom. No wise person who has been busy in the affairs of life is without innocence. This is why the *I Ching* speaks of acting *blamelessly*.

─────────── DECISION-BASE ASSUMPTIONS ───────────

Management
Act from the heart, not merely for profit.

Planning
Good intentions will find support and will succeed. Immediate, medium- and long-term results are likely to be consistently good if this is the beginning of relations. Good fortune.

Communications
If they are honest they will resonate beyond your field of action and touch other facets of life. If they are dishonest they will have a 'local' effect. This idea has vast implications.

Work and Productivity
A natural aptitude is present, as if people and resources go hand in glove. Individuals are born to their work. They do not have to intrigue or plot for results, they can generate results by doing what they do best – it comes naturally. Productivity is good. Auspicious.

Risks
Do you believe in the ideas? Do you believe that the intentions of the representatives of those ideas are good? If you do there is no risk. If not it is an unwarranted risk.

Start-Up
There may be a feeling of indecision. Your suspicions may be the result of overcaution. This is either the real thing or it is an imitation.

Investment/Finance
If the project is worthwhile then the investment is sound.

Feedback
It is either deceitful or it is the truth. If it is the truth then back it with your full support. If not then offer no support.

Marketing
Artificial efforts are not required.

Creative Judgement
Excellent. Trust it.

Contracts and Agreements
If you have the initiative, be prudent but fair.

Intuition
First impressions are likely to be the most reliable. Remember them later when doubts creep in.

Attitude
However ambiguous your feelings indications are positive. In any event act with confidence – this may mean giving the benefit of the doubt.

Advertising
If the products or services provide no real benefit they will fail to attract a market.

Backing
Auspicious.

Sources of Misfortune
Secret designs calculated to secure essentially private advantage.

Sources of Good Fortune
If ideas come naturally but are inspired by a positive attitude towards others.

——————— THE LINES (CHANGES) ———————
the Future-Links

Nine at the beginning
Follow your heart. It will work out. Good fortune and achievement.

Six in the second place
Don't preoccupy yourself with personal results. Just do it anyway, otherwise you will waste energy. Success if you do it well.

Six in the third place
Avoid heedless negligence as there are those who will take advantage of it, for private gain.

Nine in the fourth place
Don't listen to gossip. Don't worry. Just retain your integrity even when others are throwing theirs away.

Nine in the fifth place
Let it be. The situation will resolve itself naturally if you haven't interfered or aggravated it.

Nine in the last place
Success if you wait and meditate. Don't plot and scheme. Don't act at this time.

HEXAGRAM 26

The Taming Power of the Great

JUDGEMENT

Good fortune because the situation is contained for your own good. Everything is under control. Strong organization. The system is maintained and prevents costly disorders.

SPECIFIC MODALITY

Controlling the energy build-up so that it can be used in the application of wise ideas.

AMBIENCE

Momentum to achieve; action. (See Hexagram 60: Limitation.)

CONCEPT MODEL

This is the hexagram of the businessman who has mastered the art of getting the most out of his energy. Two central ideas are involved; the first is that of self-control, both over oneself and over situations (an influence able to *contain* potentially disordered situations or people); and the second is keeping oneself fresh for work each day – this concerns the ability to alternate relaxation with concentration. Keeping oneself fresh on a daily basis is the opposite of maintaining the stamina to work long hours for weeks on end and then collapsing at the end. The hexagram focuses on keeping this balance of energies in good condition so that one can be consistently effective.

DECISION-BASE ASSUMPTIONS

The following values are given subject to the information given in the Changes. Remember, the Changes take precedence.

Management
The indications are positive. Difficult situations or people can be directed. You can win the loyalty of staff and management

effortlessly, by being yourself. There is no reason why you should not be able to steer a steady course, either by a deliberate application of policy or as a matter of routine. This is an unexceptional time, but the backbone of the job is held together so that challenges can be faced and achievements are possible. Without this element present in a company nothing works, as the slightest disturbance threatens the momentum and direction of the whole enterprise. There is no fear of that here, providing you stay personally fresh and energy is maintained at a high level of response. This is a matter of renewing yourself on a daily basis.

Objectives
They will be realized in time through continuity of effort.

Planning
Long-term objectives are well favoured and likely to succeed. You can see causes better than effects. Due to matters beyond your control you are spared much time and resource wastage.

Communications
Clear and precise. Avoid pointless quarrelling.

Growth and Productivity
It is earned by painstaking work. Do not expect rapid short-term gains. Look to long term effects.

Investment and Finance
You have credibility despite the odds.

Cash Flow and Budget
Carefully fixed and controlled. There are reasonable margins. Concentrate on the strictly useful.

Start-Up
You are prepared, or you will be. Don't rush.

Feedback
Restrained, but generally positive.

Creative Judgement
Fairly good, but vision is limited. Do not be too quick to pronounce judgements on the often wider vision of others.

Creative Input
Cultivate and use valuable ideas. This brings good fortune. These ideas have their origin in ancient wisdom and it is well for you to revisit them from time to time in order to reinforce their meanings and to learn their details. The secrets of your success in influencing

and guiding others reside in this propensity, so making these ideas increasingly conscious will be significant.

Organization
Its firmness and clarity is your biggest asset.

Symbiosis
Good, despite other tendencies. Attempts to expand will be frustrated.

Advertising
Average. Not vital now. It is more important to work on quality not on projecting an image.

Marketing
A no-risk situation. Sufficient. You have the energy to do more. Go further afield. It is better that actions are restricted at present.

Backing
A plausible possibility. You will have to work for it.

Contracts and Agreements
The terms of reference at least are very clear. Logistics? Acceptability?

Sources of Misfortune
An erratic lifestyle.

Sources of Good Fortune
Maintaining consistent effort – largely a matter of personality.

──────────── THE LINES (CHANGES) ────────────
the Future-Links

Nine at the beginning
The time isn't right to push ahead. The restraining force is superior. Don't waste your energy. Wait.

Nine in the second place
You know you can't make an impression on the situation so you don't even try. Good fortune resides in patience.

Nine in the third place
The time for *cautious* advance has come. Make sure that your objectives are crystal clear so that you can keep moving in the right direction while keeping your eyes on the sidelines. Follow accepted procedures and protocol.

One cannot lessen the magnitude of great personal energy, but one can set conditions which channel that power into a form of leadership rather than destruction. If this is done early on the results will be brilliant indeed!

Six in the fifth place
Control over the situation is achieved in the neatest way. Direct confrontation is avoided by setting up a situation in which freedom of movement is restrained so that the wild force is contained. Even better, make the calm felt at source rather than contain freneticism from the outside.

Nine in the last place
Now you can act and achieve great things; there's nothing stopping you, the benefits reach out.

HEXAGRAM 27

Nourishment (Health)

---------------------- JUDGEMENT ----------------------

If you look after your health, good fortune. You are narrowing your perspective too much. Adopt a more widely sympathetic outlook.

---------------------- SPECIFIC MODALITY ----------------------

Nourishing others and nourishing yourself. Show a wider range of interests. A higher degree of positive response is called for. Take up the slack. Use your creative potential for change.

---------------------- AMBIENCE ----------------------

Maintaining an even balance between action and rest. Developing the operational practices to cater for wider possibilities.

---------------------- CONCEPT MODEL ----------------------

For those involved in the energy industries which lie at the heart of the economy: food, oil, gas, electricity, coal, solar and nuclear power, the emphasis is on quality, balance, the right resources in the right place at the right time, and the maintenance of a steady flow. If the quality of energy is poor, the machine runs down. High quality food is a prerequisite if people are to be able to function at their best. The human body is just as much a machine needing correct fuel as does a mechanical plant or car engine.

The concept of nourishment extends into the area of cultural pursuits. Intellectual and emotional needs must also be met. All this contributes towards general wellbeing and efficiency and makes the most out of available – and often non-renewable – resources.

---------------------- DECISION-BASE ASSUMPTIONS ----------------------

The following values are given subject to the information given in the Changes. Remember, the Changes take precedence.

Management
Requirement: deal with fundamental needs of staff. Look to the adequacy and quality of food in every sense. You may need to take up the slack. The effect of dealing correctly with energy fundamentals resonates throughout the whole company.

Company Image
Brighten colours internally (self-image) and give products a new look (public image). Even solidly established names in the market place need reviving. The old approach has the benefit of being comforting and consistent but, in the long run, it is oppressive and unexciting.

Communications
Uninspired. Too many platitudes.

Growth and Productivity
Potential as yet unrealized. Scan for possible improvements. Start with the grass roots. Stretch yourself more. Upgrade the present system in line with needs and demands.

Backing
Try for it. Test your faith.

Risks
What you consider to be a risk may be another company's norm. Show a little flair and imagination. The safe option is not necessarily the correct or most desirable one. Take chances on the new even if they, at first, appear radical and uncertain. Success.

Investment and Finance
You are not making the most of existing resources. You are losing when you should be winning.

Input
A fresh inflow of ideas is needed to energize and revitalize existing organizational functions. The object of the exercise is to refresh the organization. Be more flexible. You are editing out too many options and possibilities, and this is detrimental.

Feedback
Improve. Too self-centred and egotistical. You are not listening or remembering good ideas.

Education
Expand terms of reference. Provide more scope for this in the company. It is a hidden asset without which no organization can hope

to thrive. A greater interest must be taken in wider knowledge – people are not automatons.

Creative Judgement
Must be improved. Be more imaginative. Use your gifts to greater effect. Be more open-minded and receptive to alternative viewpoints.

Natural Balance
Too much nourishment clogs the works, too little reduces energy output. Too much rest causes the machine to retard. Too little causes it to overheat. It is in your interest to find a balance. If this is difficult, it may be advisable to bring in an outside consultant with the specific objective of finding a company's internal balance (a tuning job). (See Hexagram 16: Enthusiasm.)

Advertising
Perhaps the existing strategy is a little uninspired. Give the picture more zest and verve. Methods are too sluggish. Revitalize.

Marketing
If it is worth doing, it is worth doing thoroughly.

Contracts and Agreements
The subject of the agreement may be questionable. There may be moral considerations. Do not cheat the people; rather give them what they need.

International Trade
Be more flexible and far-sighted. There are a number of openings to be investigated.

Sources of Misfortune
Indigestion or under-nourishment.

Sources of Good Fortune
Balance across the board. Increase and enhance scope. Make the meeting of basic needs a priority.

THE LINES (CHANGES)
the Future-Links

Nine at the beginning
You could do better than waste energy envying the good fortune of others. Activate. Create. Assist. Do.

Six in the second place
Don't expect handouts as a let-out from doing your own work. Be self-reliant. Deserve good fortune.

Six in the third place
The wrong kind of nourishment can wear you down over a period of time. It is best to leave it out of the diet altogether as it could become a bad habit.

Six in the fourth place
Unlike the second line, the impetus to get outside support with regard to money and resources has a completely different objective. The individual has good objectives in mind but has not the means to achieve them alone. Thus his search for support may be intense but is not blameworthy because he intends to benefit others – provide jobs, resources, release new ideas and so on.

Six in the fifth place
Seek advice as to how to proceed but make sure that you ask people whom you look up to. Desist from being too ambitious in your objectives.

Nine in the last place
The position is highly auspicious for an individual of great ability and character sets out to achieve difficult things in order to benefit others. Such benefit reaches far and wide and brings with it a good deal of happiness. Supreme good fortune.

HEXAGRAM 28

Preponderance of the Great

———————— JUDGEMENT ————————

Good fortune if you change the balance of forces.

———————— SPECIFIC MODALITY ————————

Too much pressure in the wrong place. Obsession. Frustration.

———————— AMBIENCE ————————

The situation cannot persist for long; inner tensions.

———————— CONCEPT MODEL ————————

Changes are needed immediately but sweeping changes are impossible. The organization is neither top nor bottom heavy; the weight is concentrated in the middle. People and resources are trapped. This may be expressed in emotional terms as frustration brought about by an obsession (inappropriate concentration of strength in one place). When such force is concentrated in the *middle*, the situation is dangerous. Shift the load immediately. Mentally, this can be expressed as *letting go*. Total relaxation, however, is not possible because the forces keeping the load in place are equal. Deliberately drain off some of the energy – focus it elsewhere. What you do is not radical but, nevertheless, it creates a complete transition which can be realized as an increased state of freedom and enlarged possibilities.

Furthermore, it is important not to dramatize the situation out of proportion as this will only increase tension and make effective action more difficult than it already is; but underestimating the situation is just as dangerous. Unlike Hexagram 23: Separation the pressure of the situation is not part of an evolving natural force which will change by itself. Here, deliberate action is necessary and waiting is out of the question. But, difficult though the predicament is, it is not insoluble.

───────── DECISION-BASE ASSUMPTIONS ─────────

The following values are given subject to the information given in the Changes. Remember, the Changes take precedence.

Management

Overcome, as a concerted effort, the present crisis. Be prepared to change methodology, assumptions, even the quality of objectives. To not allow the fears of others to impose or influence your feelings or your judgement.

Communications

There is much static. Confusion. You will eventually impose a close order, have no fear.

Risks

This is a risk situation and a risk may well be required to bring the matter under control. There are no really safe options available just now. Take courage.

Investment

You could be in trouble. You might lose it.

Timing

You must act immediately. Might not be soon enough.

Start-Up

Take full precautions. Make sure not only that you have all the necessary facts but that the conditions and environment are appropriate. The tools must fit the job. Better still, leave it for now.

Feedback

From the suitably qualified this is valuable, even necessary. You may need to be rescued.

Information Intelligence/Availability

No extra information is required at this juncture. Act on what you have or on what is easily available. No time for research.

Creative Judgement

The problem is not without a solution. The best answers will be intuitive, spontaneous, will flow naturally from need.

Integration

Out of synchronization. This pictures an uncomfortable state of affairs – but one which is rapidly changing.

Advertising
Too many resources committed in one area of operation. Better to conserve energy at source.

Marketing
The focus is unbalanced and too narrow. The bottom might fall out of the market. Might be too late to do anything about it.

Backing
You need support. You can succeed without it but only with considerable difficulty.

Contracts and Agreements
Successful, once you know what you want. That time has not arrived, however. The position is not yet settled.

International Trade
If appropriate – the matter needs your immediate attention. Things are not going as planned.

Sources of Misfortune
Lazy adherence to old values in a time of pressure.

Sources of Good Fortune
The implementation of the highest values will bring a successful outcome. Anything less, particularly now, will be generally disastrous.

—————————— THE LINES (CHANGES) ——————————
the Future-Links

Six at the beginning
Lay your foundations with extreme care, overlooking nothing. Careful planning and testing is vital if you are not going to fall at the first hurdle.

Nine in the second place
Well-developed organizations would do well to form allies wth small organizations as the two can complement each other and bring unexpected growth. Good fortune.

Nine in the third place
Willingly accept the right help when it is offered. An attitude of 'I can do it all my way' will end in disaster.

Nine in the fourth place
A more powerful organization can indeed take advantage of its superiority over a smaller ally, but the backlash will be damaging for the larger. The larger organization's function is to *protect* and *nurture* the smaller organiza-

tion, not try to run it into the ground. A David and Goliath situation might result and that could be very humiliating. Act with calm maturity.

Nine in the fifth place

Large organizations which are only prepared to merge with other large organizations at the expense of developing allegiances with smaller, more creative organizations, develop conditions for stagnation. The situation might appear to be stronger because there is an increase in scale but, if the increase does not correspond to quality or does not admit of fresh ideas, the organization becomes ponderous and inadaptable. The unwieldiness of the situation can bring about the downfall of both companies. The impetus to such mergers is to 'grow big' and therefore (as the reasoning goes) survive more easily in a hostile market. It is a *non sequitur*. (See Hexagrams 13: Fellowship with Men, 14: Possession in Great Measure and 20: A Panoramic View.) Such mergers masquerade as 'good business decisions' but their roots are in panic. Misfortune.

Six in the last place

Sometimes, even when the heart is willing, there is no way. The conditions do not admit of any possibility of success. There is only one thing you can do; graciously submit and let the matter go, even if this means death of the venture altogether. Such a death may create room for something new. Good fortune.

HEXAGRAM 29

The Deep Waters

JUDGEMENT

If you feel successful you can be successful at anything; take calculated risks, believe in your own ability; be committed to seeing projects through. Competence. Extremely fertile possibilities.

SPECIFIC MODALITY

Taking the plunge, not procrastinating. Success even in difficult or dangerous projects. Be self-reliant. Perspicacity. Take risks. Life has everything to offer for you if you are prepared to step beyond precedents and be something of a pioneer.

AMBIENCE

Tricky, even dangerous waters. In truth, wouldn't have it any other way. Auspicious.

CONCEPT MODEL

In itself the organization is self-contained and versatile, but the waters it has to negotiate are difficult in an objective sense. It is a question of attitude. Do not delay commitments, actions and so on, but take the plunge and get involved. You are particularly suited to handling difficult situations which might easily swamp others. This is what is meant by being self-contained in an objectively difficult environment. But you have to feel confident that you are able to cope. Overcome self-doubt so that you can show your prowess in the field.

Keen powers of observation are also required. Understanding a field of action involves looking at it (with a view in this case to direct participation) for a sufficient period of time so that you know your objectives and how to achieve them. In this way, you do not underestimate the challenges but neither do you underestimate yourself. But because of your nature even an intractable situation cannot hurt you, in the same way that water plunging into water cannot hurt the water. This is what is meant when the *I Ching* says that you are well suited to these challenges and there is no reason to fear. It is the manner of *action* which is all-important.

Control over yourself brings control over your environment. This has to be well done. Therefore, a clear strategy is important and sense of the completed work. If you do not have this understanding you cannot complete it, there will always be a detail which will make the whole vulnerable. Completing work must receive your special attention and you are urged to list this as a main priority. This will lead to the development of a sound reputation in your field. Take a risk on the new. Do not hesitate.

—————— DECISION-BASE ASSUMPTIONS ——————

The following values are given subject to the information given in the Changes. Remember, the Changes take precedence.

Management

Get used to working in difficult and hostile situations so that they become normal for you, but never forget that the situation is really abnormal – act with sufficient concentration and dedication to objectives.

Identify the specialists in the team and let them handle the work in their own way. You must assume that they know best. Trust them. Attend to planning and *coordination* and keep well abreast of developments outside your own working environment. Make sure that replies are understood correctly. There is little room for error. Great aptitude for leadership is suggested.

Planning

Even so-called chance events, especially if they have a favourable outcome, arise through consciously doing what you know to be morally right. Get the inner machine working in harmony and the world will take care of the rest.

Communications

The capacity is excellent. Be imaginative, original, have confidence in your flair and attractiveness. Charisma and charm are strong and figure prominently.

Risks

You will perceive many of your key decisions as 'risks', but bringing them off is more a matter of personal confidence than strategy. A radiation of positive energy can transform danger into a controlled situation.

Investment
Nothing half-hearted is acceptable here. Believe or fail.

Intuition
The intuitive abilities of management and staff will play a large part in the decision-making process. Therefore, everybody in the company must trust everybody else. Success may well depend on anticipating what another member of the company will do; this may be particularly germane to international work, where working alone is a norm. Furthermore, communications between management and staff have to be excellent, so that symbiosis can be achieved.

Sense of Timing
Either very good or very bad. Check all the elements carefully before committing yourself. The time for commitment to particular action will come, though the overall commitment to action has already been made.

Motivation
People in the organization must be trained to work almost automatically. This will mean adequate time for practice. The will to action has to be natural and flowing. The clockwork must be well tuned and refined so that it can be relied upon completely. This is the basis of well-timed decisions. Practice makes perfect when the special talent is innately yours.

Start-Up
In general terms only, be committed. Go all the way, but be adaptable.

Feedback
Don't allow others to misinterpret your instructions, intentions and ideas and, at the same time, take care not to misread those of others.

Symbiosis
Critically important. Getting this right will enable you to provide against the unexpected contingency and to take advantage of auspicious opportunities. Always leave a little space for manoeuvre in your overall strategies. Some degree of delicacy is always appreciated by people in your position.

Advertising
Leave it to the people who are good at it. This may be an outside company. In any event, consider the situation risky. There's a good chance you do not need it.

Marketing
As with advertising, it is probably better to contract it out. If it is your speciality, be prepared to take risks and to be especially innovative in order to succeed. Intuitive improvisation could lead to originality of immense value.

Backing
It must be adequate to see the job through to completion or difficulties could be highly compromising. Don't start it unless you can finish it. Make sure potential backers know that.

Contracts and Agreements
There may be problems of trust between the parties. Do not delegate these matters. The object is to satisfy yourself of the integrity of the dealings. If you are unsatisfied, be prepared to wait for a more favourable time before settling final and binding commitments.

International Trade
Success may come through unexpected channels, through an unusual turn of events – as if by chance. No such thing of course.

Sources of Misfortune
Leaping before you look . . . or probe.

Sources of Good Fortune
A committed attitude and plenty of practice brings confidence to act correctly in dangerous or demanding situations. The natural skill, or propensity for that skill is present in abundance. Just believe in it. Don't worry about not being understood.

————————— **THE LINES (CHANGES)** —————————
the Future-Links

Six at the beginning
Sustain concentration at all costs. Remember, although you may have got used to abnormal conditions and learned to succeed in them they *are* abnormal and therefore capable of delivering unexpected challenges.

Nine in the second place
Sit tight and hold on. Nothing more.

Six in the third place
You won't like it but you have to grin and bear it without taking action to change it. But keep your eyes open for a *real* opportunity; when it appears, providing you are watching, it will be difficult to miss.

Six in the fourth place
Two ideas here. Firstly, be prepared to take the initiative. If you have something to offer, make the first move. But don't dress it up. Be direct but subtle.

Secondly, in communications keep difficult ideas simple so that people can understand them. When the building blocks are in place you can progress upon the assumption that more complex issues are communicable.

Nine in the fifth place
The difficulty resides in an attitude: wanting to do more than you can at the moment. Just hold your own situation together, that should be enough to occupy you full time.

Six in the last place
You have got yourself confused. It will take a while to unravel the knots. This is not a situation you will ever want to repeat. (The secret is to keep practising that which you are good at until your confidence returns to its usual levels.)

HEXAGRAM 30

The Clinging, Fire
(The Heart of the Matter)

—————————— JUDGEMENT ——————————

Looking after your staff, ideas and equipment brings good fortune.
The source of energy must be carefully appraised and understood.
Look also to what *inspires*.

—————————— SPECIFIC MODALITY ——————————

Making your work shine to illuminate others. Using energy
resources to maximum effect, wasting nothing. Auspicious.

—————————— AMBIENCE ——————————

Skilful manipulation and cultivation within clear limits of action.
Competent work.

—————————— CONCEPT MODEL ——————————

A company's brightness and good fortune depends upon its
resources; these may be the constant supply of raw materials in
industry, but they are also its equipment, people (management and
staff and those who work the resources) and its ideas as they are
expressed in the company's operating functions. The essence of the
concept here is understanding what lies at the heart of an organization's existence and prosperity.

The traditional image used in the *I Ching* is that of the flame. The
image is twofold. A flame cannot exist unless it is burning matter, oil
or gas, but it must also have oxygen (the flame's natural environment). Oxygen does not grow bright except through being burned.
Wood, gas, coal and oil do not grow bright except through their
expression as flame. People or companies do not grow bright unless
they feed off something which is at their hearts. In basic terms we can
say that an organization expresses itself through translating latent
forms into a new kind of energy. One form of energy must be in

proper relation to another 'potential' kind of energy – thus coal, gas, oil and so on have the propensity for conversion to fire. The same applies to every other form of energy conversion; the relationships and processes are conditioned by strict laws of nature.

———————— DECISION-BASE ASSUMPTIONS ————————

The following values are given subject to the information given in the Changes. Remember, the Changes take precedence.

Management
Look to the energetic basis of the company's *future* prospects. This may mean hitherto unconsidered or undiscovered sources of energy. These include the broad base of resources, not least people, who should not be strictly regarded as a resource but whose collective energy is nevertheless crucial in every undertaking. Are they being well looked after?

Planning
Make sure that you have energy to complete undertakings for the future. This does not necessarily mean stringent economizing, but it does mean careful calculation and the monitoring process should be reliable. Be especially aware of interdependencies in forecasting. Do not cut away the ground beneath you.

Communications
Good ideas tend to spread very rapidly by word of mouth. This will be a hidden force working in your favour. It is also the means by which you will achieve much. Auspicious.

Investment and Finance
Good prospects, likely to have dealings with other economies. The question of reputation will play a large part in future transactions, but here this is beneficial. The corresponding responsibility is to set a high standard of conduct and the difficulty will be in maintaining influences. This is a matter of planning against the widest possible criteria in the evaluation of market forces. The subject does appear, however, to be able to hold its own by virtue of its uniqueness – an immensely valuable asset.

Timing
The overall pace of work should be maintained and should not be allowed to deteriorate.

Start-Up
Be clear about your objectives at the outset. Get competent advice;

you have yet to find your market, but this is a very auspicious beginning and you should be encouraged.

Feedback
The capacity is for the best possible results, given the circumstances. There is always room for improvement but take care that a premature waste of energy is not brought about by haste and over-ambition.

Creative Judgement
Excellent, but you *must* consult with colleagues and be willing to be led by sound advice if the ideas are to be put into practice with any hope of their 'shining' in the market place.

Growth
Steady, don't slip back on what has already been achieved. See Timing above.

Advertising
Capability to release products far and wide.

Marketing
Be adventurous; if you haven't exhausted your resources in the past, you should be able to achieve unusual results of a positive nature. Auspicious.

Backing
If everything is on paper and well organized proceed with confidence. If no joy at home, seek foreign backers but see that your presentation is good.

Contracts and Agreements
Avoid a sell-out, do not underestimate your worth to others. Agreements ought to be well augmented.

Research and Development
Auspicious for the development of new energy concepts.

International Trade
Prospects are excellent and products and services should be well received if they are well presented. Everything may become visible.

Sources of Misfortune
The chief difficulty is pacing; avoid using up all your resources too quickly. One has to assume that they are finite.

Sources of Good Fortune
Acknowledge your sources of energy for what they are. Do not

attempt to abandon your roots. Be content with maintaining your existing profile. Take care of your operating base and it will take care of you.

THE LINES (CHANGES)
the Future-Links

Nine at the beginning
A key idea is set forth here, the application of which extends far beyond its localized meaning: 'The beginning holds the seed of all that is to follow.' This is true of a project which may take many years to complete and of a life of a person whose early years are well nurtured with care and love. But it is also true of the work of each day. (See Hexagram 26: The Taming Power of the Great which underlines the importance of daily self-renewal.) In busy times it is important to organize at the beginning of work and to clarify the mind. A poor start is hard to rectify. Better to start again rather than to extrapolate from a false start. Start well and the chances are good that it will end well also.

Six in the second place
A brilliant time. Keep it all burning bright. Shine on.

Nine in the third place
A transcendent attitude is set forth. The transience of life is an idea we all personally encounter. There are two common attitudes to this awareness, especially when it comes in times of good fortune (in times of decline the idea of the passing of all things is equally poignant): we can either enjoy it while it lasts or feel sorry for ourselves. Both are extremes. The best way is for each individual to discover for himself the golden mean.

Nine in the fourth place
The expression of energy must be regulated to last the distance. Some people can, in a sudden and majestic burst of energy, rise to fame and fortune, but they don't have the strength to endure. A certain seriousness of purpose has to characterize those who mean to bring a lasting benefit to the world. The light that burns steadily according to its source is greater because it endures. There are many examples of such luminary figures and ideas that live through the ages.

Six in the fifth place
The peak experience can be the platform for a real transformation to a higher cycle of experience. Here you can change your view of the world and understand the phenomena of life afresh. It is hard to be objective about the experience at this level without erring on the side of cynicism or over-excitement. The true flame burns straight and steady.

Nine in the last place
If something keeps going wrong you must look to its source, it's cause. The *I Ching* gives a compelling example: if a group of people are bent on

destroying society and laying its culture to waste, one must look to the leader of that force, the source of power. If the leader is stopped the whole force is stopped.

A second idea, closely allied to the former, also deals with the method by which fundamental or *source* faults are brought under control or eradicated. Having identified the source of 'corruption' or 'disease' it is not necessary to destroy the whole if it can otherwise be saved by pruning. One must do only what is necessary in order to maintain the flame. In a business this might be cutting away a policy, sacking a director or getting rid of useless material. It is not necessary to go to extremes to rectify isolated wrongs or faults.

HEXAGRAM 31

Influence and Natural Attraction

------------------------------ JUDGEMENT ------------------------------

If you are receptive, good fortune. The medium and long-term view may prove your caution unwarranted. There are great possibilities in the seemingly insignificant or bizarre. Take the line of least resistance and all will be well.

------------------------------ SPECIFIC MODALITY ------------------------------

Communication is the key. Be willing to receive the opinions and presentations of others with an open mind. This will be greatly appreciated and may lead to auspicious changes and good fortune. *Understanding* between people is not intellectual, finally. It is a matter of feeling. Every good teacher knows that all communication is a matter of resonance and empathy as well as sympathy.

------------------------------ AMBIENCE ------------------------------

Favourable for friendly relations and for agreements. Set up a congenial and relaxed atmosphere away from the work place if this will help a meeting of minds.

------------------------------ CONCEPT MODEL ------------------------------

Even people and organizations which are, by virtue of their size or strength, in a natural position of advantage have to be receptive to influences from people and organizations which are not so well placed. This is well favoured as there is more than a common objective interest between the parties. They may join together in a spirit which transcends the purely formal attraction of a business agreement. Something warmer and more personal is at work here, but it can only be given any meaning if the stronger of the parties realizes that the initiative lies with him and not with the smaller or weaker. He must, as it were, open the door to communication and show himself receptive and willing to listen to ideas and propositions.

In this way meetings of mutual benefit and potential are made possible. Magnitude of strength, size and power does not necessarily (as here) mean correspondingly greater wisdom or knowledge. It is often the case that people who are not so highly placed have an attraction for those in higher places because they have something valuable to offer. It is therefore in everybody's interest to admit such people in a spirit which is without prejudice. In this way the circumstances accord with the times and good fortune arises.

DECISION-BASE ASSUMPTIONS

The following values are given subject to the information given in the Changes. Remember, the changes take precedence.

Consultation
Make yourself available and receptive to the advice and opinions of others before taking important decisions; if the advice comes from a quarter which does not usually command your attention, be careful to listen to it. This may be the occasion to fly in the face of policy – policies do not necessarily cover every contingency. There should always be the option to place an unusual construction on laws where it is plain that following a precedent creates a manifestly absurd, unjust, even dangerous nonsense out of policy. One must never follow in such cases because precedent demands. If the position is absurd it is because the precedents are not sufficiently well understood.

Feedback
Be especially sensitive.

Communications
There will be no lack of them. They must be considered, however, with care and in an atmosphere of congeniality and relaxation.

Planning
Do not overestimate your strength in every situation. Do not underestimate the opposition. There are missing ingredients to the whole picture and, therefore, intuition is needed as fact finding has its limitations here.

Growth
The potential certainly exists. Auspicious.

Productivity
An increase is possible though you will have to be flexible in your approach. It may involve the setting up of a new department to deal

with new product or service ideas. This means a genuine commitment.

Investment and Finance
It is a risk if you cannot afford to lose. You must keep up with the needs of the times.

Backing
The support will be intangible at first, given in principle only. This has yet to be translated into figures. Provide all the information you can to support your application.

Management
Avoid a know-it-all attitude. You don't know it all and a presumptuous attitude is not warranted. If something is too quickly discarded this may be a mistake. Look at everything with care. Take time.

Information
Be thorough but careful about the conclusions you draw on your own. See what conclusions others come to without any deliberate suggestions on your own part. Write them down in positive, middle and negative terms then refine them through analysing the *reasoning* processes involved.

Advertising and Marketing
It would be unusual to present a modest profile in the media but this will be more effective than the loud blowing of trumpets. Good ideas have power to communicate without much pushing. This implies the existence of complementary resonance between ideas and objects which is *natural*.

International Trade
Unusual and imaginative transactions can succeed if you follow intuition. Auspicious for the middle and long term.

Sources of Misfortune
Bigotry. People always sense and avoid it.

Sources of Good Fortune
Allow new ideas into your considerations. Avoid following as a matter of policy the well-trodden route. Be original, let the unexpected play a prominent part. Give credit where credit is due.

THE LINES (CHANGES)
the Future-Links

Six at the beginning
A subtle twinge of 'other', intuitive, influences. But is it enough to move you to action?

Six in the second place
You feel the motivation to go forward but because the action you will take does not come from the heart (you are not really convinced!) it does not have the necessary energy to bring success. Hold your position.

Nine in the third place
Hold your position, not out of lack of confidence to act but because the situation is not objectively right for action. You may desire it, however. You would not fear to act, however, if it were right, would you?

Nine in the fourth place
If you set out to influence others deliberately by calculated means, there will be no general power. Universal influence does not arise this way. It is sincere feeling (which does not cast about looking for whom it may influence) which really has the power to influence. It comes straight from the heart and its magnitude is determined by its 'unmeasured' sincerity. In this sense the action blindly follows the heart, and that is right.

Nine in the fifth
People who are impervious to the influence of others rarely become confused in their actions. They therefore act without regret. But such people never influence others at heart. People follow, imitate and are guided by those who *feel* a connection with others. This is the secret of real influence. This is why ideas are, in the end, more powerful than personalities. It is ideas which set the tone and resonance between people even though those ideas might not be crystallized in words or images. Ideas can influence down the ages when the idea of resonance is the concept tool.

Six in the last place
Talk alone doesn't influence as much as some people would like. This is merely a statement of fact.

HEXAGRAM 32

Duration
(The Power to Subsist in Time)

JUDGEMENT

Success: a state of equipoise. (See also Hexagram 63: Completion.)
The course is correct. Relationships are in order.

SPECIFIC MODALITY

Once the centre is found, control through self-control. Progress is
made by keeping operations on an even keel. There are no stormy
waters immediately ahead.

AMBIENCE

Like breathing, the pattern sustains its regularity through changing
conditions. Good fortune.

CONCEPT MODEL

Equipoise: this is the point of balance, of natural harmony in the
whole scheme of change. It is conceived of as maintaining life and
position by breathing. The position is still, yet it is dynamic. The
stillness is not stagnation or retrogression, it is, like breathing, life-
sustaining, strong and able to maintain its place by merely continuing
to be itself. The important point is that it is central.

   The reference is not to the lungs of an organization but more to
the effect of their functioning in relation to the whole organism. It is
this point of balance which itself subsists in time, and the extended
meaning is that *through* this point other things are made to last. The
positioning is a controlling position by nature in the same way that
breathing controls the well-being of an organism or a fulcrum sets
the ambit of action around it. This is the position through which all
the changes pass in order to reach other positions. It is, like the
position designated by Hexagram 63: Completion, a *key* position.

   From this position the organization cannot grow, neither can it slide back. It is in an unassailable position. It holds its own in a state of dynamic equilibrium, but not in the sense of treading water (see Hexagram 5: Patience) when special effort is required in expectancy of change. Here it is simply held. The forces on either side, although qualitatively different are, in the whole scheme of change, equal in force. Action and the way you do it are matched.

From within the organization (from the viewpoint of staff and management), everything will appear to be clearly defined; all the specialist parts are working distinctly, but harmoniously. A state of pure function exists. This is why good fortune and misfortune are not appropriate judgements, but *success* (smooth function) is apposite.

This is a good time to observe objectively all the relations of the company infrastructure. Rarely will you see them functioning in such balanced harmony; everything has, as it were, found its own natural and comfortable level of operation. It is well to get a clear picture of this state of affairs as it may be a valuable measuring rod in times to come.

The company is right on course. This is not the time to consider policy changes, make radical reshuffles of management or impose changes of production. This is not an actively creative time. As a general rule, any dramatic changes would be disastrous (unless the moving lines indicate otherwise), throwing the alignment of past and future out and creating waves which will manifest later as obstacles. Such obstacles can often be traced back to swerving off course during times of equilibrium.

The holding of a state of equilibrium is also determined by maintaining communications. There is no suggestion that, in avoiding steering off course, you must be a stickler for traditional patterns. What is required is that you inform your organization and make adaptations which keep the dynamic equilibrium stable. This may seem paradoxical but it is a matter of measure. The need is to change naturally with the times rather than to force strident and changeful policies. In order to do this you have to be aware of trends in the market place; these should be considered in the light of past experience against future expectation. Far-reaching vision in the sense described in Hexagram 20: Contemplation would be looking too far for present purposes. So between these poles, the right perception can be maintained.

————————— DECISION-BASE ASSUMPTIONS —————————

The following values are given subject to the information given in the Changes. Remember, the Changes take precedence.

Management
A steady course is maintained through the strength of an independent position. Keep things moving, but be alert. This is the balancing force which can be maintained and procedures generally preserved.

Risks
Take no risks where the internal functioning of the organization is concerned. Entertain ideas which keep the company up to date with what is happening with the rest of society.

Planning
Make no changes of a fundamental character. Don't look too far ahead. This is not the time to make decisions for the long term. The medium term is appropriate.

Communications
Good. There is a general consensus of agreement in principle and in practice.

Feedback
Good. Honest. Reliable.

Creative Input
Consider as a matter of policy. It is impossible to make the correct positional adjustments, however slight, unless you have your finger on the pulse of the times.

Contracts and Agreements
Routine agreements are in order.

Investment
Sound. It will hold up without too much monitoring.

Backing
The exciting and the new won't attract just now. Anything which requires too much imagination will be better held in abeyance for a while. But there is no judgement on the ideas which seek backing.

Advertising and Marketing
This is not the time to sell the market a new company image. The one which is established will be trusted.

Creative Judgement
It is not being put to the test here. It is adequate and sound for the decisions you have to make.

Growth and Productivity
Take the last six months' figures as a reliable guide to the average over the next six. Otherwise, steady growth.

Sources of Misfortune
Distraction; sudden changes in policy; changing direction. None of this is advised.

Sources of Good Fortune
Continue to do what you do best. If it has worked for you in the past you can confidently expect it to work for you now.

———————————— **THE LINES (CHANGES)** ————————————
the Future-Links

Six at the beginning
In order to find out what is the correct pace (that which can be maintained indefinitely), let the extremes be discovered. What is the fastest pace of work? What is the slowest? Let these be judged by experience rather than in theory, you can only know for sure by carrying out a period of testing. When the truth of capability is established you can be sure not to take on too much in any given time. The warning advises against taking on too much. Accept work at the rate which can be maintained as if the process were not going to stop. It has to be *working comfortably* if all the elements are to function symbiotically.

Nine in the second place
You are made for greater challenges but don't let the thought of this inhibit your energies in this situation. Just use the energy that this task requires and no more.

Nine in the third place
Are you in control of your moods or are your moods in control of you? If your moods are in control you attract situations in which you are unable to cope. Finding your centre of gravity means controlling your moods so that you are not moved by eddies and currents which tend to swirl fiercely around perilous places.

Nine in the fourth place
Finding the right opportunities requires a sense of what is appropriate; to tune in needs a sense of pitch. It would be demented to attempt to score hits in clay-pigeon shooting using a fishing rod. You have to do the right kind of thing in the right field of action. It depends upon what you want to do. It

does not matter how persevering we are in upholding our intentions, what is important is to seek the right avenues and contexts in which those intentions can be meaningfully realized.

Six in the fifth place
You have to do what you believe to be right without always deferring to the opinions of others.

Six in the last place
Will to action is stronger and steadier if it comes from the heart. Instability of temperament is not as effective as dynamic equilibrium. The former is out of control. The latter is in control, things are done well.

HEXAGRAM 33

Retreat (Strategic Withdrawal)

— JUDGEMENT —

Success if you do not try to achieve advance. Retreat to a position of safety. Commit no resources in the field of action. You cannot make any progress at this time.

— SPECIFIC MODALITY —

Preserve resources by strategic withdrawal in the face of advancing forces. Act immediately and carefully. Retreat. Good fortune. Know when to say no.

— AMBIENCE —

Pressure to preserve your resources. Urgency. Pressure to preserve independence of choice and action in the face of an aggressive bid to take over.

— CONCEPT MODEL —

When it is dangerous to advance, one must know how to retreat so that the opposing forces cannot exploit the situation. In contrast to Hexagram 24, here it is right not to push against the forces but to recognize them for what they are.

Retreat is appropriate when the oncoming force is in opposition to your own direction *and* threatens to harm your position. The opposition may not, of itself, be stronger in terms of brute strength, but it may be strategically stronger. Thus, retreat must not be all-out flight, but strategic as in a game of chess, calculated to win safety and also to inhibit the advance of the opposition.

The opposing force is not yet in a position of advantage. There are other hexagrams which picture situations where one is helpless to avoid the consequences of an outside force. This is not the case here – there is time to adjust.

To gain a more comprehensive understanding of the idea of

retreat, one must not think in exclusively militaristic terms. Retreat can also mean preventing an obnoxious influence from destabilizing one's composure: retreat into oneself, as it were, becoming unavailable for communication. In this situation, the attitude one adopts is important. Vengeance, dislike or aggression will not lead to success. Such negative emotion clouds one's judgement and strategic sense and is one which the opposition can exploit with ease. Especially in dangerous situations, clarity of mind must be maintained; there should be no fear. One's best actions are objective, being dictated by circumstances. Backing down, losing face or embarrassing compromise only arise if retreat is not carried out effectively and strategically.

——————— DECISION-BASE ASSUMPTIONS ———————

The following values are given subject to the information given in the Changes. Remember, the Changes take precedence.

Feedback
Give no information which could be used to erode your position. If in doubt, say nothing.

Growth and Productivity
Take a cautious attitude and cut back for the time being. Make a stay on plans to develop your place in the market place. It could be wasted expenditure as you do not know the plans and extent of the competition. Retreat is an important idea only if it becomes germane to plans for growth.

Timing
Retreat immediately. But make each of your actions correspond to the movements of the market. Withdraw gradually, though as speedily as possible. The distinction is important because cutting a position dead can make your next moves predictable, and the opponent can plan for them.

Planning
Change plans for the time being, but keep the changes a secret.

Marketing and Sales
Do not commit expenditures in any foreward drive in the field.

Advertising
It could now work against you. Your ideas might be used to help competing companies rather than attract support for yourself. Com-

mit no further resources until you have had a chance to reassess. Put an immediate hold on currently uncommitted plans.

Creative Judgement

Not unremittingly poor. Used to retreat, it is an asset which is immeasurable by the opposition. You use this resource to great advantage if you are so disposed.

Personal Initiative

Do not interfere with central ideas. Take a back seat on this one.

Start-Up

This is the time to review your ideas and perhaps consider another approach later on – if germane at all. Certainly commit no funds and ratify no agreements.

Investment and Finance

No new investments must be entered into. You may have to recall or consolidate existing commitments to avoid losses.

Backing

Seek no commitments, expect none.

Agreements

Sign nothing. Ratify nothing. Just hold with an option to vary or rescind if already agreed in principle.

International Trade

Return to base. If possible, recall resources in the particular field of action which is under scrutiny.

Risks

None.

Sources of Good Fortune and Misfortune

Consolidate your position by withdrawing resources. But do not do so rashly. Make each move a considered one and do not make the mistake of holding ground, come what may. You could incur heavy losses through such inflexibility. Giving ground does not necessarily mean losing resources; it may do, however, if you hesitate in retreating from current positions.

─────────────── **THE LINES (CHANGES)** ───────────────
the Future-Links

Six at the beginning
Here retreat means *keeping still*. Take nothing, give nothing. Words and

actions must be trimmed to effect a non movement. This gives the opposition no point of immediate advantage.

Six in the second place
Here the pursuing force is relentless. This is not necessarily unfortunate as some good comes out of a strongly felt need to be helped.

Nine in the third place
A problem arises when it is right to leave a situation but one's exit is impeded by the cloying needs of people who refuse to let one move on. In order to retain control you are compelled to consider making some use of these people even though they are not properly qualified. Do not let them spoil the work, however.

Nine in the fourth place
It is safe and appropriate to move on now. Yours has been a beneficial and salubrious influence, and things will not be so fine in your absence.

Nine in the fifth place
Only by keeping in touch with your own affairs in the wider social group can you hope to make the right preparations and give warnings, so that people are not offended. Giving notice enables one to tidy up one's affairs and also gives others the opportunity to try to persuade you to change your mind. But you mustn't be dissuaded from leaving if the time is right to do so.

Nine in the last place
You can leave with a clear mind without doubts, recriminations and attachment. Your view of the situation is exactly right and the new path to be entered upon is unimpeded.

HEXAGRAM 34

The Power of the Great

The deliberate use of advantage to achieve just and good things. Success. Very auspicious. (See Hexagram 13: Fellowship with Men.)

——————————— SPECIFIC MODALITY ———————————

The power of initiative in the service of justice. Loyalty to high social principles rather than to individuals. Political evils arise when the reverse prevails.

——————————— AMBIENCE ———————————

Great energy appropriately directed for the benefit of *others*.

——————————— CONCEPT MODEL ———————————

This hexagram is linked with Hexagrams 20 (Contemplation) and 2 (The Receptive). This hexagram concerns itself with the ability to manipulate and use higher ideas and, in this case, to act according to an understanding of fairness and justness. When power manifests in an individual, it is all too easy for him to use it for his own ends. This temptation is strong when the constraints of office are weak. Therefore, those in power must be accountable for their actions, not so much to other people as to exemplary *ideas* such as 'goodness' and 'justice'. Thus the specific meaning of the hexagram lies in the central idea of allegiance to higher principles which govern all social forces and cultural growth.

Only through such an expressed allegiance can fame – social visibility – be sustained. The power to rise to such positions is a matter of nature's power, and not a matter of strategy. Thus sustaining such positions is a matter of what lives best in the light, such as openness, honesty, justice, fairness. A society and its individuals are measured by the ideas they uphold. The higher and brighter those ideas, the more enlightened the society, and so the world is uplifted. If those values are not strongly held, however, then when a natural decline of energy sets in they lose value and power also. Lip service is self-deluding. These ideas can only be *sustained* in periods of energy decline by the force of conviction. Developing this conviction is the goal of collective humanity. The Power of the Great means the great power of nature to act through man's intelligence to achieve great good.

—————— DECISION-BASE ASSUMPTIONS ——————

The following values are given subject to the information given in the Changes. Remember, the Changes take precedence.

Management
Newly promoted people should think not only in terms of their pragmatic responsibilities to company and employer, but also in terms of the wider significance of their decisions and the values which govern them.

Motivation
The time is very auspicious for carefully considering your future commitments and strategies. What you do now and over the next few months will establish a pattern which will affect future choices. Take care that you are absolutely clear.

Communications
The power to achieve with the minimum of cooperation is implied here, but this is also a good time to make your intentions known to those who will show an interest or be of help in the future.

Investment and Finance
Good fortune if you favour ideas which anticipate or create trends. The established organization is safe.

Risks
As this is a time of improvement in fortunes (either expressed in growth or as the lessening of restraints), there is no risk. Only those ideas which go with the times (answer the visible needs) will be successful. Beyond these, you will be taking risks which will not pay off. Take care to listen, read and observe. Listen to, and follow, your intuitions.

Initiative
This is accented. Minimalize the time it takes to arrive at collective decisions. The time should be used in *action*. Do not

confuse protracted meetings, however creative, with 'getting things done'.

Timing
Take a time frame of no more than two months to apply decisions. Clarify key directions in not more than two weeks, otherwise impetus starts to drain off.

Advertising
Images which reflect the time are those which portray sky and earth in harmony and action. Universals are memorable, especially images of spring, favoured for high response.

Marketing
Strategy will pay dividends if you aim to be as visible as possible.

Creativity
A wider understanding always implies a possibility of more creative solutions and methods of procedure. There will be opportunities to bring fresh insights into old and established practices and to change and modify them in keeping with the demands of the time.

Purpose and Intention
There will be a general drive to establish a new, or a series of new, platforms of activity and new ambits and contexts of activity – for example, the creation of new departments within an organization to meet certain emerging or anticipated needs. Energy is present in abundance and procrastination should not be allowed. The objectives may well be long term but immediate effects will be felt in the short term.

Recruitment
This is the time to take on new people with clearly defined responsibilities. Both management, staff and experts should find a place in the new build-up of action. Those who are most suitable will be marked out by their awareness of wider issues, their willingness to accept personal responsibility and their ability to act on their own initiative, with the minimum of supervision.

Contracts and Agreements
Those which should be ratified will be ratified in the near future. New agreements 'in principle' should be sought now, for future planning.

International Trade
Increasingly favourable, providing deadlines and appointments are kept. There is some flexibility, but not much.

Start-Up
An excellent time to begin new things. Good fortune.

Backing
Provided your intentions are clear and well presented, further interest will quickly follow. Backers who are not prepared to act quickly, however, or see the project completed should be abandoned. Cast your net quite widely. Adequate resources must be available and, at the planning stage, these must be established in some detail, with margins.

Sources of Misfortune
If the wrong people and ideas are encouraged in a time of growth, they will come to have the upper hand in a time of decline. This can lead to tyranny and oppression instead of care and sustenance.

Sources of Good Fortune
The attitude should be to grow towards *worthy* goals. Only these will bear fruit in another season, only these will be visible, only these will be appreciated and endure.

———————————— THE LINES (CHANGES) ————————————
the Future-Links

Nine at the beginning
Do not force things at the beginning. All the processes need to be gone through naturally.

Nine in the second place
What has been well done begins to show positive signs already. But don't count your chickens before they hatch.

Nine in the third place
Power and responsibility should be used to increase benefit and enhance the work. Showing off only causes people to think how unworthy you are to hold power. Only a despot is fooled by a superficial show of strength. A wise leader measures his strength by the benefit it brings.

Nine in the fourth place
People begin to cooperate and difficulties are overcome. People who are self-contained (work quietly) and consistent (with clear goals) are also effective, whereas brute force and shouting from the tree tops achieves nothing. Power resides in character and not in outward display. The higher the ideal the greater the potential power. If those ideals embrace the higher aspirations of mankind and conform to his natural evolutionary tendencies they will be a source of immense guidance and strength. The drive for power and wealth for its own sake, however, cannot subsist in time.

Eventually it consumes itself (naturally) because it cannot manifest in higher forms (See Hexagrams 1: The Creative and 2: The Receptive.)

Six in the fifth place
If you can become more personable you will achieve with greater ease and relaxation because your energy is not being exhausted by anger or negative emotions.

Six in the last place
Realize the intractability of your predicament so that you desist from aggravating it. (See Hexagram 6: Deadlock.)

HEXAGRAM 35

Progress

————— JUDGEMENT —————

Great good fortune; great progress; the nod of assent from fate. An implicit cooperation of natural and empathic forces. Ideas understood now will have great benefit in future times.

————— SPECIFIC MODALITY —————

The rapid development of projects and ideas which are of wider importance to society rather than personal gain. This is an auspicious time for understanding the reasons *why* certain ideas work well and others do not.

————— AMBIENCE —————

Purposeful, unintimidated development. Progress in generating successful relationships.

————— CONCEPT MODEL —————

This hexagram points to the realization of powerful, stimulating ideas which have a significance and importance extending beyond one's personal good fortune. The work is going well and creatively. You will feel a sense of being guided by a higher force. Feedback from the outside world will come eventually, but now it is the ideas themselves, and the form in which they are envisaged, which are of paramount importance. These must be developed because they are valuable, though their true significance may not be realized at once. Communicate – and when the right people are told of the work they will be very supportive.

   The other intimation here is that the individual concerned is not in a strictly independent position. He cannot develop the full potential of the ideas alone and unaided. He does not have sufficient resources (finance, expertise, administrative and management experience) to carry the project to fruition. But without his ideas and ability to coordinate efforts along a particular line, the project cannot work either. However, when the right time comes, all the necessary resources and help will be forthcoming (but see any conditions attached in the lines where appropriate and the future hexagram, if any, in order to know how best to proceed).

Ideas and projects are 'on the right lines' and that is sufficient to make a clear case. Ideas seem to be 'coming from above'. The individual concerned is acting as a catalyst or 'receiver/transmitter' and, without this ingredient, the so-called logic of the situation would not be meaningful. The hexagram says 'Carry on, you are doing well, don't worry about whether people will follow or understand.'

When these kinds of conditions prevail – giving confidence to continue – the right help will inevitably come.

―――――――――― DECISION-BASE ASSUMPTIONS ――――――――――

The following values are given subject to the information given in the Changes. Remember, the Changes take precedence.

Management
Take the widest possible view. Do not discard any ideas, plans and possibilities. The most positive and confident attitude must be in evidence. What happens now will definitely have positive consequences for the future. Make headway under your own steam as internal forces are cooperating nicely. External cooperation, by which is meant outside companies and organizations, is forthcoming, but any delays in this regard should not be taken as a judgement on personal progress.

Planning
The time is auspicious for making clear plans. Keep careful notes and, where particular concepts come through loud and clear, make certain to connect them within a larger scheme.

Creative Judgement
Your creative judgement at this time is unusually brilliant and you can rely upon your intuitions and conclusions, provided your perception is not clouded with thoughts of material gain. Develop these ideas but be patient; take a long view.

Investment and Finance
Auspicious, if not now, then later. But the outcome is certain when the right cooperation is found.

Backing
Auspicious. Seek and you shall find.

Growth
The short-, medium- and long-term prospects are excellent, but this is strictly conditional upon understanding the whole picture. An illuminating influence is gaining ascendancy.

Cooperation
Inevitable, but make sure your ideas have clarity.

Feedback
Unless otherwise conditioned by the lines or the future hexagram, continue along present lines with confidence. Any negative feedback is not a judgement on the ideas.

Wealth
In both the widest and the material sense, wealth will come through these ideas. Auspicious.

Advertising
Bright ideas abound. Make use of them.

Marketing
Successful but not necessarily immediately.

International Trade
Especially auspicious if proposals support a fully developed project. Otherwise, the future prospects are generally sound.

Contracts and Agreements
A warm atmosphere prevails and the situation is reliable. Both parties in any current negotiations will benefit enormously and the proposer need fear nothing. Generosity is in order.

Sources of Misfortune
What is being described here is progress from the darkness of selfish aims to wider aims which benefit and illuminate others. How they signify in the tangible world will depend upon aptitude and ability. But *progress is into the light*. Transcend selfish aims.

Sources of Good Fortune
Material considerations are secondary to the development and clarification of these newly emerging creative ideas.

THE LINES (CHANGES)
the Future-Links

Six at the beginning
You are doing the right kind of work. Others may not, however, understand or appreciate the significance or value of the work and things would go better if they did. But do not change course. If you have to work without the cooperation of others, so be it. Good fortune will result, perhaps from an unexpected quarter.

Six in the second place
Times may be hard just now. Keep working though. Soon, a person who understands your predicament gives help because the work is good and worthwhile and is not offered with any underhand or ulterior motive.

Six in the third place
With the solid support of others you are able to venture onward with the work.

Nine in the fourth place
This is a situation which must be strenuously guarded against. It is as follows: an individual (or more than one person) attains wealth and power either by his own work or through favour, deserved or otherwise, coming to him from another. An inferior person sees in his new wealth and power an opportunity to abuse his position, to break the rules, as it were; to go against the spirit which should accompany wealth and influence. This spirit corresponds with a true stature of mind, ability, heart, understanding and real nobility. In the hands of the selfish, mean, cruel, ignorant and cowardly, wealth and power do indeed become evil. In the end there is no escape from the consequences of abuse.

The main thrust of the line, however, is not to accuse, but to warn against the trappings that great progress may bring when it manifests as an office of wealth and power. Simply that. But it is a warning which has no greater significance than in the world of commerce and politics. Warnings of this nature are ignored at great cost.

Six in the fifth place
Sometimes a person does not have sufficient energy to wring every ounce of advantage out of a time of progress. But don't waste time worrying about what you could have done, and 'if onlys'.

Nine in the last place
It is acceptable to make vigorous progress when correcting past mistakes, though it is important not to overdo it. Forceful behaviour is not usually justified, but here some action is necessary to prevent matters from getting out of control.

HEXAGRAM 36

The Darkening of the Light

---- JUDGEMENT ----

Do not flaunt your abilities and virtues and you will come to no harm.

---- SPECIFIC MODALITY ----

The object of the exercise is to lie low in the face of dark, difficult or tyrannical circumstances. Untrustworthy influences are in the field. Be careful.

---- AMBIENCE ----

Darkness is coming but the dark conceals not only evil but good.

---- CONCEPT MODEL ----

An organization whose people act malevolently cannot be fought *here and now*. The only way to offset such influences is to remain quiet and unprovocative. This is the time of the bully, and the bully needs a visible object.

Attempts at 'making a stand' are absolutely doomed now and so no forceful effort should be made. The 'darkening' effect which this hexagram describes works for the tyrant or bully and not for talent, ability, cooperation.

This dark influence has many manifestations. It may take the form of people gossiping and spreading rumours (all untrue) and doing everything to undermine a 'good name' and 'reputation'. People may be deliberately attempting harm out of sheer malevolence, jealousy, even hatred. Indeed, in business, an individual might like to know why his work or communications seem to fall mysteriously upon stony ground. If he consulted the *I Ching* and received this hexagram his mystery will be explained. It is because he has aroused negative reactions (quite undeserved, and quite unjustly) in others, and he has called attention to himself at a time when it is better to remain silent and let the 'darkening' turn to light again.

All the positive elements of the previous hexagram are therefore reversed, and no cooperation can be expected or should be sought at this time. Better by far to carry on with the work and continue to make *personal progress*, 'hiding one's light' as one does so. Do not offer to help people who do not want to be helped, for this is a time when they are unreceptive to guidance and willing to harm those who show this disposition. This is a time for turning the other cheek, keeping a careful note of everything that occurs (do not ignore malefactors), while being unresponsive, taking up no issues and starting no arguments. This is what must be done until the time changes. And then, if you have been attentive, you will know what to do.

The picture here must be taken on its merits. Some circumstances will be severe and therefore have to be taken very seriously, other circumstances might not be so severe but, nevertheless, harbour the seeds of tyranny. The individual must appraise the 'energy' of the situation and use his intuitions accordingly. Each situation, by a natural law, nourishes its opposite so be watchful.

─────────── DECISION-BASE ASSUMPTIONS ───────────

The following values are given subject to the information given in the Changes. Remember, the Changes take precedence.

Management
Every good influence will be turned against you. Lie low. Do not arouse enmity. Do not attract attention.

Staff
Exactly the same applies here as for management. You will only have received this hexagram if you, yourself, are the *object* of the darkening influence. You are not the darkening influence and you must take care not to become a part of it by falling in with its ways. If you were to do this, you would find that when the light influence begins to ascend as in Hexagram 35: Progress, your fortunes would be on the downward instead of on the upward spiral.

Investment and Finance
The situation is untrustworthy, do not invest. The investment is likely to yield no fruit for one reason or another – fraud or theft or just a bad venture.

Backing
Not at this time.

Start-Up
Make no proposals, do not suggest any ideas. Keep everything quiet.

Creative Judgement
Not necessarily poor but, once again, to avoid having violence done to it, it is better to say nothing at present.

Advertising
Wait before making commitments. If you have not already reaped rewards from recent expenditures do not expect to in the near future. Certainly do not add to expenditure at this time.

Marketing
Keep marketing initiatives to a minimum to avoid unfruitful and wasteful responses.

Feedback
Do not seek it as it would be negative and damage motivation. (But do not be discouraged inwardly.)

Contracts and Agreements
Inauspicious. Best not to follow through at this time, even if pressed.

Growth and Productivity
Outwardly in decline. Inward development is possible; indeed, these are times when inward growth flourishes.

Research and Development
This is not a time when breakthroughs are likely. No blindingly brilliant discoveries and insights can be expected. Do not make the mistake, on the other hand, of misjudging the value of previous work or destroying it.

Product Choice
Do not settle on a decision at this precise time.

Creative Input
You may be forced in upon yourself and thereby draw upon inner resources for ideas; in this way you could be re-working old impressions and memories which will not have much bearing upon external matters but may nourish the inner light considerably. In this sense creative input is important. External input is not to be valued – merely noted.

Sources of Misfortune
Insisting upon making your views known; making yourself visible, pushing yourself forward, generally being incautious in all communications. Responding to provocation.

Sources of Good Fortune
Attempt to make no outward progress, preserve inner calm; do not
under any circumstances give way to allurements which find no
ground in excellent and tested precedents. Take absolutely no risks.
Self-development is always valuable when the outside world yields
little light; the *I Ching* often emphasizes this activity in dark
times.

THE LINES (CHANGES)
the Future-Links

Nine at the beginning
Your situation is inhospitable. You are compelled to move quickly as there is
nowhere safe nearby to rest. The people around you are unhelpful and you
should not make them your confidantes as the information will certainly be
used against you. They are already dragging skeletons out of cupboards,
twisting the truth, telling lies, placing false constructions upon events,
deliberately misrepresenting your position/attitude/opinions and so on.
Their behaviour is utterly and completely reprehensible, but this is no time
to dwell upon it. You just have to suffer in silence and find a place of refuge,
though it will cost you in the things that matter most. Even those who have
sympathy with your situation, in principle, cannot here help you. The
thought of support at the highest level is warming, but that may not be *felt*
where you really need it.

Six in the second place
A conflict of opposites. (Another perspective is offered in Hexagram 6:
Deadlock.) You help others without thought for yourself. This is laudable
and praiseworthy and invites good fortune. In a dangerous situation such
action is the height of real nobility.

Nine in the third place
A conflict of opposites is pictured, but here the situation is different from
the opposition of forces pictured in the preceding line. The office of the
bright and good is engaged in restoring order while the office of chaos and
evil which has made malpractices habitual is also about its wicked business –
but, good wins over evil by taking it by surprise without actually meaning to.
They run into each other by a happy chance. Caught redhanded.

Six in the fourth place
Now you understand the evil intent, you realize (without being discovered
yourself) the extent of it and the limitations upon your, or other people's,
power to make an impression. This is lamentable and the whole organization is about to collapse. There is still time to get out without coming to
harm, and this is exactly what you should do without further ado and without
looking over your shoulder.

Six in the fifth place
Everything around you has gone crazy. This may refer to your organization, your immediate environment or to society at large. But there is no escape. If you let your 'sanity' become a known fact you will be in danger. So, like many of Shakespeare's Fools as, for example, King Lear, you *act* crazy in order to blend in with the general craziness; bringing order against such impossible odds is out of the question. Nevertheless, you know exactly what is going on. Do not present a vulnerable face to it under any circumstances. This is sometimes the only way of coming through in one piece when mad tyrants rule the day.

Six in the last place
When evil people rule, everybody suffers without discrimination, good and bad alike. This is what is meant by Darkness. But when there is nothing left to prey upon it slowly expires. To gain a better understanding of this *natural process* (though, in the affairs of man, being higher, it takes on a moral significance), read the Concept Model of Hexagram 30: The Clinging, Fire.

HEXAGRAM 37

The Family

----------------------- JUDGEMENT -----------------------

Success if proper relationships within the organization are maintained and respected. Family matters are a conditioning factor. It is
in the intimacy of the family that strength resides,

----------------------- SPECIFIC MODALITY -----------------------

Everyday functioning and communication as if within a family unit,
so that all know their respective places and are content within that
framework of responsibility.

----------------------- AMBIENCE -----------------------

The situation is an abstract of intimate but ordered relations,
therefore pleasant and happy. Auspicious.

----------------------- CONCEPT MODEL -----------------------

The idea that work is inspired through a natural and spontaneous
affection among staff and management is uppermost. Even in the
absence of clear and rigid structures of authority and responsibility it
is still possible to generate events. People who like each other tend to
work well together and cooperate. The basic empathy and interaction of complementary personalities working together in an amen-
able and conducive framework produces a meaningful as well as
productive set of possibilities. It is the duty of management to
recognize this.

The highest level of symbiosis, contact and relationship possible
in a society is that which the family ideally admits. Business
organizations which emulate and function as a family have an added
dimension in which many difficulties are overcome. Cooperation
becomes a matter of special duty, special friendship. The atmosphere is one of higher trust and greater *personal* responsibility. The
attitude of *people coming first* is illustrated best where organizations

behave as if they were a family. (But see Hexagram 7: The Army; Hexagram 13: Fellowship with Men; Hexagram 11: Peace; Hexagram 30: The Clinging, Fire. See also Hexagram 45: Gathering Together.)

─────────── DECISION-BASE ASSUMPTIONS ───────────

The following values are given subject to the information given in the Changes. Remember, the Changes take precedence.

Management
Practise what you preach. If an example cannot be set words will lose meaning and, in time, respect breaks down and with it social cohesion and work. The links between these ideas are clear and necessary. If the head isn't right, the rest tends to go wrong also, but see Hexagram 13: Fellowship with Men. Be especially careful that what is expected of people is clearly relevant and recognizably so, otherwise there will be a problem of quality or function. Explanations are always called for and questions answered satisfactorily. The idea of 'I give the orders and you follow them' is itself out of order *here*. By nature people cannot indefinitely conform happily to situations in which contradictions and disparities prevail. The human mind abhors disorder and confusion. If this requirement for explanation, order, reason, is well catered for through training programmes and daily practice the secret of equilibrium, consistency and duration is made manifest (see Hexagram 32: Duration). Every organization requires an everyday *modus operandus* and these factors are the basis of its smooth continuation. Cash flow is a secondary consideration here. Order begins in tranquillity. Exellence arises from meditative calm.

Planning
The direction already set is adequate to the purpose.

Feedback
All the usual lines of communication must be kept open. Feedback is positive and regular.

Communications
Conventional but positive and regular.

Growth and Productivity
This is an ongoing situation. There will be no sudden rises and no sudden falls. The wheels keep turning and progress is not halted.

Investment and Finance
Beware of overindulgence. Pet areas of interest must not be cultivated at the expense of wider considerations.

Start-Up
The backing of family and friends is required. If rights and obligations have already been established through filial connections this could be an auspicious start with few internal problems.

Backing
You have to show a track record as well as a plan. A demonstration of committed individuals will impress backers most.

Contracts and Agreements
Do not compromise family interests; otherwise favourable. Affection can be powerful integrative forces in business matters.

Integration
A prerequisite. Family organizations are favoured.

Risks
You will not be called upon to take undue risks. Most situations can be understood in detail; unknowns are minimal and not especially crucial. Use the facts which are available.

Advertising
What is the appeal to the family? Use familiar images of happiness and mutual support.

Marketing
The family is the most fundamental social unit. The expression 'market' depersonalizes the real idea of appealing to the family. Underline the idea of the family in any strategy to win the general assent of people in the sales situation.

International Trade
Auspicious if family feeling is strong. Strict commercial practices without the extra investment of trust are not particularly well starred.

Sources of Misfortune
Bland indifference to family bonds.

Sources of Good Fortune
Forging stronger family ties will have a salubrious effect and will be rewarding, especially in the long term.

―――――――――――― **THE LINES (CHANGES)** ――――――――
the Future-Links

Nine at the beginning
The ground rules have to be established firmly at the beginning and include codes of conduct. They must be crystal clear. It has to be understood by one and all that these rules must be universally accepted and obeyed. The rules have to be self-evident, reasonable and comprehensible. New people must have time to learn them. Systems of communication and reference have to be clear and available. All this is vital for the beginning and is right for any unit, family, business, organization. Failures to act on these strictures always cause trouble later, sometimes much later, but the trouble is inevitable. So this is the time to get it right: at the beginning.

Six in the second place
It is natural that the wife and mother should be the centre of the family and be responsible for keeping the family together and running. The wider meaning, however, is that, by carrying out daily and immediate actions rather than constantly stepping beyond those responsibilities (presumably to dilly-dally about), brings good fortune.

Nine in the third place
Clear lines of conduct have to be drawn. They must be reasonable and fair. (See Hexagram 60: Limitation, for greater clarification of this important idea.) People need to know what they may do and what they may not do in any given situation. As a general principle this is natural, but here the reference is specifically understood in its disciplinary context. (See Hexagram 21: Decisive Action.) Freedom of action and movement is only meaningful if limits are drawn – the idea of limitation does not refer to 'constraint' but to boundaries which are appropriate to the field of action, as in football or chess. An employee cannot be reprimanded for breaking rules which he has previously broken without being reprimanded. Limits enable people and situations to be defined, reference points of conduct and action to be set up; people know where they are and can therefore be effective. This idea is fundamental to all concepts of law and order in society. The legal assumption that a member of society is presumed to know the law (understand the limits of his socially acceptable conduct) cannot be reasonably relied upon unless the educational system provides that information *specifically*. How can the law be reasonably enforced *without* that assumption? This central idea finds its first home in the family and gives rise to a network of ideas.

Six in the fourth place
In the family it is traditional, perhaps natural, for the wife to be responsible for the household budget. In the company it is the accountant who regulates and monitors income and expenditure. In Government it is the Chancellor of the Exchequer or the Treasurer. The important point is that this is a

specific duty, an office. The regulation of resources, specifically financial resources, should establish a balance between income and expenditure and, by so doing, provide for the needs of the household/company/country/ continent/world. The values of balancing and provision are, in nature, enshrined in the receptive or feminine aspect. Feminine qualities are therefore appropriate to the office. A maternal feeling must govern this idea of money otherwise, as is well known, it soon grows horns.

Nine in the fifth place

A good leader, a good father inspires a feeling of confidence, trust and affection. His authority is not derived from the big stick but from his nobility of character, his excellence of mind. Organizations which lead with a punishing edge in order to maintain discipline invite sabotage and chaos. But here, the leader is good.

Nine in the last place

Do not wait to be awarded responsibility by convention. The power of feeling and the awareness of aptitude and knowledge naturally require one to assume leadership. This is true both of families and organizations which require a guiding force and a source of wisdom. See Hexagram 62: Inner Truth. It is the power of this inner feeling which is the natural corollary of leadership. Its absence in people of special responsibility is conspicuous and lamentable as, without this quality, order cannot be maintained in pressured situations. The quality of *inner truth*, invested in the right person, can pervade the whole company and order can be maintained.

HEXAGRAM 38

Opposition

JUDGEMENT

If no attempt to achieve anything decisively important is made, success. Hold back. Avoid commitments.

SPECIFIC MODALITY

Two people within the same organization have different objectives and different loyalties, but there are grounds for agreement.

AMBIENCE

Energetic; stimulating; disharmonious.

CONCEPT MODEL

Two points of view, though not reconciled into a decisive pattern of action or codified into an agreed plan, have the merit of positing the limits of the situation. The two positions represent different ends of the same spectrum. These positions are held by two people, or two parties, or two factions within the same general system of organization. They cannot work together towards a common goal with any real chance of success, especially when that goal demands great unification of forces.

Thus no attempt should be made to achieve great progress or to start new ventures which require concerted effort. But this is not a situation in which one side cancels out the other by an equal force. The nature of the opposition is not neutralizing or destructive but, rather, weakening.

The secondary meaning of Opposition is that the two forces are different in nature and therefore have the propensity to complement each other and produce a synthesis of qualities. This is the propensity for transformation and creation. The difference can be expressed as a function of nature which shows how things can, by degrees, assume different forms.

——————— DECISION-BASE ASSUMPTIONS ———————

The following values are given subject to the information given in the Changes. Remember, the Changes take precedence.

Feedback
Not necessarily negative. The situation is one of mutual fascination, even temporary and fleeting beauty.

Management
The mix throws up new possibilities, but the real aims of the company in the long term should not be contemplated in this combination. It is a learning situation but you should not allow yourself to be carried away by enthusiasm.

Investment and Finance
A mild fling might not bring harm, might even bring some reward, but any major commitment of funds would be disastrous in the long term. Don't commit the company or its resources here.

Risk
Yes, this is a risk situation, but one which is not necessarily harmful. Show some restraint; treat the situation with some sense of humour and there could be benefit, but this is not the place to consider long-term options.

Start-Up
Not really. This is more an interlude, an interesting exercise in exploration. You need not pass it up, but a company should not be founded on this idea, combination of resources or management. Quite definitely, you should not think in permanent terms.

Backing
You could get backing from a very unusual source, but don't tie yourself down to close relationships or long-term repayments. The situation is fickle but could help get you over a difficulty if it's small and short term.

Profits
They could be short and sweet if they are commensurate with investment. But it won't change your life overnight unless you have thrown everything in, in which case you could be ruined. It is, however, unlikely that the context of the situation even allowed you to make such commitments.

Creative Judgement
Be careful not to delude yourself. The interest is keen and under-

standing could bring its rewards in another context, but *not this one.*

Growth and Productivity
A minor rise in fortunes, but the situation is unstable and there will be fluctuations. Since you have to change your operating assumptions eventually, you may as well start thinking about that now.

Planning
Only plan for the short term. Medium- and long-term plans require a different combination of people and possibly resources too. You cannot rely on continuing funds and cash flow under these auspices.

Communications
Stimulating, interesting, rewarding and the elements have a curious attraction. But keep your distance. Enjoy it while it lasts. The predicament is essentially fickle. It is important not to impose opinions; watch for this in others also.

Advertising
Unstable approach. Methods contemplated should not be carried forward into practice, it could give the wrong impression.

Marketing
The wrong presentation, the wrong image, therefore attracting the wrong market.

Company Mergers
The merger is not really meant to be. Some good can come of it but it cannot be expected to subsist in time. It is not advisable to make such a match. Only by creating a third company out of the elements of the two would it work but, even in this case, do not expect to set up something big or especially profitable.

Operational Management
A choice of leaders. Points of view and temperaments are opposed; loyalties lie in different directions. Although this may not be conflict (see Hexagram 6: Conflict), neither is it unity.

Takeover Bids
If a bid is made to take over your company strenuously resist it. If you intend to make a takeover bid – hold back. Other players in the field could cause a rough ride.

Sources of Misfortune
A merger is out of the question as the medium- and long-term prospects would be mutually destructive and confrontation would be

unavoidable. The whole tenor of the above should give a clear indication of the nature and limits of the situation. If you understand this you can retain control without coming to harm. (See Hexagram 44: Coming to Meet. Some of the inherent dangers are presented in that hexagram: dealing with newcomers in trustworthy *and* untrustworthy situations.)

Sources of Good Fortune

Show some restraint but be prepared to learn something valuable. Make no long-term plans; commit no major resources. There is no indication that it will be difficult to extricate yourself from the situation but be prepared to move on if necessary.

——————— THE LINES (CHANGES) ———————
the Future-Links

Nine at the beginning
It is the law of resonance which governs attraction between people. Because the laws of attraction are based upon natural principles no coercion should be necessary when seeking cooperation; no special schemes, designs, arguments or force are necessary. Avoid people who employ such behaviour, they can turn nasty. It is best not to arouse deliberately such people as they will plot and scheme even though the result will be that they get their fingers burned by being persistent in forcing themselves on the *wrong* people. The cue to what is appropriate should be taken from natural responses. People who belong with one another need make no effort to transmit this information in any unnatural way. This is a case of 'let it be', if progress is to be made.

Nine in the second place
The so-called 'chance meeting' sometimes brings together people who belong or who have a natural affection and empathy. Due to complexities, diverging life styles, different ambits of action, people appear to meet by chance but in truth they do so because of the invisible yet natural force of mutual attraction.

Six in the third place
Frustration; nothing you do seems to bring about a positive result. But the situation is not what it seems. This is not, as elsewhere, an intimation from fate that you are on the wrong road. Despite the difficulties, do not be disheartened as things will turn out well for you. Libels and slanders should not be taken to heart though your sensitivity to the situation is not wrong. Don't forsake the right loyalties.

Nine in the fourth place
Even in company one can feel a stranger because one is with the wrong people. Everybody feels like this sometimes. But here there is someone with

whom one feels a real link and the loneliness can be overcome through this association. There will be success without compromise.

Six in the fifth place

You are not aware of any special feeling for a particular person, but this is because you do not see the connection, the natural attraction. Fortunately for you the other person does feel this attraction. His behaviour makes a strong impression and you realize that any feelings of doubt and mistrust were groundless. You should combine as there will be success in joint undertakings. Do not look for obstacles and impediments once you have recognized your friends. Keep the future in mind. A good start-up situation.

Nine in the last place

You are wrong. They are your friends. Their intentions are impeccable and they are well disposed towards you. It is unnecessary for you to be on your guard or to be aggressive. An inner condition of constraint is overcome in this sudden realization of kinship. Good fortune will result.

HEXAGRAM 39

Obstruction

JUDGEMENT

By following the explicit guidance of a more experienced person you can extricate yourself from difficulties. Good fortune.

SPECIFIC MODALITY

Surrounded on all sides by difficulties and obstacles. You have to get out; you must overcome, but there is a way. Keep your head.

AMBIENCE

Concentrated difficulties. The requirement is calm energy.

CONCEPT MODEL

Knowing how to overcome difficulties and obstructions is a special art. Problems and setbacks tend to become increasingly insurmountable and do much damage to one's motivation, will to action and impulsion to go forward. There is a challenge here which everybody encounters in some degree in their lives, and which must be faced. The equation which has to be understood is that external difficulties, obstacles and problems correspond with inner blocks on self-awareness. The Christian idea that difficulties are sent to try us is, indeed, meaningful in this context. We need our inner reserves of energy, patience, perseverance and calm, strategic and careful thought.

This present situation is particularly hazardous and cannot be negotiated alone. Help is needed from a person of greater experience and, in the circumstances, greater ability, if the way over the impasse is to be found. To attempt such a feat without help would be disastrous.

—————— DECISION-BASE ASSUMPTIONS ——————

The following values are given subject to the information given in the Changes. Remember, the Changes take precedence.

Feedback

The feedback you are giving is negative. The feedback you are receiving is positive. Realign your reactions and responses by taking a few moments of quietness.

Communications

Be willing to communicate, but be twice as willing to listen to others. One particular person will take a keen interest in your situation if you are prepared to take him into your confidence. Heed the counsel given. If communication is volunteered do not turn away from it. Help can come from the most unexpected and unlikely sources.

Risks

Definitely not.

Management

Do not be quick to jump to conclusions or conform to usual practices. The situation calls for some new element. A degree of ingenuity and fresh insight is necessary. If it is not offered, seek it from a trusted and objective source, such as an experienced and trusted consultant. But an answer does exist. This is not a 'muddle along as best we can' situation. The way forward is specific and methodical and until that way is clearly understood and adopted the resolution will not be successful.

Growth

Arrested. Implement no schemes to force growth and productivity.

Investment and Finance

Do not invest at this time. Advise upon the conditions, providing they are realistic *and* attainable, where investment is a feasible idea.

Start-Up

Difficult but get the right advice. Do not attempt to go it alone. The situation is impossible to negotiate alone.

Backing

You need it and so you should seek it, though this is not a new venture situation in itself but, rather, a necessary course of action.

Creative Judgement

Not good. Do not act upon it.

Advertising
Indications are negative. Further investment is ill advised.

Marketing
Probably difficult, if not impossible to do effectively. Concentrate upon internal management and corporate structure.

Planning
There is a need to review plans, realign perspectives in terms of long-term goals, as short-term goals are self-evident and pressing.

Contracts and Agreements
You are not in a strong position to strike a fair deal. Sign nothing at this stage and get advice when the time comes. There will be a need to renegotiate the whole agreement from scratch as the *framework* of the agreement is wrong. The fundamental terms need to be changed, the main ideas behind the agreement do not accord with priority intentions. It is a question of redrafting after considerable thought. Expert help is called for.

International Trade
Inauspicious at this time. There are insurmountable problems of communication.

Sources of Misfortune
Narrowminded, egocentric, know it all, aggressive pushing forward will be disastrous.

Sources of Good Fortune
The adoption of an attitude of some humility in the face of superior challenges. With the right help the right way out can, and must be, found.

―――――――――― **THE LINES (CHANGES)** ――――――――――
the Future-Links

Six at the beginning
Go back. Survey the problem again. Bide your time. Wait for the right moment.

Six in the second place
Problems have become compounded. There are two ways of overcoming a problem: go round (or under) it; or go over it. The strategy of avoidance is always preferable. But here you can do neither. Dire necessity compels you to meet the obstacle head on. This is looking for trouble but there is no choice because the nature of the problem means it cannot be resolved in any other way.

Nine in the third place

You cannot afford to take risks in the field of action. The people who rely upon you cannot survive without you, so stay put. Good fortune.

Six in the fourth place

There are unseen difficulties if you follow this line of action. You cannot trust to a lucky break, it won't happen. Neither should you go alone. Hold back and wait both for the right people and a time when the way forward can be scrutinized calmly.

Nine in the fifth place

This is your calling; your responsibility. You have the ability to sort out the situation and call upon others to help do so under your leadership. You might be tempted to turn your back but, if you do, the answer to the situation may not be found without you. Stay and help. Lead.

Six in the last place

Just as in the situation depicted in the last line a special person is called (perhaps by conscience) to lend help in a difficult situation. It is a moral imperative because a) he does not have to; b) he is quite safe anyway; c) he has no fear for his own destiny and life. The only reason he turns to help people in difficulty is because they need him; their chances of success increase immeasurably because he *can help* when others can't. A person of similar ability and stature joins a man with this resolve and the result is great good fortune. In this case a new force can transform a situation. The situation is auspicious and success is assured.

HEXAGRAM 40

Deliverance

---------- JUDGEMENT ----------

Successful resolution of arduous problems. Good fortune.

---------- SPECIFIC MODALITY ----------

Return to normal routines and conditions as soon as possible now that the main period of struggle is over.

---------- AMBIENCE ----------

Recovery, convalescence; continue as normal in a calm way.

---------- CONCEPT MODEL ----------

During times of difficulty and tension extraordinary energy must be used in order to resolve situations. The return to normal patterns of working is, however, the general aim. No organization can exist perpetually in a state of high tension, there have to be periods of 'normal working'. If this were not the case there would be no slack to take up when extraordinary times prevail. People are most alert when relaxed. The possibility of increased tension brings about the possibility of increased efficiency. But a perpetual state of full tension would lead to immediate breakdown if new pressures were added.

What is pictured here is a situation following a period of maximum tension and maximum concentration which was required in order to overcome pressing difficulties. Overcoming such obstacles has been a priority. What kind of obstacles have been overcome? (See Hexagram 39: Obstruction.) Obstacles could be a deadline, a tight situation, a serious emotional imbalance, confusion, anger, fear, turmoil of some kind. These predicaments require immediate energy, immediate resolution as they necessarily preclude progressive action. Now the obstacle is passed.

───────── DECISION-BASE ASSUMPTIONS ─────────

The following values are given subject to the information given in the Changes. Remember, the Changes take precedence.

Planning
Once satisfactory order has been achieved in everyday events they should be allowed to run in gently. There is no need to force an artificial or unnecessary pace. Let the reinstated elements find their own level and allow details to emerge. All planning must take account of a monitored performance rating over a period of time. For a company this is a year. For an individual life and the world system this is a ten-year period. The natural level has the quality of endurance and difficulties can be met. The varying energy requirements have to be built into the original planning. The object of the exercise is to maintain a condition of general recovery. Consider the initial period as a period of convalescence.

Management
Once a routine practice has been *found* it must be objectively agreed and systematized so that it can be seen to provide for all reasonable and naturally expected contingencies. (See Hexagrams 20: Contemplation; and 32: Duration.) The capacity to increase speed and to accommodate depressions has to be inherent. The situation must work normally *as if* there were no extraordinary elements with which to contend. Treat the situation as 'experimental and new'; people must not be overworked, situations must not be overloaded.

Creative Judgement
Not quite stable. Wait a while before making intuitive assessments or acting on them.

Start-Up
Anything requiring vigorous new energy should be avoided for the time being. But continuing with an already established project is in order providing methods and procedures are already in working order.

Backing
The situation requires further stimulation and maturity before backers are approached.

Investment and Finance
Commitments are reasonably safe providing there is an acceptable track record. Entirely new ventures should be watched for a while yet

– a year. The prospects are generally favourable and there is nothing specifically unreliable. Common sense prevails.

Agreements and Contracts

Providing you are willing to renegotiate difficult points from scratch and establish a more equitable working relationship (also forgiving past mistakes) there is no reason why steady progress cannot be made. Nothing dramatic should be attempted, however, and time should be given for new foundations to settle before placing heavy demands upon them.

Growth and Productivity

A climate of steady development is present. Can it be maintained without chopping and changing all the time? Stick to the plan.

Advertising

Nothing flashy or loud. A modest profile carries further at this stage.

Marketing

Keep it straightforward and simple. New markets will show themselves if past experience has shown some measure of success. If not, there are still fundamental changes to make in style, direction and plan. These should be drawn up quickly and with the minimum of fuss as the indications should be clear by now.

Communications

Differences of opinion should be forgiven and forgotten, and some tangible indication of a new mood should be communicated as soon as a favourable opportunity presents itself – but make that soon. In any event, an atmosphere of congenial cooperation develops. Keep events in the open and avoid being in any way presumptuous or pushy.

Feedback

At first urgent and then more relaxed.

Sources of Misfortune

Dwelling on the mistakes of the past; holding grudges; wasting new energy on useless misgivings; maintaining a level of tension; looking vengefully over the shoulder – this will cause retardation and possible disaster. Keep your eyes on the future and think positive.

Sources of Good Fortune

A change in conditions calls for some feeling of optimism and elation when the change is a release from long tension. But the energy must be used to complete unfinished work and to establish a routine in order to stabilize the situation so that progress continues to be made

– but not in an atmosphere of rush and hurry. Then the new time can be consolidated (see Hexagram 24: Return) and perpetuated.

——————————— THE LINES (CHANGES) ———————————
the Future-Links

Six at the beginning
You are through the worst of it. Now is the time to consolidate the successful transition of attitude and condition. Rest. Sleep. Empty the mind. Breathe. Relax. Do not rush around playing with schemes and plans and getting priorities confused. This is a period of convalescence. The scale of the earlier disorder will give some indication of how long the period of convalescence should be. The general rule is that a period of quietness should equal a period of confusion. A mild outburst of a few hours should be settled by a few hours' settled rest. A few years of madness should be tempered by a few years of quietness. And so on.

Nine in the second place
Sometimes rescuing a situation from disaster means sacking people who are sycophants, don't do much but are full of false praise, enjoying the spoils of privilege and power. The individual who brings about this order is someone who is not given to violence but is calm, rational and spiritually strong. The influence transmits as power of character. Such a person is dedicated to bringing the situation to a new order and consolidating success. He knows there is no room for people who cannot be trusted to maintain the vision. There are not less than three such hangers-on.

Six in the third place
Success has brought with it sudden material comforts. It takes time to adapt to a new standard of living. But the warning is crystal clear: don't flaunt it or let it go to your head. Others love to steal from vain people.

Nine in the fourth place
The situation has changed. There are things to be done. Some of the people around you have no real attachment to your path in life. For their own reasons they persist in hanging on but, so long as they do, those with whom you should be working keep their distance and the future becomes less certain. You cannot change the fate of your life. But if you have some conscious intimation of the drift of events then make a few decisions of your own. The absence of decisions on your part can be construed as dragging your feet and success seems to be slower in coming. The right people are available and they should be allowed to approach. (See Hexagram 19: Approach.)

Six in the fifth place
Be self-reliant. If obdurate people won't leave your field of action ignore them completely. Sooner or later, they get the message and leave of their own accord.

Six in the last place

It often happens that the wrong people hold positions of power. They have values which are not in keeping with their responsibilities. These people are obtuse and self-opinionated, often hinder progress and inhibit the birth of a new time. They hardly know the damage they do. They have to be moved out of the position of responsibility. If necessary they must be sacked at the right moment. They certainly will not go away of their own free will as they are not susceptible to good influences, and do not take hints. Indeed, it will do no good to try to cooperate with them. They have to be stopped. This is one of the few instances when the *I Ching* speaks of a decisive break with certain types of people (but see the lines in Hexagram 29: Deep Waters).

HEXAGRAM 41

Decrease (Poverty/Taxation)

'Amass a store of gold and jade and no one can protect it.'
Lao Tsu, *Tao Te Ching*

JUDGEMENT

Certain sacrifices have to be made at this time of a financial nature in order to provide for future times; if this can be done in an excellent spirit: supreme good fortune.

SPECIFIC MODALITY

Wealth passes from the people to government through taxation, levies, duties. In the proper measure and at the right time, the exchange is successful though some hardship might be felt. But the time for *decrease* passes. Certain values must be observed, however, if tyranny and demoralization are to be avoided.

AMBIENCE

Lean times. Ornaments and even the trappings of worship, if necessary, must be sacrificed in order to preserve fundamental needs of provision and order. Sound administrative principles have to be practised at these times.

CONCEPT MODEL

Even when resources have to be redirected so that there is not much in the way of luxuries certain values still shine through: sincerity (see Hexagrams 11: Peace; 25: Innocence and 12: Standstill) and self-sacrifice. There are always times when these are called for. This hexagram's counterpart is Hexagram 42: Increase. Both have certain rules. If the period of decrease is not properly administered the power to generate wealth and work at another time is wasted. The period of decrease is therefore also the time when one stores energy, makes cutbacks so long as they do not affect morale and so long as it is understood that the sacrifice is necessary and temporary. A continued condition of relative deprivation destroys morale. If a fixed time limit is not set at the outset, the resources which should be saved are used in pilfering, worry and secret hordings, and the spirit of storing up energy for creation of wealth is undermined.

This is therefore a situation which must be carefully explained; plans must be made, promises given, conditions described, resolutions offered and upheld. Otherwise trust diminishes and abuse can flourish. For this reason the *I Ching* constantly underlines the requirement for openness and frankness when dealing with public amenities, wealth, taxation, special resources and benefits in general. One cannot rely upon people to cooperate during lean times if leaders have been stealing and lying in times of abundance. Secrecy is always noticed. When the time for cooperation comes people remember they suffered hardships while others prospered. But if the natural cycle and correct inner values have been maintained (this is the time to fortify them), then generating power in times of decrease is successful. Less correct values lead to longer hardships. One cannot take from the land what the land is not able to produce. One cannot take what has not been put in. The cycle of nature must be preserved if it is to be capable of sustaining itself.

─────────── DECISION-BASE ASSUMPTIONS ───────────

The following values are given subject to the information given in the Changes. Remember, the Changes take precedence.

Management
What is lessened in outward prosperity can be counterbalanced by training and learning and spending time growing prosperous inwardly. In nature this is the purpose of the time of decrease. Pushing against the time by trying to maintain the same output is a mistake. This is not the time for success in the outward aspect. Success can be had in inner cultivation and storing up outward resources for a more propitious time. The fortunes of the company are going to fare better if you don't cream off and exhaust its existing assets.

Profits
Don't even try. The lesson is 'to preserve'.

Start-Up
Not now. Wait for an auspicious time such as in Hexagrams 1: The Creative; 24: Transition; 34: The Power of the Great; 35: Progress;

42: Increase, or 50: The Cauldron. This is not the time to venture forth with new ideas. It is a good time to evaluate the value of an idea carefully. Energy devoted in that direction will reap rewards when the time comes for action.

Investment Finance
Only invest in fundamentals. Luxuries and products will not flourish at this time and so investment should be in those ideas which sustain people – these will flourish when they answer basic needs.

Planning
Large plans must not be contemplated at this time. Do not organize for relatively large expenditures. Prepare to economize and preserve but think in terms of the useful application of preserved resources. Do not spend on anything which is not vital to keeping the situation alive.

Advertising
Cut back.

Marketing
Only ideas whose needs are visible can be marketed successfully – these are basic and obvious. Read the times and direct accordingly.

Creative Judgement
Fairly good, but will you remember your thoughts of today in a time of increase? A wealthy person should always remember a time like this and take careful note of impressive ideas, especially for products and services which might eventually be useful when people have more capital and disposable income. During times of Increase these ideas are not so visible. Ask, 'What is needed now?' This will be a basis for future success.

Intuition
If you are not busy spending but thinking your intuitions will sharpen up. They will become increasingly sharp in the next two or three months. This is the best time to develop intuition. It is very difficult to sharpen intuition during times of increase and plenty. Rightly, other matters will occupy your attention at that time.

Growth and Productivity
No. Expenditures will be wasted. Inward development will profit. For the businessman who is always preoccupied with money and profits this is a lesson on what it means to keep his actions in synchronization with natural forces. Those who do not know how to adjust at these times go under or fail to make progress when the time

is right. The same applies to government expenditure. The situation is a testament to man's illusory control over nature. He cannot change these forces, but if he adapts to the time how can he fail? Nature is with him and not against him.

Contracts and Agreements
If they are not really equitable and just, i.e., if benefit is not truly aimed at those who have the greatest need, the lashback will be disastrous later, for it is here that the real wealth of a nation, a company staff, a team is nurtured. Starve morale in a time when support and need is highest and you destroy yourself. This is not an easy idea to grasp, but the lessons are there.

Risks
Inauspicious. Future prosperity is at risk if expenditures are not properly directed now.

How to Get the Best from People
Help them when they are in need. You cannot tax what they have not got when you need the investment in a time of opportunity. What is sacrificed now in extraneous matters (luxuries *et al.*) will return later.

Sources of Misfortune
Showing off; stealing and causing misery by keeping up appearances with no corresponding spiritual value; unjust deployment of resources in a time of scanty provision; behaving without any conscience towards the needs of others. Selfish greed. What you waste now will cost you later.

Sources of Good Fortune
Simple sincerity is appropriate when the glitter and trappings of wealth cannot be had. There is no shame in this. People always understand it and resent a show of wealth at the expense of their poverty. (See Hexagrams 49: Revolution; 59: Dispersion of Wealth and 14: Wealth.)

--- **THE LINES (CHANGES)** ---
the Future-Links

Nine at the beginning
It is a good man who steps forward to help someone else when there is no private advantage by so doing. But even he cannot give endlessly. It is for the person being helped to perceive if the help he receives harms his helper. Such a stricture applies to Government expenditures especially when funds are weighed according to need. It is insane, unnatural and irresponsible (see Hexagram 7: The Army) to spend vast amounts of money on protecting a

system which is engaged in oppressing its people. No government is respected for such maladministration and it is, indeed, an evil government which neglects the fundamental needs of its people. At a time of decrease a good government knows how to meet contingencies and where to direct funds quickly and swiftly to areas of greatest need (see Hexagram 13: Fellowship with Men).

The principle here is that when we have enough in a time of decrease we can give to others in full measure without bringing the economy to its knees. Helping people in need always pays financial dividends later, but its rewards in friendship, good-will and cooperation are a million times more valuable. It is a duty to give to those in need. The corresponding duty is that a good man will not take more than he needs from another in the way of voluntary help.

Nine in the second place

You can help best by being strong yourself and being the embodiment of exemplary values. You do not need to compromise your self-esteem to be of help to others, and what value would there be in gains acquired that way? You do not stoop to conquer, you raise people up by the power of your inner strength and only when people are raised up in this way are they helped.

Six in the third place

The right person will come at the right time if you have no close kinship. But in a time of decrease three is a crowd and there will be squabbles.

Six in the fourth place

The environment is bad for you. It reinforces the wrong elements in your nature and your better friends know it and keep their distance. But if you show that you are willing to change your ways your friends won't tarry in reinforcing and supporting you.

Six in the fifth place

Nothing, absolutely nothing can prevent you from embracing good fortune. It is a matter of fate.

Nine in the last place

This is the line of the Man of Excellence. He does things which benefit everybody. This is genius and brilliance of a very high order.

HEXAGRAM 42

Increase
(Spiritual and Material Wealth)

---------------------- JUDGEMENT ----------------------

Great good fortune and great achievement if you realize that the power of leadership is to serve and not dominate. A time of increase in personal good fortune.

---------------------- SPECIFIC MODALITY ----------------------

A special time for achievement but sacrifices must be made. Careful discrimination is required in expenditure.

---------------------- AMBIENCE ----------------------

A powerful drive forward which could be misused and energy wasted if self-discipline is not used.

---------------------- CONCEPT MODEL ----------------------

Here, we see a picture of management and leadership which deliberately makes its power and resources available 'from the bottom upward', as it were. Creative energy, rather than assuming its natural lofty position, sublimates into more earthly regions. In organizational terms this means leaders and managers who serve rather than dominate. They are people who use their extra energy to increase the wellbeing of those not so highly placed. But in order to do that they have to understand and feel confident of their own abilities and strength.

---------------------- DECISION-BASE ASSUMPTIONS ----------------------

The following values are given subject to the information given in the Changes. Remember, the Changes take precedence.

Planning

Before any plans to expand or develop are implemented it is necessary to make sure that those resources and people who have drawn in their belts during earlier periods of need are now adequately remunerated and replenished. Plans for future prosperity stand or fall on proper preparation. Finite resources must be reorganized for the long term. All expansion must be considered in these terms. Begin by focusing on the fundamentals. (See Hexagrams 30: The Clinging, Fire; 41: Decrease and 47: The Well.)

Management

Benefits which accrue to management before they accrue to staff and basic resources are misspent and are an unbalancing force. Good management raises up people and resources in need to a position of greater wealth. This is a time of great energy and efforts will go a long way. The requirement is immediate as there is a time limit within which such 'increasing' activity is meaningful and germane to the time. Your own increase is a part of the process. The giving of rises in salary is only a limited application of the principle. The increase and benefit must be broad-based and general.

Creative Judgement

Excellent, but do not dissipate energies by becoming distracted. This is definitely a work first, play later situation.

Feedback

Begin with the grass roots and work upward. The quality of feedback is usually a condition of the time. Here there is an *aptitude* and *imperative* for positive feedback. Things will not work properly later unless appropriate and tangible feedback is given in all directions.

Communications

Excellent. Aim for clarity and make intentions categorical providing they are in keeping with the wholesome demands of the time. One will only meet with negativity from those who have selfish motives.

Investment and Finance

Invest in those who have invested in you and are still in need. Stocks of basic raw materials need to be replenished and stored. People want a reward on their past investment before future investment in the new is entertained. The cycle of investment must be maintained at this point or the chain will break. But invest you must. This is not the time to hold back or save. This is the time also for a return on investment.

Growth and Productivity
At the very minimum, parity must be maintained but there should be development in some areas. Deal with areas of greatest need first. This will be a long-term investment you cannot afford to ignore.

Advertising
Deal first with internal company needs before new or extraordinary budgets are given the go-ahead. Auspicious.

Marketing
Step it up.

Start-Up
Very promising. Present proposals with confidence and clarity.

Backing
If general equilibrium is being maintained in the wider commercial field, this should be no problem at all. Seek it with confidence.

Contracts and Agreements
The agreement must show a fair apportionment of profits. A measure of generosity can be expected and is in order. Consider the position of *being generous* as a prudent investment in the future.

Risks
The comprehensibility of the available facts, properly considered, should eliminate the risk element. Arrange the facts according to the principles described and they will reveal an internal logic which should point in a clear direction. It is a matter of extrapolation.

Sources of Misfortune
Failure to nourish, replenish, raise, repay for past sacrifices will cause a polarization which may require drastic restructuring later. Such a requirement will be unnecessarily costly if the needs of the present are not met immediately.

Sources of Good Fortune
Increase those who have been decreased. Expect or appeal for increase if you have made sacrifices which have benefited the whole organization. This is the time to raise, replenish, fill, complete. In organizational matters this may express itself as a high moral priority. Viewed in nature it is a necessity. Auspicious.

THE LINES (CHANGES)
the Future-Links

Nine at the beginning
You have been given the means by which you can achieve something of immense value. It is not everyone that is granted such a power. Use it well and to great effect while the time is propitious. You can make great progress in whatever you are doing. Do not think about what you will get out of it in terms of personal wealth; and do not shirk the extra work-load the position brings. Just think in terms of the benefit the work brings. That is its true reward.

Six in the second place
You will receive great benefit and nothing can prevent it. But the reason for this is that you are learning to understand how everything works and you yourself have become a valuable catalyst for that natural process. When such a thing happens it is impossible not to be increased. This is a very special situation for an individual who is singled-out. Continue to be so dedicated and the whole process augments itself naturally.

Six in the third place
People of conviction can turn the tide of events away from calamities and distress and transform them into prosperity and well-being. This means that the power they possess is so in tune with nature that they can perform what appear to be superhuman feats.

Six in the fourth place
You are a catalyst, a receiver-transmitter. You work to make comprehensible the higher to the lower and the lower to the higher. This activity receives its assent in the clarity and honesty of your actions.

Nine in the fifth place
The laws of nature, when they are working properly, appear to have the quality of a human virtue – the conscious and moral equivalent of balance in a time of increase is generosity, beneficence, kindness. But this is not something which is meticulously planned but, rather, is something which occurs as a corollary of understanding how things work. Mencius speaks of 'a politics of kindness'. This springs from a natural obedience to the Golden Mean, as perceived by the ancient Greek philosophers, notably Aristotle. The two ideas, kindness and balance in a time of increase, dovetail and make sense of nature.

Nine in the last place
Somebody who should bring increase to others but who does not is selfish and greedy and the effect is that cooperation and good will also desert him. Such people end up being the object of dislike and justly so, for they are happy to take when there is little and hoard in order to protect themselves at the cost of others' misery. This is irresponsible, reprehensible and unnatural behaviour and spoils future good fortune. For believers in luck this is the way to lose it.

HEXAGRAM 43

Breakthrough (Determination)

—— JUDGEMENT ——

The herald of a new time which is better, higher, more rewarding if you make a pledge to yourself to complete the change of attitude.

—— SPECIFIC MODALITY ——

A new way of life waits in the wings. The wealth is shared, not hoarded. Do not tolerate malpractices any longer from any quarter in your field of action. The value of past work is now becoming apparent.

—— AMBIENCE ——

Achievement. But you do not rest on your laurels. You complete the change with a resolution towards perfection.

—— CONCEPT MODEL ——

There are changes which are brought about by the time, as the situation in Hexagram 24: Transition signifies; in that hexagram, a better time dawns and comes naturally without being forced. But here the change to new conditions comes about as a result of a decision. It is difficult, however. A firm resolve and great effort is needed because the temptation to let the situation go is strong. But the drive and the will is there to make the change. How do you achieve it? If you force matters the effort might backfire and the result will be without grace. What is required first is the personal admission that the work is not complete and that a special energy and effort is required.

Organizations might feel that certain questionable practices do no harm and that their continuation can be tolerated. But this is probably self-delusion. The whole act needs to be cleaned up; those practices which are known to be unacceptable should be brought under control. New rules have to be made.

─────────── DECISION-BASE ASSUMPTIONS ───────────

The following values are given subject to the information given in the Changes. Remember, the Changes take precedence.

Management
The system of management is inadequate and needs to be radically overhauled and reviewed objectively because an inherent inefficiency is causing the resources of the company to stagnate. The result is manifest inefficiency and deprivation for some members of the organization. But there is still time, if the decision is taken immediately, to begin the review. Once a new system has been agreed to increase the use and flow of resources, however, it must be constantly monitored and a department or job role set up, either within the company or by hiring an outside consultant specialist, to this end.

Feedback
In the face of negativity don't be disheartened. Quality will win through.

Planning
Integration problems. Long-term plans will fail if basic operating assumptions are not changed.

Advertising
Premature. Success is strictly conditional on the quality of the work.

Marketing
Long-term success is strictly conditional.

Investment and Finance
Take a wider view. Organizations which move resources around, rather than 'fixed assets' like property, are favoured.

Start-Up
Auspicious if you are determined to generate wealth beyond your own needs. The situation is particularly strong if matters of good principle are involved. Prospects are excellent.

Backing
Auspicious, but choose organizations which are prepared to take risks and who know how to communicate difficult ideas.

International Trade
The right ideas and the right structure could be very successful. Be prepared to take a risk on higher values.

Growth and Productivity
There will be either an imminent collapse or a change which will precipitate growth.

Creative Judgement
Can you write the reasons down clearly and comprehensively? Do you understand the stages involved? Can you make a decision? Are you prepared to stick by it because the reason for it is sound? Can you be resolute in the face of setbacks.

Communications
More understanding is needed. You may be missing hints. Demand greater clarity and reasons for systems.

Sources of Misfortune
No resolution for change and work, no creative growth. Selfish hoarding of wealth equals disaster at any level.

Sources of Good Fortune
A firm decision to act upon sound reasons which have an inner consistency and which are meaningful beyond the parameters of your own bank balance. Auspicious.

———————— **THE LINES (CHANGES)** ————————
the Future-Links

Nine at the beginning
The decision is fine. But be careful. Test your abilities with problems cautiously. You don't want to be stopped by an indigestible problem when your resolve is fresh and energy high.

Nine in the second place
Trust your reason but tether your donkeys, as they say. Keep your ears and eyes open. The situation may or may not be straightforward. The situation requires you to be relaxed, but alert, confident but not incautious. To be equal to the task is a condition of personal strength as well as of ability.

Nine in the third place
Difficult. The situation is embarrassing because you run the risk of having your reputation called into question (quite unjustifiably) because of your association with people who have bad reputations. What can you do? If you openly disown such people they will live up to their own bad reputation and try to drag you down with them. If you don't, the people whose respect you deserve withhold their willing cooperation. But if you know the truth and hold to it you can live through this without irreparable harm. The object lesson is to avoid association with organizations and individuals who are not prepared to acknowledge your standards of conduct.

Nine in the fourth place
Stop – or it will cost you dearly. You are wrong. The *I Ching* is right.

Nine in the fifth place
He is wrong. You are right. Do not give up the fight.

Six in the last place
The hardest thing is to examine yourself for tendencies to weakness when everything is almost in order. But it is important for you to make a real and heartfelt effort. Be aware of the situation. There are one or two important matters still to be cleared up.

HEXAGRAM 44

Coming to Meet

―――――――――――― JUDGEMENT ――――――――――――

If the wrong people are not encouraged, success. Be careful who you employ or allow into your confidence. Watch for the 'undermining' influence and for false appearances.

―――――――――――― SPECIFIC MODALITY ――――――――――――

If you cannot go in person, send an envoy. Be fully informed of the effects of your decisions so that you know the right way to proceed in the future.

―――――――――――― AMBIENCE ――――――――――――

Some danger that the initiative of the wrong people or individual voluntarily enters the field of action. They should receive no power.

―――――――――――― CONCEPT MODEL ――――――――――――

The overall situation is generally strong, progressive and creative. But this does not define it. There is a new element coming into play which has to be taken into consideration. Often, when things are going well, there is a force of temptation, usually recognizable as an individual, which threatens to put a shadow on events. It is important to be aware of this force for what it is. Its effect is strong only in so far as it is in direct contrast to everything else. Its symbol is the yin line in the first place (the Changes). It is the only yin line in the presence of strong yang lines. Its place at the bottom indicates its subtle, creeping nature.

In the foregoing hexagram the weak yin line occupied the top place, in the presence of five strong yang lines. It was an insidious force because it had to be overcome although its strength could not easily be measured.

———————— DECISION-BASE ASSUMPTIONS ————————

The following values are given subject to the information given in the Changes. Remember, the Changes take precedence.

Management
Take care who you promote. To understand the motives of an attractive force you have to understand your own. This calls for some personal examination. If you are incapable of this you cannot prevent the wrong influences from taking hold for the simple reason that you do not recognize what they are. The aptitude to make an evaluation is not necessarily absent, but it must be used. The idea also extends to what ideas or values are promoted also, and how far afield.

Creative Judgement
Creative judgement is always limited by the degree of one's self-knowledge. That is a plain fact. Here, its value is crucial in the long term. You must view ideas and people not superficially but as a whole, as the consequences go beyond what is immediately present. Some effort, therefore, has to be made to look to effects as well as causes.

Advertising
What are you promoting? Exactly? What other ideas are suggested by the images used? What are the concepts of association which are favoured? There is a hint that the successful image will have a universal appeal if it reflects a universal value, a value which is already resident in the market place rather than one invented or imposed.

Marketing
Auspicious.

Communications
Powerful and effective.

Investment and Finance
Auspicious, but look at the track record carefully, think about the ideas behind the achievement; don't look only at the fiscal value. If you invest in ideas which tend to weaken creative self-reliance you are investing in ideas which will, in the end, collapse. It is the propensity for creative change which must be enhanced.

Start-Up
Auspicious. But be patient.

Backing

It is early days yet. Do not be too quick off the mark. The tendency is very positive, but let it mature. If you have careful regard for all of the foregoing and act accordingly, you should actively seek backing from people. The usual requirement to present your ideas in a clear and comprehensible form (simple, unambiguous – the hallmarks of clarity and success) is emphasized. If there are doubts in your mind, do not act. You cannot lift off until crystal clear in your own mind. This is a basic condition for starting anything. Clarity has to be developed through constantly reviewing the situation, means *and* effects. Remember that a backer will not always look at the wider effects of a proposition, only at the profit-making potential and the cooperation which can be brought to bear to that effect. You, therefore, have to be aware of the effects and they must be equally emphasized. If such an approach is not well met by prospective buyers, that is a judgement upon them, not upon you. They are the wrong backers. The right backer will always have a wider view, and his intentions will be excellent, perhaps more so than your own. If you begin by looking through this lens you will see any deceptions, if they are present.

Feedback

Difficult to interpret at first. Let others take the initiative. Do not seek feedback in an overly eager way. Do not be seen to encourage it, and do not encourage it. It should be spontaneous if it is to be of real value.

Planning

The measure of a good planner is his perception of the effects of action in the long term. A good planner is not required for the short term – just good instincts and intuition which may or may not be invested with a wider view. A good intuition can equally work for the greedy as for the altruistic. A good long-term planner knows the seeds and where to plant them. (See Hexagrams 1: The Creative and 2: The Receptive.)

Growth and Productivity
Auspicious.

Contracts and Agreements
Auspicious but see Start-Up and Backing. Agreements should be long term but, if you are not sure, short-term agreements should not be made.

Meetings

Ask searching questions, listen to the answers. If answers are ambiguous then motives and intentions are being hidden. Why is this? Only those who are clear and open in the face of searching questions (which also have to be framed openly and clearly) can be trusted in the long term. Do not make commitments at the meeting. Always wait until you have digested what has been communicated.

Risks

None.

Operational Management

Take care who you recruit, or invite to positions of responsibility. Be careful about those with whom you entrust valuable ideas and work. There may be a current of influence which, when cultivated, saps energy, misuses confidences, attacks creativity, forestalls strength and purpose, undermines confidence and whittles away at determination. It is a steady and creeping power. Do not invite 'vampiric forces' into one's own life. Be discriminating. The wise and judicious person recognizes insidious opposition at its beginning. Note first impressions; those who seem untrustworthy at first may turn into staunch friends.

There are ways of dealing with such situations. Consult the *I Ching* on the specific way to deal with the situation. See Hexagrams 21 and 43.

Attitude

Unlike Hexagram 43: Resolution, where the undermining influence is clever and immensely devious – here the undermining influence is not so consciously devious. It appears devious because of its sham innocence, its pretence of weakness. Its *position* makes it devious rather than its intention. It is possible to set a seed into events which will grow and cause confusion, obeying the law of its own nature. After it has been planted it does not have to be monitored and masterminded. The architects can leave it to do its pernicious work for the process is automatic.

Once consciousness of such a conscious force has arisen, however, that seed and its offspring can be destroyed at the optimum moment by the creative force. Becoming conscious of that *seed* is most difficult, for it is all too easy to grow used to its presence and pass it off as normal, a 'fact of life'. This lack of awareness nourishes the evil and enables it to seize control at the decisive moment and threaten to, even succeed in, bringing down the house. (See Hexagrams 23: Splitting Apart; 49: Revolution.)

Sources of Misfortune

Look for a divisive influence. It could be nothing more than a tendency to accept a situation which is just acceptable because it is still weak. That would be the mistake you will rue. You have to control it or it will control you, sometimes without your knowing.

First, one must learn to recognize such times. Then one must learn to recognize such people. They work over a period of time - you must not get the impression that this element comes into being and is then squashed. It can be in the atmosphere and prolong its existence through temporary attachments. It is even possible to get so used to the presence of such an influence that, after a while, one comes to accept it as normal, no longer a threat. But when it (whether in the form of an individual or certain values) rises up through the organization to assume a position of strength or authority it can show itself for what it is. This is the influence which can corrupt. It can destroy good work.

It must be stressed however, that, in order for the chain of events to be set off, there has to be an invitation from the strong and creative elements present. Such an invitation is therefore not advised even though your position might, to all intents and purposes, appear impregnable. What is allowed to advance with a free hand now, will have to be contended with later when it has become stronger.

Sources of Good Fortune

The object of the exercise to organize events into a coherent order. Other people will be involved in carrying them into effect.

THE LINES (CHANGES)
the Future-Links

Six at the beginning

If an influence is not checked when it is weak how are you going to control it when it grows up? (See Hexagram 37: The Family.)

Nine in the second place

How do you control an unruly but weak force so that it learns to control itself? Not with violence. The individual concerned should not be allowed to represent the company's interests. Keep this person where you can see what he is up to at all times.

Nine in the third place

You want to submit but you cannot. You should not submit but you want to. Confusion, but the potential harm is restricted and contained. The inner discomfort is unenviable.

Nine in the fourth place
They may be useful so avoid angering them.

Nine in the fifth place
Your control over people and the whole situation results from the effect of your character and personality. You don't even have to say anything. Order returns because the processes of nature make it look like fate. What is the difference?

Nine in the last place
If others dislike you because you won't get involved, that is their problem. You can take it.

HEXAGRAM 45

Gathering Together (The Group)

JUDGEMENT

The whole is greater than the sum of its parts. When people join together with a common aim and in a common feeling: success and good fortune.

SPECIFIC MODALITY

The individual is enhanced by his membership of a larger organization so long as it has an honoured and respected leader. New talent should be encouraged.

AMBIENCE

Strength and fortitude. The future generation can be secured through the past.

CONCEPT MODEL

The natural disposition of people is to form themselves into groups. The idea is not restricted to organizations which form in order to create profits, although the gathering together of large numbers of people who share a coherent identity allows them to achieve luminous and visible results. The basis of the idea is the impetus to work with others. Behind that impetus is a spiritual idea: the whole is greater than the sum of its parts.

But what joins people together? In Hexagram 8: Holding Together, people are held together by a strong leader. Here there is more: a strong leader *and* a strong idea. The two together give rise to a purpose. The members of the group feel empathy not only with other individual members, but with the aims of the group. They gather in order to achieve something which has the effect of enhancing the identity of the group.

————————— DECISION-BASE ASSUMPTIONS —————————

The following values are given subject to the information given in the Changes. Remember, the Changes take precedence.

Management
Definitive requirement for strength and self-possession. You have to have your own act together if others are to have confidence in you. The opposite of this is indecisiveness and lack of self-discipline which communicates itself to those who would follow and repels that all-too-important ingredient called 'confidence' from which morale is generated.

Planning
The possibilities are very great. Are the aims and intentions clear?

Creative Judgement
Use it to take preparatory measures.

Advertising
Big ideas are under consideration. If there is enough cooperation they can succeed.

Marketing
The scale contemplated is relatively large; coordination is therefore a key factor. Otherwise, all other things being equal, auspicious.

Feedback
Everybody in key positions has to be approachable. Cooperation is not possible without a positive aura of action. Auspicious.

Communications
Excellent.

Growth and Productivity
Things are in their beginning. The full potential has by no means been realized. Auspicious.

Investment and Finance
If there is a strong sense of unity, nobody can lose. There is everything to gain. Auspicious.

Start-Up
Gaining the cooperation of people is the first step. No problems are envisaged but, if you have any doubts, see Hexagram 8: Holding Together.

Backing
Auspicious, but it is a matter of the scale of benefit. Resources have to be vested in a wide range of activities. It is probably better if there is more than one source of investment and support.

International Relations and Trade
The position is positive. If sound objectives are shared in the open the achievements could be luminous and great. Auspicious if you think in terms of the wider community.

Agreements and Contracts
Since they are based on a judgement of the whole group there is less emphasis on any specific aspect. The whole vision is contemplated and a sense of participation by all concerned is felt as the guiding force behind agreements. Therefore they are auspicious and successful.

Sources of Misfortune
Watch for divisive tendencies, envious behaviour, jealousy and selfish motivations which work against the concept of 'gathering together'. Resources can be wasted, squandered, stolen (as in a lake bursting its banks) if this is allowed to happen; some perception of the whole project and its limitations has to be understood at the outset. This is why so much emphasis is placed upon correct leadership as it is the responsibility of the organizer to provide against such eventualities by understanding the limits of the whole in relation to its parts.

Sources of Good Fortune
Here we see the beginnings of cooperation on a larger scale. Many people could become involved when the project achieves momentum and matures. The forces behind such initiatives tend to find a direction of their own once they have grown to a certain size. If people pull together the overall situation will be immensely improved.

───────── **THE LINES (CHANGES)** ─────────
the Future-Links

Six at the beginning
Uncertainty and insecurity prevail. How can they be overcome? People must ask for clarification and help. The leader recognizes the need and reinforces the collective position. Uncertainty arises when the beginning of the venture is not brought about by a clear decision but by an indefinable desire to do

something, nobody knows quite what. The situation is capable of clarity and action, however.

Six in the second place

You feel drawn towards certain people. Let that attraction work. You do not have to scheme. The attraction or empathy is a natural feeling which works through the principle of resonance which governs change and direction in life. This idea of resonance working at a global level is still a mystery, although its existence is indisputable. When it is further understood (see Hexagram 16: Enthusiasm) the laws of attraction in nature and in the affairs of men will not be regarded as arbitrary. The laws of attraction are quite specific.

The *I Ching* itself may provide a coherent language for contemplating the dynamics involved in the attraction between people, the laws of empathy, since the *I Ching* is itself a resonance system.

Six in the third place

You do not feel so integrated with the whole organization as you would like. To some extent you know that the matter is out of your hands. The organization has to recognize you. Do not be put off, however. There is someone, integrated into the group, who can help. You have to make a conscious decision to communicate with this person. But do you know who it is? The process of thinking along these lines, however, will reveal the right solution.

Nine in the fourth place

Altruistic action. Great good fortune. People are naturally attracted to the cause and to the work. No problems, the outcome will be successful.

Nine in the fifth place

Some people are attracted to a leader for 'personal reasons' which are superficial and undoubtedly selfish. These people are in it for what they can get out of it. The leader, however, is aware of this, though he does not make a big production out of it. Instead, he continues in the spirit of the work; the effect is that the attitudes of those who joined for their own reasons are gradually but definitely transformed.

Six in the last place

Misunderstanding. You should see eye to eye but you don't, although it is not your fault. The person who has misjudged you sees that you are upset, realizes his mistake, and acceptance and reconciliation are finally achieved. This brings about a new and more positive climate for activity.

HEXAGRAM 46

Pushing Upward
(The Beginnings of Ascent)

--------------------- JUDGEMENT ---------------------

If you try hard: great success.

--------------------- SPECIFIC MODALITY ---------------------

There are no obstructions but you have to work hard. The rewards
are objectively measurable. A sense of real achievement and accomplishment. Very auspicious.

--------------------- AMBIENCE ---------------------

Easy if you take it little by little until it is finished.

--------------------- CONCEPT MODEL ---------------------

The picture here is simple. It is that of growth. This is the time when,
if you invest time and energy, no obstructions or inner difficulties
stand in the way of achieving what you set out to do. There is a higher
correlation of energy to production. There is a matchless impulse to
work and achieve. This is why the Judgement is so good. In nature it
is a characteristic of the time. If no energy is expended nothing will
happen even though the soil is fertile and capable of yielding much.
Here, the volition is unimpeded, but the *will* has to be engaged.

Cooperation also arises from the situation. You have the added
support of well-wishers who respond to your efforts *after* the work is
completed. Not only this: the effect of the cycle is to elevate you to a
position of still greater effectiveness. Again, this is why the Judgement is so favourable. The time is excellent for achievement and
there is nothing more to be advised other than to work hard and
make the most of it.

—————— DECISION-BASE ASSUMPTIONS ——————

The following values are given subject to the information given in the Changes. Remember, the Changes take precedence.

Management
The pace of work can be stepped up naturally. Much will be achieved if you direct your mind to achievement. Any apparent obstacles can be accommodated with ease, providing the will to do so is present.

Planning
Past effort will pay dividends. There may be a change of plans when the measure of success has been evaluated. You may find that you are able to be more imaginative in your aspirations and that you won't be going it alone so much. Auspicious.

Communication
Be active. Make many suggestions.

Advertising
Auspicious.

Marketing
Go further afield, make more effort. The results could be amazing.

Feedback
Brilliant. You couldn't hope for better. The time favours you. Take advantage of the situation to show what you can do.

Growth and Productivity
If the figures do not show a vertical rise you haven't been working hard enough and the fault will be yours. There is nothing in the way.

Creative Judgement
Excellent. Use it to the full.

Investment and Finance
This is not a quick in-and-out affair. This is a result of consistent effort of the will. Continued application will bring in handsome dividends.

Start-Up
Very auspicious. You can make great strides forward, even establish yourself.

Backing
Go to see them and ask for what you want. You will find that people are happy to be of service. Such a welcome reception augments the whole process. But do not entertain misgivings.

Contracts and Agreements

No obstacles, but be choosy, don't just accept anything and everything because it is on offer. You can do well out of a time like this if you are prepared to do your homework and seek the right arrangements. There are no objections to special demands as they fit in with the overall ethos.

Timing

Maintain a rhythm. You can put yourself through your paces. Unless impinged upon by circumstances (described elsewhere), stay put – that is, maintain your base of operation in order to maximize results.

Risks

None. The situation is self-contained and is entirely within your control. What you perceive as a risk is the amplification of your own timidity. Forget about it.

International Trade

If contacts are being approached for the first time, cooperation and development are favourable. Expand the scope of joint enterprises.

Sources of Misfortune

They reside only in a complacent attitude. Otherwise there are no sources of misfortune.

Sources of Good Fortune

Consistent hard work, good communications, rhythm, positive energy.

THE LINES (CHANGES)
the Future-Links

Six at the beginning
Your motivation comes from an empathic feeling with those who hold a more fortunate position to achieve results; you therefore work to bring yourself into alignment with them. This brings good fortune because you know where you are going and why and all other things are equal.

Nine in the second place
Show your work. Be willing to put yourself forward. Do not worry about the 'right' credentials or appearances. People can still respond favourably to evidence of determination and ability, even in a highly institutionalized framework of recognition procedures.

Nine in the third place
Clear, uninhibited progress. This is the time to pull out all the stops because there is no telling when times will change. Entertain no doubts. Do not even

think about the actual or potential negative elements as this would waste precious time.

Six in the fourth place
The work is successful. Fame. Recognition. Acknowledgement. Achievement. You will be working with new people from now on.

Six in the fifth place
Excellent and fortunate. You cannot cut corners. You must not let it all go to your head. This would lead to abuse.

Six in the last place
Burning up energy for the sake of it is not right, you have to have an aim, a plan, a clear set of mental reference points by which to guide and measure your progress. This way you can pace energy, make it count and control distracting whims.

HEXAGRAM 47

Oppression (Exhaustion)

JUDGEMENT

You can make a success out of this situation even though your confidence and worth are being undermined and the conditions are oppressive.

SPECIFIC MODALITY

The wrong people are in positions of authority and this makes matters more difficult, especially as they are unreceptive to approaches.

AMBIENCE

You are tired, but your relationship with yourself is capable of transforming an outwardly depressing circumstance to one of personal contentment. You should recognize the limits of your own energy. Know when to switch off. Rest, but do not worry.

CONCEPT MODEL

Only a certain kind of person (one who has determination and also philosophical detachment from the ups and downs of everyday life) can make a success of a situation where the name of the day is Oppression. It is all too easy to be miserable. Certainly there is cause. People who are without vision, kindness and an awareness of the higher possibilities of life are in a position where they can oppress the majority – politically, a time of the tyrant. Energy seems to be wasted, effort comes to nought and goes unrewarded and unhelped. Motivation drops to an all-time low. Progress is impossible. It is in times like this that spirits are broken. How do you win in a no-win situation? You refuse to be beaten. You make yourself flexible. You waste no energy. You speak little. You move slowly. You project yourself to the absolute minimum. You give the minimum.

——————— DECISION-BASE ASSUMPTIONS ———————

The following values are given subject to the information given in the
Changes. Remember, the Changes take precedence.

Management
Waste no energy in complaint. Show fortitude in retreat.

Planning
Pointless as an outward show. Keep silent as to plans, though this is
not the time to contemplate the future.

Risks
Take none. Inauspicious.

Creative Judgement
Do not tax it.

Energy
Save it.

Growth and Productivity
Minimal if not zero.

Feedback
Negative.

Start-Up
No. Inauspicious.

Backing
No. Inauspicious.

Advertising
On no account should you make your position public.

Marketing
Do not draw attention to yourself.

Contracts and Agreements
Inauspicious. Agree nothing.

Timing
This is not the time.

Communications
Silence is the best policy.

Sources of Misfortune
Giving up.

Sources of Good Fortune

Doing as little as possible to help the oppressor. Non-cooperation.
And doing as little as possible at present.

――――――――――― THE LINES (CHANGES) ―――――――――――
the Future-Links

Six at the beginning

You have become depressed. Try to resist this feeling, otherwise it will
dictate to you and you will become powerless.

Nine in the second place

Everything seems alright as to appearances but you have a feeling of
profound dissatisfaction. You feel low, worn out, hopeless. Help is on its
way. So hang on. Be patient and try to cultivate a positive feeling. What is
that positive feeling? *Be grateful.* This will lift your spirits and give you the
power to endure; then you can learn to change the time.

Six in the third place

A mess. You have lost your self-reliance, your inner poise, your strength.
You have to sit down and give the matter some serious thought. Stop the
restless condition by stillness and quiet. You cannot achieve anything at the
moment. Meditate or learn to do so.

Nine in the fourth place

You can help but you're afraid to put your back into it in case you expose
your intentions. But this timidity is what attracts difficulties. In the end your
original impulse takes hold of the situation, but you should have the courage
of your convictions and not hold back.

Nine in the fifth place

You have the power and the will to alleviate the oppressive situation. You
have a clear vision but, without help from others who have the office and the
power to turn the vision into reality, you can do nothing. They should help
you, but they do not. Their behaviour is, of course, utterly despicable and
blameworthy, and offends the spirit. But that is their bad karma. Even those
whom you would help, the powerless and the oppressed, are blind to the
needs of the time and do not recognize the saviour in their midst. You are
alone. But you will prevail. Expend no effort therefore in attempting to
persuade and endear. This is not the time for it. Rather, take solace in your
meditations and built up strength until the right time comes of itself. All you
can profitably do at the moment is pray for their understanding. They
cannot get anywhere either. Their sense of progress is the worst kind of
self-delusion.

Six in the last place

You are suffering from inertia and judging your present situation by the
criteria of the past. Open your eyes, get an update. Test the restrictions, you
can now break them. Make the decision to do that now – and you can get
free.

HEXAGRAM 48

The Well

JUDGEMENT

If the resources of wisdom, knowledge and information are used to bring a comprehensive understanding then everything is in order. If these resources are not used, misfortune.

SPECIFIC MODALITY

No matter what the prevailing conditions: transcultural, transpolitical, transsocial, transideological, this concept embraces and is fundamental to them all. The truth is still the truth though its manifestation and expression may change. (See Hexagram 17: Following.)

AMBIENCE

Neutral insofar as the Well is available. But will it be used? Positive, if one thinks of the treasure of life itself and its meaningful correspondence to human endeavours, spiritual and temporal.

CONCEPT MODEL

The Well is a form which is useful if it contains water which is fresh, clear and drinkable. If the water is freely available and people come to it as a source of priceless nourishment and relief from the pain of need then all can flourish. The Well is a metaphor for the form which contains the truth. If the truth is not available because the Well is hidden people suffer in ignorance. If the Well is not hidden but people do not recognize it then how can they take from it? The result is that they suffer in ignorance once again. The Well must be made accessible to everybody who has need of it.

───────────── DECISION-BASE ASSUMPTIONS ─────────────

The following values are given subject to the information given in the Changes. Remember, the Changes take precedence.

Management
If the system works it will be central to your success. It has to be sufficiently comprehensive and not over-specialized. By and large the line of thinking is auspicious. (See Hexagrams 12: Standstill; 13: Fellowship with Men; 17: Following and 20: Contemplation.)

Planning
There may be some ambiguity, but the best criterion is usefulness rather than aesthetics. How much benefit do you think it will bring?

Feedback
It is conditional, but the indication is certainly positive.

Advertising
Badly needed.

Marketing
As wide as possible. Auspicious.

International Trade
You will need a great deal of cooperation; franchise agreements, licences might be in order. Trade is capable of global appeal, but is likely to remain local.

Telecommunications
Possibly the most interesting option here. Follow these up.

Start-Up
Be cautious. There will be need of solid financial support.

Backing
If they can be convinced of the vision, backers will go all the way. Can you make them see it? Be prepared to present ideas in their modern application; give the state of the art so long as this does not belie functionality.

Creative Judgement
You are speculating; your considerations are far from facile, but perhaps very ambitious. This is not a criticism in this case. Do not think in the immediate term but in the medium and long term. Build it up.

Growth and Productivity

Auspicious, but anything is possible. The effects could change everything, the very assumptions upon which social organizations are based. Can such ideas be privately owned? It is doubtful on moral grounds, but that may be the only way to introduce such ideas in their beginnings.

Investment and Finance

You will have to be prepared for a large commitment and will have to believe in the ideas. Auspicious.

Contracts and Agreements

Make sure that all aspects are covered. You will almost certainly not have thought of every contingency. Think ahead. What form will these ideas take in, say, ten years? What are the principles involved? The point is to be comprehensive in considerations so that a full meeting of minds is possible. If you don't go far enough the value of the whole might be rendered useless.

Risks

Yes, in a sense. There is a lot to do, but it is certainly worth it in this case. The alternatives are not any more promising, though they may be safer. Are the alternatives so far reaching? Are they better?

Sources of Misfortune

The key question you must ask is this: Does this answer a sufficiently wide need? If what you do answers such a need, you are doing the right thing. If not there will be misfortune, the energy will have been wasted. It is a question of making facilities available. That is the issue. Practical application – usefulness.

Sources of Good Fortune

Be inventive – help people help each other. Contribute everything you can to providing them with the *means* to put these ideas into the world so that a real benefit arises.

─────────── **THE LINES (CHANGES)** ───────────
the Future-Links

Six at the beginning

This person has nothing to offer and should not be consulted. His nature has become degenerate. Leave him alone.

Nine in the second place

The ability is there but it is not being put to the best use. This comes from inadequate mental exercise and mixing with the wrong people. If you do not use it you tend to lose it after a while, and what you could have given becomes harder to give. To change this state of affairs, you have to sharpen up. (See Hexagram 43: Resolution.)

Nine in the third place
Here, the person concerned is endowed with great ability, he has a great deal to offer, but the situation is sad because nobody sees with sufficient clarity how to make use of such a person. This is a loss for everyone. Fate intervenes, however, and opens up a few doors if the predicament does not soon change. Society needs to make use of such people, it cannot afford not to.

Six in the fourth place
One is engaged in self-perfection, personal development, preparation, practice. One is building up one's abilities for the time when they will be used. Make use of this time and get the most out of it.

Nine in the fifth place
There are some people who are naturals. They have a special gift for mankind and their words should be heeded. A great deal of benefit will be bestowed if they are taken seriously. But, in order to bring them into the right relationship with the needs of mankind, certain conditions have to prevail. It is a duty to assist and help such people. They are the Well itself and what they give is more than good for people, it is vital.

Six in the last place
See the Concept Model. Here, the Well is actually available and is an eternal source of nourishment. Its nature is such that, no matter how much use is made of it, its abundance is increased by increased use. The benefit keeps spreading and everything is sustained and fertilized. This situation is brilliant.

HEXAGRAM 49

Revolution

--------------------------- JUDGEMENT ---------------------------

Every revolution starts with one man with the vision. Now people begin to understand. Supreme success, but you must persevere.

--------------------------- SPECIFIC MODALITY ---------------------------

A great change is going to take place; it is a good and natural change and one long intuited and awaited. But the matter is serious and is not to be considered lightly, as there is some work to do. Concentrate on the key changes only. Let the residual changes take care of themselves.

--------------------------- AMBIENCE ---------------------------

Great energy, but see that your timing is impeccable.

--------------------------- CONCEPT MODEL ---------------------------

There will be change in the balance of power; a change of leadership. The power of initiative will shift. The effect will be to restore equilibrium through all the major structures of the organization. This radical change is brought about naturally though its exponents will be acting in conscious harmony with the conditions prevailing at the time. Revolution answers a need in the people.

--------------------------- DECISION-BASE ASSUMPTIONS ---------------------------

The following values are given subject to the information given in the Changes. Remember, the Changes take precedence.

Management
This is a time of powerful and far-reaching reorganizational measures. These should be seen whole before the first move is made. A clear vision of the whole has to be complete. But the measures must be implemented as there is clear need. Basic

assumptions have to be brought into line with the new time; they have to change, to be enlarged, focused and space created. The conditions are right and all the key decisions have to be made. Do not become ensnared in detail or in the academics of policy formation. The time must be seized for change.

Planning

The plan requires careful integration. If an overall pattern does not emerge there is something wrong. It also has to be simple in its basic layout. Key needs must be identified, and the means and mechanisms for meeting those needs form the validity and backbone of the time. Check and double-check that needs will be met in the structure. Areas of unmet need will have the effect of unravelling the 'knitting' at a later stage. The other dimensions of operation can then be laid on top of this basic structure. And so on. Is there a pattern?

Growth and Productivity

Establish the direction of change. You cannot hope to realize substantial benefit, public or personal, until you concentrate energies in the direction indicated by the time. Auspicious if you can read the time and go with the change.

Investment and Finance

The terms of reference are changing. This is either a great loss-making situation or a time of great possibility. If you have anticipated the trends then the logic of the change will be apparent and you will know what action to take. List the key ideas under two heads: key personal changes (expansion of possibilities) and key social and political forces. Is there a pattern? Be prepared to draw your own conclusions; the 'qualified' opinion of others may be at variance with your own. Look to your own reasoning.

Advertising

Change the image but not merely cosmetically. If it represents a real change of heart, auspicious.

Marketing

Change the approach.

Government

Change, either of government or of the form of government. Radical changes of policy are needed to meet the changing demands of people, beginning with those in greatest need and working upward through the scales of plenty.

Feedback

Natural and productive. But do not abuse it or misuse confidence.

Start-Up
Auspicious if you are prepared to depart from traditional patterns of thought and practice. Out with the old and in with the new. But this must be selective. You must be discriminating as there is much that is still worth keeping.

Backing
Auspicious and natural, but be prepared to persevere and resist the doubts of others.

Contracts and Agreements
Forms need to be changed. New rights and obligations have to be created. Otherwise auspicious.

Creative Judgement
If you are right for the job you can trust your judgement.

International Trade
There will be changes of policy and agreements, but cooperation can be expected from sources hitherto unwilling to cooperate.

Communications
Direct and honest. This is not a time for secrets.

Risks
The situation will appear risky but it is not; it is a time when changes are demanded and are expected but, because of their far-reaching nature and because many of the ideas are unpractised, the challenge is set. But you must, nevertheless, go ahead and introduce new systems and policies. Stick to key structural and policy changes, however.

Timing
Vital. You should be in the preparatory stages now, but the actual time of application and implementation is not far off. Time must be judiciously spent in preparation and review therefore. Maximize consultation. Clarity in communication is emphasized.

Resources
Radical redirection is required in keeping with the time.

Sources of Misfortune
A time of revolution does not call for extremes, violence and partisan attitudes. If the changes contemplated do not improve conditions substantially then they are either not far reaching enough or they are wrong in themselves. Enough must be changed, but in the right way (see Concept Model).

Sources of Good Fortune
Be prepared to adapt existing resources to new ends. Providing such a redirection is addressed to fundamental needs they will be successful.

─────────── **THE LINES (CHANGES)** ───────────
the Future-Links

Nine at the beginning
Change of any kind should be brought about by necessity, not out of anger. It is important not to impose ideas for which the time is not ripe. The means by which such changes are implemented has also to be considered carefully. If the changes are in line with the needs of the time there will be the right kind of assent. If they are not so well tuned, powerful opposition will make itself felt, from people who want to protect their own position. Such people can be dangerous to the whole enterprise; moderate behaviour and cautious changes are required therefore.

Six in the second place
Sometimes a gentle suggestion to the powers that be that change and reconstruction are necessary is so persistently ignored that the only way is to act to bring about a major and radical re-evaluation of policies and values. This is called revolution. In order to achieve this, the first requirement is strong and clear-minded leadership. Supporting such a leader is correct. Secondly, waiting for change is inappropriate. After a period of careful planning, one acts with determination and vigour. It is important to anticipate the new climate of living before it is created, otherwise how can you know that you have done the right thing?

Nine in the third place
The time for change has come. What is to be changed? What should remain unchanged? What is the basis for change? What is the need to be fulfilled? What are the reasons and policies? Is the case for change clear *in each case*? Where certain practices have repeatedly failed, or consistently brought misery, where there has been a history of grievance in a certain area, then they must be changed at the level of policy and implemented without delay. Fresh grievances must be examined with care. Do they fall in with the general category of need?

Nine in the fourth place
A change of government; a change of leader. The changes must reflect the higher needs of mankind. There must be a visionary approach. A leap forward into lighter, fairer, kinder times. People's needs, from the most basic to the highest spiritual and creative, must be catered for. A new government should not consider how best to improve the lot of sections of society, but must be prepared to make sweeping changes which alter attitudes for the uplift of the people. Their happiness and wellbeing as a

whole must be the tangible effect of change. If such measures as are taken do not reach this high standard then selfishness and blindness is at work and is not adequate to the demands of the time. If the new policies and their implementation do not really change matters *substantially* for the better (look to structure as well as policy – do they complement each other?) they will fail.

Only policies which allow people to feel differently about their everyday lives – better cared for, with more freedom, more creative opportunity, less restrictions, higher standards in everything – are correct. These can be *seen*, they are *tangible*, they are *felt*, they are *comprehensible* and *meaningful*. Obscure policies will not achieve the changes required. Good change so directed always has a quality of utmost clarity and simplicity. People know when they are being lied to; they know when promises are nothing but empty words; they are perfectly well aware of the truth. These things cannot be hidden.

The corollary of this is that a new government must be prepared to reorganize its methods and assumptions, practices and systems to reflect a more wholesome and intelligent set of values. These values, clearly underlined in the *I Ching*, always reflect nature and are always relevant to the demands of the time. What the times demand is never a matter of an artificial construction of events but is a matter of truth, nature, balance which penetrate into the heart of man. Anything less is self-delusion of the most dangerous kind. The consequences of inadequate understanding are everywhere around us. This is why people who possess the quality of clear, penetrative thought can really achieve change. They can see the need at heart and they can see the steps that lead to the satisfaction of need. The system must serve the people and not enslave them in its complexity and distortion.

Nine in the fifth place

You are understood even before you ask. Excellent. Your perceptions are wholesome, full of insight, correct and well-proportioned. This way of acting is immediately acceptable and welcomed by others and there are no doubts about your ability or intentions. When you bring about changes people recognize your policies and the philosophy which supports them. They actively support such a change and good will and great good fortune go with you. You could wish for no better indication of the favourableness of the position. The change in you is serious and brilliant.

Six in the last place

When great changes are brought about they have the quality of being fundamental and far reaching. It takes time for these changes, however, to influence every stratum of society. One must not be over-zealous or impatient. Such major changes of policy and action have a way of permeating into the structures of society and the details gradually work themselves out naturally. It takes time for the effect of changes to sweep through the land but, if they are well tuned to the time and to the needs of the time, they will have the correct readjusting effect. At first the effects will appear superficial but gradually they will deepen and become a part of the new scheme of things.

It is not necessary to reinforce these changes in microscopic detail. What is appropriate will find its own level once the overall structure of new relationships and possibilities has been designed. It is like a musical composition: once the new key and basic melody have been established, the orchestration and variety of sound arise naturally. We are not, therefore, talking of minor adjustments to an existing system but of a new system altogether, a new ambience, a new framework of values which have emerged to answer the requirements of the time. When the time is right for such a change the old structure does not serve and is therefore incorrect.

HEXAGRAM 50

The Cauldron

JUDGEMENT

Changes in values and assumptions lead to a new culture; the detail. Cultural gifts. *Supreme good fortune.*

SPECIFIC MODALITY

Producing work; the building up of culture, art, education, entertainment; the manifestation and public proclamation of high ideas. Everything which cultivates the free expression of natural impulses and creativity is deemed great and good.

AMBIENCE

Wonderful; the atmosphere is fertile for all forms of creative expression and lends shape and meaning to the basic values which underline social attitudes and aspirations.

CONCEPT MODEL

As if following on from great social change (as depicted in Hexagram 49: Revolution) a natural flowering comes in the form of the manifestation of ideas. There is a direct relation to the higher representation of the ideas described in Hexagrams 1: The Creative and 2: The Receptive. Art, literature, music, theatre, design of all kinds, film, sculpture, painting, everything, indeed, which can now be described as cultural expression is emphasized here. This is the time when ideas assume form and are communicated. The translation from ideas as abstracts to ideas as visible expressions is extended into an even greater idea of cosmic knowledge – the invisible accumulation of knowledge and experience which cannot be lost once it is born.

———————— DECISION-BASE ASSUMPTIONS ————————

The following values are given subject to the information given in the Changes. Remember, the Changes take precedence.

Management

Concentrate on cultural and creative output. Staff and company should be encouraged to develop this side of their interests even though it may not be the main thrust of the work itself. It is always a complementary area of concern and should, therefore, never be neglected.

Planning

Auspicious for artistic and cultural ideas, products, shows, exhibitions, fairs. The accent is on innovation and change, imagination and inspiration. These must be given space in any forward scheme.

Communications

A central consideration. All cultural endeavours must eventually be put on show or communicated to those whose interest is in the fostering of development. The consistent keeping of records, the faithful upkeep of ideas lends power to history and ideas, and feeds the bank of available ideas for the future. Communications are well favoured in this category of interest.

Investment and Finance

All cultural objects attract investment and interest. Commercially, there are good propositions on the table or in the offing. Auspicious if you take these seriously. Development is auspicious.

International Trade

The cross-fertilization of cultural ideas and objects is vital to the overall condition of the world social body. Seek to make relatively well-aimed and committed strides in this direction. Auspicious.

Feedback

Gradual but positive. Do not expect immediate reactions. The spread of ideas takes time to permeate and percolate but, nevertheless, has a lasting value.

Growth and Productivity

So long as growth revolves around the dissemination of wider social and cultural ideas, or in some way supports these endeavours, the time is propitious. Specific attention to issues which communicate or inform, record and portray brings a general benefit and success.

Advertising
Generally favoured because it involves direct communication with the public. But, in keeping with the theme of the hexagram, advertising which promotes ideas of real cultural value is particularly favoured.

Creative Judgement
Excellent. Make good use of the time to be as creative and as innovative as possible. (See Hexagram 22: Grace.)

Marketing
For high ideas, auspicious.

Risks
Yes, but only in overcoming timidity of communication or concern for sticky issues such as commercialism *v.* art. The value of art is that it makes ideas available for wider appreciation – national and international. It lends understanding and toleration between peoples and so is valuable. Auspicious if you take a positive and less self-centred view.

Start-Up
The prospects are excellent for new projects. Cooperation can be expected if the project demands it for completion.

Backing
Auspicious if it is specifically required at this stage. Support should be sought from both public and private sources.

Contracts and Agreements
Auspicious. They are merely a conduit for the wider dissemination of cultural ideas.

Sources of Misfortune
Neglecting the wider needs of the culture brings misfortune. Adequate and substantial support must be given to this social category of self-expression as it represents the visible achievement of society and is a valuable interface with other cultures. Treating this as a secondary priority is a misunderstanding of its relative value. Cultural interest is a priority for the budget and leads to expansion and growth in all areas of commercial concern.

Sources of Good Fortune
Specific attention to art, education and cultural ideas brings great good fortune.

—————————— THE LINES (CHANGES) ——————————
the Future-Links

Six at the beginning
Despite basic disadvantages you can succeed if you are prepared to clean up your operation and your life. An opportunity will present itself through which you can demonstrate your talents and develop them. People will show an interest because you are sincere in your approach.

Nine in the second place
Take on a significant project, one that draws out your abilities and represents both a challenge and a contribution to the culture. Do not spend too much time day-dreaming about the possibilities: get down to the work; neither should you boast or wear yourself out with self-praise. Your cultural worth is measured by what you have completed. Pretending to achievements which go beyond your real work attracts disfavour.

Nine in the third place
You are disconcerted because you have much to offer of great value but the right openings have not made themselves available to you. This can get in the way of your continued work and spoil your attitude. Try not to let it. The time will come when your work will find its outlet. Do not, then, make the mistake of directing too much self-criticism at your work to date. It is fine.

Nine in the fourth place
You are wasting your opportunities, talents and resources. For this reason the work fails. Such a predicament is not praiseworthy because you have the opportunity but do not use it.

Six in the fifth place
The position is strong. The work (contemplated in a period of high civilization and culture) attracts the right kind of support. This is profoundly auspicious as it means there is every chance that the work will be completed to a high standard. The general benefit is therefore obvious.

Nine in the last place
Yours is the brilliant cultural achievement which brings understanding, illumination and benefit. Enhance and develop the work for it is exactly what is needed and is, in a higher sense, great. Great good fortune.

HEXAGRAM 51

The Arousing (Shock, Thunder)

——————— JUDGEMENT ———————

When you understand what is behind the force of life you can act fearlessly and guide others. But sometimes that awareness can come as a terrifying shock. It will pass, but remember the lesson.

——————— SPECIFIC MODALITY ———————

Spiritual insight is what makes an individual fit to lead. Only real understanding brings with it a knowledge of the deeper, more serious significance of life, without which it is impossible to act with wisdom.

——————— AMBIENCE ———————

First the shock of deepening awareness and then the calm of understanding which makes activity possible.

——————— CONCEPT MODEL ———————

Even though you might have been brought up sharply by a series of poignant new insights into your own relative position, you do not, as a result, lose your bearings. The effect of the situation is to deepen your awareness in such a way as to enable you to take a much wider view. You also feel a spur to action. The importance of things becomes clear. Any lazy attitude will be swept away by such insights as you now know it to be delusory. The murky edges of perception now assume a definition and clarity which provide for some degree of certainty. The impetus towards clear, well-defined and well-directed activity is welcome. The import of this hexagram is vital and generally positive. It represents a test for those who either have, or will one day assume, initiatives of guidance and leadership. Such leadership is based not on speculation or so-called 'informed opinion' but on an insight into truth and the human heart leading to basic and categorical imperatives about the real nature of things.

Such people can be relied upon to make qualitative distinctions which lead to the adoption of correct policies and plans. Therefore the value of the experience depicted here – always private, always rare, always significant and personal – is of the first order.

DECISION-BASE ASSUMPTIONS

The following values are given subject to the information given in the Changes. Remember, the Changes take precedence.

Management
Apply what you have now learned to the affairs of the company. If you do not, you will receive repeated reminders. But the tendency is positive if you align with it. Auspicious.

Planning
Auspicious. If there is a need to make some adjustments in the forward thinking of your scheme do not hesitate to make such changes. They will bring great rewards.

Communications
Good. If the line of action is right, cooperation will follow.

Feedback
Accurate.

Growth and Productivity
Now there is every likelihood of getting somewhere.

Advertising
Be patient. New insights will emerge of their own accord at first but later will need work.

Marketing
Allow any new ideas to digest a little longer. Further discussion with colleagues is in order.

Investment and Finance
Be fearless once you are clear. Be persuasive and vigorous. Your ideas though daring are probably the best you've had.

Creative Judgement
Clarifying by degrees. Let the mist clear completely.

Start-Up
The time is surely coming soon. Be positive and ignore misgivings.

Backing
More solid now than you had hitherto expected.

Contracts and Agreements
Any changes will bring improvement.

Sources of Misfortune
Take time to examine your motives. Here you will find the source of all misfortune; it can be avoided if you change your 'reasons for acting'. This may take simple faith.

Sources of Good Fortune
The rules relating to culture are as clear as those relating to fundamental needs (see Hexagrams 48: The Well and 50: The Cauldron). There is a scheme to things and sometimes you have to follow your heart if your head is not clear. The result will be good fortune. You cannot oppose the wider order with any hope of lasting success.

————————————— **THE LINES (CHANGES)** —————————————
the Future-Links

Nine at the beginning
You have not lost your footing but you feel as though your position has been altered by circumstances beyond your control. The readjustment, however, is in order and you will feel better for it, have no fear.

Six in the second place
The situation is akin to that described in Hexagram 33: Retreat, which requires one to seek safety in the face of loss. But the loss here is temporary and no unnecessary action should be taken. The matter is not within your effective control, so take refuge and wait. In the end you will find that you have lost nothing. The sudden event has only temporarily knocked things out of alignment. In order to retain the possibility of picking up the position where you left it, you have to protect yourself, but do not alter the scheme by making insistent demands.

Six in the third place
The shock of events – the forces of fate – are at work. If it moves you to action all well and good. If not you will miss out. Compose yourself, then act – this means keeping your wits about you. If necessary, be adventurous along the line in which you have been prompted.

Nine in the fourth place
It is difficult to know what to do or what can be done in this predicament. Despite the persistent pressure your innate resilience enables you to maintain equilibrium and even continue working. Fortunately, you retain control of the situation.

Six in the fifth place
Despite the barrage you do not lose your centre of gravity. This is excellent

because it means that the initiative is still squarely in your hands. Use it and act.

Six in the last place

A state of shock. You need rest and recuperation until you are yourself again. Don't worry about what others might think. How can you be of any use until you are in equilibrium? Withdraw and rest.

HEXAGRAM 52

Keeping Still (Mountain)

─────── JUDGEMENT ───────

Good fortune if you know how to get the best out of people and out of yourself; this is the same as knowing how to use relaxation practices as a means of generating more invigorated work and gaining a more wholesome perspective.

─────── SPECIFIC MODALITY ───────

The achievement of serenity as a normal working framework is by far the most effective personal statement. Concentrate on the work in hand.

─────── AMBIENCE ───────

This is not stillness itself, but the need for it, the means to it. The actual position is one of tension generated by egocentric attitudes.

─────── CONCEPT MODEL ───────

This hexagram concerns immediate working conditions. The common-sense idea at the heart of the concept is that people work best when they are relaxed; when they are not busy defending their ego; when they are not worrying about the future; when their minds are attentive. In other words, provision for happy working conditions, adequate remuneration, a balance of work and rest periods sets the individual up for maximum concentration and effective work. This applies to any working condition which requires an everyday approach. The absence of any one of these factors unbalances the whole and leads to a chain reaction. Inadequate rest periods and inadequately *paced* work (too fast or too slow) have the effect of increasing tension which, in turn, reduces concentration. Reduced concentration leads to unproductive behaviour and general dissatisfaction.

Secondly, if the relations between company personnel are not mediated by a relaxed and informal style, i.e., that which directs effort towards common goals, people become over-concerned with status preservation. Oneupmanship and other puerile symptoms begin to pollute the emotional balance; the result once again is dissatisfaction and the falling off of quality and productivity.

Thirdly, adequacy of remuneration – not only as a motivating factor but as a means of relieving individuals of the burden of financial worry – is also a vital and key factor, if quality and productivity are to be maintained. If remuneration is not truly adequate or fairly organized, people resent their position and the downward spiral starts off again.

So the balance between these three key points gives rise to a happy, productive and qualitative working team, in which peace of mind is central. Only from such a spiritual state can real understanding spring. These principles prevail regardless of the scale of the organization. If the environment is not fit for human comfort or geniality people won't stomach it willingly and happily. The pressure of fighting for adequate remuneration can compel people to swallow what is wrong and unfair but, as has been exhaustively explained elsewhere, this is not work but slavery. An agitated environment leads to bad decisions and downfall. Nature's balance is abused thereby, and even the misguided principle of 'each man for himself' fails. On the other hand, if the collective team is well looked after then quality and production are proportionately enhanced. The overall responsibility of balancing these elements lies with the organization's structural planners. (See Hexagrams 20: Contemplation; 27: Nourishment; 32: Duration; 48: The Well and 49: Revolution.)

DECISION-BASE ASSUMPTIONS

The following values are given subject to the information given in the Changes. Remember, the Changes take precedence.

Management

The question to be asked at the end of quarterly, biannual and annual balance sheets is: *at what cost this profit?* In this case, the cost is human misery, tension, a host of industrial diseases, heart failure, unhappiness *et al.* Taking care of the comforts, ambience, remuneration and the rest/work balance should be the first priority of organizational planners. Decisions must be made – if quality and production are principal aims of a service or commercial organization – on the basis of a comprehension of the natural dynamics which find their expression in human nature itself. Without such a balance the problem of tension spirals out into misfortune, a misfortune of many faces.

Planning

See Hexagram 20: Contemplation. In that aptly named hexagram, a view is found only through quiet thought. This hexagram, however, speaks about physical stillness as a prerequisite to effective and profound thought. The two ideas coincide in the area of *planning* for this process requires clear, uncluttered thought and the ability to penetrate problems. Projections can safely be made as self-interest and ego are naturally displaced when people think deeply. Thus, good and effective planning is here regarded as necessary for spiritual as well as physical health. Stillness.

Growth and Productivity

Nothing immediate, but gradual preparations can be made.

Investment and Finance

The matter requires further thought before commitments are made.

Advertising

The images used may be dynamic but do they best carry the ideas about the company? Perhaps there is something too 'loud', 'macho', 'boasting' and generally off-putting about them. Take time to review the quality of the image.

Marketing

Tense relations. A quiet period is required.

Feedback

Perhaps too defensive (self-protective).

Communications

Not *all* the information is getting through. It is unwise to make decisions without a complete picture. What is preventing reception? Sometimes tension can create 'dishonest' relations leading to mistrust. The spiral generated from the falling-off of trust spells death to any company. Cooperation is the crucial ingredient of success in the commercial world.

Risks

Dangerous, inauspicious.

Start-up

In order to start well you first have to be relaxed. Momentum cannot be generated from a position of *tension at rest*. Rest must be relaxed in order to provide for the possibility of *tension and movement*. These relationships have to be preserved in nature or there will be malfunction, expressed in individual physical, mental, spiritual and, later, in organizational terms. When considering breakdowns of any kind, these are the terms in which it can be fundamentally understood. Other factors, details and specifics flow from these basic ideas.

Backing

When the fundamental dynamics are in order, seek it, but not yet. More work is needed. There is therefore no judgement of good or bad fortune at this stage.

Contracts and Agreements

The emphasis is misplaced. Too inflexible? Parts will have to be redrafted to get everything into perspective. Do not sign until this has been done.

Sources of Misfortune

Tension, inappropriately induced, either through ignorance of the natural dynamic or deliberately – in the latter case there is a mental problem.

Sources of Good Fortune

The ideas of rest, relaxation, movement and tension must be understood as relative states – physical, organizational, wholistic. If these dynamics become confused in the overall organism the efficiency of the whole system will be seriously impaired. If they are naturally balanced the organism will work well and effectively (see Concept Model).

THE LINES (CHANGES)
the Future-Links

Six at the beginning

You have not yet begun. Do not do so yet. You understand the situation and the values which move things naturally. You have some understanding of the relationships involved and, although this is by no means complete, it is enough for you to see how the wrong moves made now, at the beginning, will lead to compounded mistakes later on. This is the time to stop and think carefully – before you do anything at all. In this way you can have the intuitive certainty that you will be doing the right thing. (This is the primary function of intuition; more widely available tools of intuitive development, regardless of the *forms they take* (see Hexagram 17: Following) can only be good. You may like to consider the implications of an 'intuitive technology'.)

They are needed in up-to-date, state-of-the-art forms, so that they are acceptable, relevant and palatable to the needs of the time.

Six in the second place
The organization trips up and falls over because it has taken the wrong path and achieved momentum in that direction. When it encounters an obstacle, it therefore trips up. Unfortunately, although you can see the situation as plain as day, you are not empowered to prevent such an occurrence. The lesson for management is that they should listen, not only to each other but to others who may well know better. But wisdom comes, in this case, after the damage has been done.

Nine in the third place
It is very dangerous to force turbulent movement into a state of rest. If you try, the inner pressures begin to break up the surround and the structure begins to crumble. The combination of force and environment is such that it will be better if the movement is allowed to slow down; giving this advice is all you can do. Putting the brakes on will be disastrous.

Six in the fourth place
You are well on the way to gaining mastery over the self – that is, the drive of the ego. You are not there yet but, by understanding the state of affairs, you have a still greater chance of achieving the desired state of stillness or, more accurately, equilibrium (clarity of vision). The tendency to outbursts of agitation is still there, but the control is stronger.* You ought not to feel doubt.

Six in the fifth place
You talk too much – why? Because you are not sure of yourself. This is bravado without substance. Save your energy. Be quiet.

Nine in the last place
You are now *at rest*. Excellent. From this position you can handle every small detail without exhaustion. This is highly auspicious. You act with great effect because you act from the heart.

---

*The higher self which the *I Ching* reflects in each individual is not the lapdog or the sycophant of the lower urge. It does not necessarily give the answers you may seek (if it is the lower self which seeks a particular answer). It gives the superior answer. It addresses itself to the Superior in your own nature. When you and the *I Ching* are in accord, then the superior man is in control and the natural cycle is in tune. When there is a conflict, it is always a conflict between the lower and the higher in your own nature. In such situations it is safer, as well as correct, to defer to the *I Ching*. In a very real sense, the *I Ching* is the ego's task master. In this sense it is an evolutionary tool of the most impeccable kind.

HEXAGRAM 53

Development (Gradual Progress)

—————————— JUDGEMENT ——————————

Good fortune if you do not try to go too fast (see also Hexagram 24: Return), or too slowly (see Hexagram 12: Stagnation).

—————————— SPECIFIC MODALITY ——————————

The setting has been agreed; now let development proceed gradually so that the outcome is strong and well established.

—————————— AMBIENCE ——————————

Lovely, calm spirit so that you do not jump the gun, and keenness so that you go forward.

—————————— CONCEPT MODEL ——————————

It is possible to destabilize the position within the organization by rushing forward to 'grab the future' before its time has come. Similarly, over-caution is also bad because change is taking place all the time and one must, as it were, keep up with it. You should move forward and steer, but keep a tight control over objectives and pace. No unnecessary and unnatural stimulants required.

—————————— DECISION-BASE ASSUMPTIONS ——————————

The following values are given subject to the information given in the Changes. Remember, the Changes take precedence.

Management
The fundamental drive is to enhance and improve people's relationships *in general*, as well as in a management setting, with each other. The work of gradual development is really directed towards this end and the generation of commercial success – profits, business, markets *et al.* – is regarded in this context as a valuable by-product of

the process. The idea is that, if influence from management creates solid trust and communication between people, then they are likely to function better in *any arena* of activity, and the best principles will be upheld to everybody's benefit.

Planning
Quick turnover and fast production can quickly dwindle into nothing. Plans must be addressed to long-term objectives. Solid business ventures which are capable of subsisting in time are favoured. This means that they must be adaptable, and management must be adaptable to the demands of the time. The implication is that there is the propensity to be a leader in the field; that is, you influence the growth of other concerns.

Investment and Finance
A quick 'in and then out again' investment is badly augmented. Such an approach will avail little. You should be thinking in terms of ideas which will form a backbone to the future. The idea is not so much to look around for businesses which have been established a long time as to look for ventures which have the capability of becoming solid and well established. Such an investment will be sound and is auspicious. The ideas may be brand new, but may mark a whole trend of development. This trend touches the formation of culture and so should be cultivated. People will follow the times if the arenas are set up through real investment and commitment. There is more than a hint that some kind of tangible, visible, architectural firmness is required.

Growth and Productivity
Unhurried but definite and strong.

Feedback
Follow established procedures but new objectives. If in conflict prefer the latter to the former.

Advertising and Marketing
If products or services are new, do not launch them with a big bang. Large investments in advertising and marketing will not be returned. Let the new ideas take hold gradually. If they are of good quality they will find their place without too much public pomp and ceremony. Some introduction is necessary, of course, but the style of introduction has to be modest, rather than loud.

Communications
Auspicious.

Start-Up
Not on your own. Seek a parent company. Be polite and courteous.

Backing
Auspicious.

Contracts and Agreements
Is there a fair and comfortable apportionment of responsibility? Is the agreement based on cooperation and is this an explicit understanding? If it isn't, make it crystal clear as people often become very confused about this issue in practice. They often end up sitting around expecting results without doing any work.

Creative Judgement
Providing it has a moral orientation it is likely to be sound.

Sources of Misfortune
'Anything for a quick buck' fails.

Sources of Good Fortune
Steady long-term objectives put the matter into proper focus.

─────── THE LINES (CHANGES) ───────
the Future-Links

Six at the beginning
The ideas are formed. The general direction is set. But you are alone without help or cooperation from others. This may check your advance. An assurance of gradual growth is, nevertheless, made and what you can achieve becomes a solid base for the future. Do not worry about the small-minded chatter which is unkindly directed against you. The judgement is against them and not you. Good fortune.

Six in the second place
You have made a good beginning. You have a natural proclivity to share what good fortune you have earned. Excellent. Confidence is building up. A pleasant social environment is created.

Nine in the third place
This is not the time to make dramatic moves or change address. Let things evolve. Have faith in the general direction of events. You may feel restless but the direction is, nevertheless, correct and avoids arguments. Preserve your own position with strength and make certain of it. Good fortune.

Six in the fourth place
This is not your 'place', your natural habitat. You cannot rest in comfort but you can keep an eye out from a relative position of safety. Consider the situation as temporary but, for the time being, make the best of it without

giving away too much. You will have to change this situation later, at a more auspicious time.

Nine in the fifth place
People who are thrown together or are together by choice, heavily conditioned by prevailing circumstances, feel alienated and unable to settle a point of view. The period is transient, but lasts some time – two or three years. The outcome, however, will be positive and favourable and the right relationships will be established harmoniously. Good fortune.

Nine in the last place
Perfection. The example you have set will be followed and will subsist in time. You will leave behind you something of value which is not only commemorative but also exemplary. A grand and brilliant thing.

HEXAGRAM 54

Relationships Governed by Law

————————— JUDGEMENT —————————

Good fortune if you act in the knowledge that relationships between people in earthly life are finite and transient.

————————— SPECIFIC MODALITY —————————

Creating legal *and* voluntary relationships. Legal relationships are those like marriage, company mergers or employment contracts. Voluntary relationships are those of friendship, guidance and help.

————————— AMBIENCE —————————

Take care not to create confusion of position and identity.

————————— CONCEPT MODEL —————————

The stronger party takes the initiative here in the formation of a legal relationship, a marriage, a merger, an employment contract. The relationship has certain rules of conduct which are established either by the written rule of law or are culturally assumed. Such relationships have to be clearly defined. But in order to avoid an unworkable situation arising, certain ideas have to be considered. Firstly, no relationships can succeed, whether legal or voluntary, unless some affection exists between the parties. People cannot cooperate strictly by rules and regulations. Some degree of mutual understanding or empathic resonance must exist, otherwise the 'rule book' would be endless: it could not cover every single exchange. There has to be room for initiative and the acceptance of general prnciples. Secondly, no relationship can exist in a vacuum; it must be understood in terms of wider ideas, not least that of death. The *I Ching* states clearly that if people 'keep their eyes on the Big Door' they can maintain a true perspective on all relationships. Within that framework, success is possible.

─────────── DECISION-BASE ASSUMPTIONS ───────────

The following values are given subject to the information given in the Changes. Remember, the Changes take precedence.

Management
Terms of employment have to be clear, but these are not the basis of loyalty and trust. (See Hexagram 7: The Army.)

Planning
Plans can only go so far. One should not expect plans to cater for every contingency. Are the relations between people considered in the scheme of things?

Advertising
Inauspicious.

Marketing
Inauspicious.

Investment and Finance
In the matter of a merger or of a takeover, do not invest.

Growth and Productivity
Do not press for it.

Contracts and Agreements
Inauspicious.

Start-Up
Not at this time.

Backing
Unlikely.

Communications
If they are spontaneous they can be believed. If they are calculated, do not plan too much.

Feedback
According to established practice. Otherwise not special.

Sources of Misfortune
Misunderstanding through misconstruction.

Sources of Good Fortune
If real feeling backs it there is something to be glad about.

THE LINES (CHANGES)
the Future-Links

Nine at the beginning
Advisers and administrators may not be in the limelight, but their position in the background may be honoured by real friendship and trust from the people they serve and help. This is fine and good work can be done. If such helpers become presumptuous, however, there will be a conflict of duties and problems of a personal nature.

Nine in the second place
Ideally, people should work together and help each other. One of the parties is not keeping up his side of the bargain. But the other remains loyal to the cause even in the face of difficulty.

Six in the third place
Maybe you are winning your pleasures in a way which compromises your character. Only a person who is alone and bears unshakable responsibilities can justify the predicament. Anybody else is chancing his luck.

Nine in the fourth place
The right position comes because you have waited without 'losing yourself'. Good fortune.

Six in the fifth place
There is a responsibility to find somebody a suitable position without being asked. Even though, to all appearances, the person deserves better, the position is nevertheless acceptable and good fortune comes.

Six in the last place
The effort is wasted because it is not sincere, and that cannot be hidden from view. There is nothing to be done.

HEXAGRAM 55

Abundance

JUDGEMENT

Success; you have everything you need at present but, even now, it is not enough for you. Let the feeling of dissatisfaction go. Revel in your time while it lasts.

SPECIFIC MODALITY

Cultural activity. You can and should take the initiative. Aim for a high achievement. Give full expression to your creative abilities. Do not be over cautious. Be forward thinking.

AMBIENCE

Ambiguous. The sun shines but the clouds are in your head.

CONCEPT MODEL

This is about leadership, cultural initiative, ability and controlling moods of despair. The requirement is to take advantage of the time to make the most of all your gifts. Note your ideas; your plans at this time will be enlightened and inspired but nagging doubts and feelings of gloom have to be dispelled. They can take many forms for different people. The awareness that everything passes – the realization of the transience of life and achievement – can leave a hollow feeling if you get on the wrong side of it. The flip side of that coin is the feeling that everything is worthwhile in itself, but philosophical justifications may not be enough. It is a question of leaping out of the dark and choosing to see the positive side if only because it is more helpful and productive.

The objective situation is actually very bright and everything is going well. The fact that things may not always be so auspicious in the future need not worry you at this stage. It is a matter of level; your achievements are relative to your past, not the world at large. What is great for you may not be so great for someone else; what is a slump for you may be another person's high point. Such comparisons may be very poignant in your mind at the moment.

────────────── DECISION-BASE ASSUMPTIONS ──────────────

The following values are given subject to the information given in the Changes. Remember, the Changes take precedence.

Management
The potential you see now should be allowed to condition your plans for the future. Your vision is almost certainly based on genuine insight. Let this play itself out in the running of the company and, if necessary, in redirecting it. These are not hunches, this is real vision.

Planning
Auspicious provided you believe what you are doing is worthwhile.

Feedback
Motivate yourself, do not rely too strongly upon outside promptings. People outside your circle cannot have your vision at this stage. Later, they might understand the wider meaning of your ideas.

Advertising and Marketing
More auspicious than you think.

Investment and Finance
It is more a matter of the investment of your time than of hard cash at the moment. Use it as productively as possible. The inclinations towards future financial investment are likely to be spot on. Innovation is in the air.

Growth and Productivity
Much better than you think. You have no idea of the value of what you have done or how far it can reach – or rather you do, but the picture you see is greyer than reality.

Administration and Paperwork
This is the time to get it done.

Start-Up
Hard to do, but do not be in a hurry. Listen to new ideas.

Backing
Inevitable, but perhaps from nominated sources. Others will show their hand to be favourable if you make your ideas known.

Communications
Give it two weeks, then make a special effort to bring all your communications into line with each other. Auspicious.

Meetings
Auspicious. Arrange many.

Creative Judgement
Brilliant, but do not overdo planning. Be spontaneous. Let yourself flow a bit. Sometimes the best work comes like this.

Contracts and Agreements
You may think the terms are bad but, if there are good precedents, do not make waves. Ask for what you want and give reasons. Be prepared to negotiate but settle everything within the next six weeks – at least with regard to details of principles. Blatantly unfair terms should be ignored.

Sources of Misfortune
Stopping in a mire of melancholy. It will not last, though. The picture is very favourable as a whole.

Sources of Good Fortune
Largely a matter of being positive when you do not feel inclined to do so. You might take a few chances, they could well pay off, however bizarre those proposals may seem, however cautious you might feel. It might be exactly what is required of the time.

─────────────── **THE LINES (CHANGES)** ───────────────
the Future-Links

Nine at the beginning
The proposition is excellent and will succeed. The partner is exactly right for the venture. Work together with confidence. He has the right kind of energy.

Six in the second place
Your ideas and the proposition are certainly right. The negative reaction you are receiving is due largely to greed and selfish envy. This is hardly helpful as it effectively blocks progress, but if you retain a positive outlook it will transform the attitude of others and the true brightness of the idea will shine through in time.

Nine in the third place
The wrong people are getting in the way of cooperation and progress. These people are not well informed or of high ability or integrity. They can be used by others intent on destroying matters. Your position is powerless. It will pass, though.

Nine in the fourth place
You have the power to do the job, all you need now is someone to direct the work. This person now joins forces with you. He has the right experience.

Six in the fifth place
Success on a high level of attainment. This is universally recognized.

Six in the last place
You have been fortunate in opportunity, achievement and help. Now that you have what you want you do not want to share it. You hoard it and even look down your nose at others. This is a position of loneliness brought about by a conceited attitude towards good fortune. It is a form of imprisonment.

HEXAGRAM 56

Travelling Business People
(International Trade)

JUDGEMENT

Success. A traveller is always a stranger so he must behave without presumption if he expects people to be well disposed towards him.

SPECIFIC MODALITY

Foreign travel; the travelling salesman; the diplomat; the international businessman. Matters must be dealt with efficiently. One should not stay in one place too long. The guest behaves respectfully to his hosts.

AMBIENCE

Friendly relations, but one acts with reserve and maintains an attitude of reasonable caution. The traveller is always vulnerable to wrong influences.

CONCEPT MODEL

In a world where international trade, travelling for business and pleasure has become the norm of developed nations, there is an increasing need to be open minded and friendly. In each country or city to which one travels, one is a guest. The hosts are always the people of the country as well as the specific host company or organization. One behaves therefore with respect and decorum, and one expects to be treated with respect and decorum also. This is the way to develop friendly relations. As a stranger and guest one is always vulnerable to unlooked-for influences, some good and some bad; therefore it is important to hold some reserve. It may not always be possible to tell whether one is in friendly or hostile company.

––––––––––– DECISION-BASE ASSUMPTIONS –––––––––––

The following values are given subject to the information given in the Changes. Remember, the Changes take precedence.

Management
Unfamiliar territory, circumstances and people – even though you may be a seasoned traveller, international businessman or experienced travelling salesman at home or abroad. You win cooperation and welcome from people if you are yourself well disposed to your hosts. If you are willing to fall into their ways and follow the home rules you can be successful.

Planning
Auspicious.

Growth and Productivity
Auspicious.

Feedback
This depends on your own original attitude. Warmth can be expected if you, yourself, show warmth.

Communication
Constructive and positive.

Investment and Finance
Auspicious in foreign parts.

Start-Up
Be modest in your proposals.

Backing
Auspicious if you are prepared to go further afield for support.

Contracts and Agreements
Auspicious.

Creative Judgement
This is a time when you will come into contact with many new ideas. Be open minded and receptive. Share information and ideas. The possibility of expanded awareness for future creative judgement is auspicious.

Advertising
Go further afield than usual.

Marketing
Be adventurous, but be courteous. Do not go bursting into other

people's lives without showing some respect for the way they customarily live. Tune your strategy to the place. Be careful of assuming that new ideas are automatically welcome. Introduce new possibilities gently and with due consideration. An understanding of the local humour is vital.

Sources of Misfortune
Over-presumptuous, disrespectful and pompous attitudes while travelling.

Sources of Good Fortune
Recognize the transience and ephemerality of the position and recognize that you are a guest in somebody else's 'home' in every sense. Be prepared to take your shoes off, as it were.

THE LINES (CHANGES)
the Future-Links

Six at the beginning
Adopt a suitably serious attitude if you hope to be taken seriously yourself. Take care of the important business of the trip.

Six in the second place
You find somebody who can assist you in carrying out your business. It is apparent to your hosts that you have something of value to offer and, with their help, this can be augmented to greater benefit. You are made welcome and common courtesies are offered: a place to stay, facilities to carry out business and meet people. Auspicious because you do not presume beyond the invitation.

Nine in the third place
If, through your attitude, you alienate yourself from the kindness and companionship which has been offered, you bring difficulties upon yourself. How can you achieve anything worthwhile without the cooperation and assent of your hosts? Have you forgotten that you are a guest in somebody else's country and home? If there is danger, it is your own misguided conceit which has created it. Can you make amends?

Nine in the fourth place
You have the right attitude in so far as you behave properly towards your hosts. You also have something valuable to offer and can expect cooperation from your hosts in augmenting that value to wider benefit. But you still feel generally mistrustful, and cannot quite make yourself at home. You are defensive. There is no suggestion that this is not advised and, therefore, no criticism is offered. So long as you act with due decorum, you can keep your ambition in proper bounds and so not give offence.

Six in the fifth place
You have done well. You give what is most needed and provide a new field of interest and activity for your host. Everybody has been impressed by you and you are consequently rewarded. It is possible that you will be asked to stay and be offered a job and position in keeping with your abilities. This is highly favourable and auspicious, even though this is not your home country. The praise is well deserved.

Nine in the last place
You are making light of important matters. Your security at home and abroad is based upon a place to rest and keep your things. If you do not have sufficient respect for these things, you may not feel this is important, but you will only regret your attitude. It is vital that you readjust your perspective because you might be throwing out something of immense value to you personally. Realize that before you jest about it as if it were nothing.

HEXAGRAM 57

The Gentle and the Penetrating

─── JUDGEMENT ───

You may not express your understanding in public or in dramatic terms but it goes deeply into the nature of things. Use your insights, however great and penetrating, to some end. They must be focused; then you will be successful.

─── SPECIFIC MODALITY ───

Work on your understanding, quietly and unobtrusively. Be consistent about this. This is a process of discovery. Your work forms the background to culture; the ideas are influential, powerful, even charismatic but they are so all-embracing that they can easily be taken for granted.

─── AMBIENCE ───

Intense concentration. The narrow beam of focus penetrates deeply into the darkness and shows it for what it is. The veils of mystery draw back slowly and yield their secrets for good.

─── CONCEPT MODEL ───

The mind has the power to probe deeply into the darkest regions. Here, we are concerned with the power to awaken ideas long dormant, to bring enlightenment in a time of obscurity, to uncover the secrets of darkness and to reveal fresh insights into the nature of things. This is not only a dynamic of the power of perception but the way by which perception penetrates, like a narrow and concentrated beam of light, into the darkness. It is the mind acting with the precision and focus of a laser beam; the mind working with the brilliance and clarity of enlightenment. This is the power to uncover secrets and to make hitherto unrealized connections.

--------------- DECISION-BASE ASSUMPTIONS ---------------

The following values are given subject to the information given in the Changes. Remember, the Changes take precedence.

Management
Be patient; introduce new ideas with care; avoid over-burdening and startling with new ideas or breakthroughs; be prepared to accept the guidance of one who knows how to deal with these ideas. Consistency is the key to giving the right impression and making the influence effective. If there are practices which do not meet with the open and avowed interest of the company's ethos the 'practitioners' should not be caught red-handed or put on their guard. Rather, they should be quietly stalked until they can be brought out into the open. The natural reaction of someone up to no good is to keep a sharp look-out and, at the first sign that they might be found out, they are off into the most obscure and difficult to penetrate place they can possibly find.

Planning
Pursue your present line without deviation. Be prepared to work slowly but, above all, remind yourself and the company of the key objectives. The gradual building up of work can be so slow that people lose direction. Constant reinforcement of the direction (without increasing hurry) is the correct way to carry forward plans. Avoid indecision.

Research and Development
Illuminating insights at this time. Very auspicious.

Investment and Finance
If the work involves the development of ideas, products or services, the investment will be sound and a long-term solid commitment should be entered into without reservation. The investment will be proven.

Start-Up
Slow but sure.

Backing
Seek it with confidence. Be decisive. Do not be vague about your intentions; there will definitely be a tendency to vacillate and waver. A backer may not see that you are prepared to stand by your ideas. He may feel that your apparent non-committal style shows a lack of faith in the project. He couldn't be more wrong. So be prepared to prove the true weight of your conviction.

Feedback
It will seem ambiguous. The answer is that it is either better than it seems, or it is a completely false façade. You will know without too much thought on the matter.

Growth and Productivity
Steady but sure.

Advertising and Marketing
This is your weak point in this position. There may not be much need to work on this aspect, however. The tone of your presentation should not be inconclusive or lack definition. Be clear and precise, judgemental, unequivocal about ideas. This is not showy confidence with little substance behind it – this is the meaning of the substance. Do not belie the substance through a weak company image.

Communications
Great aptitude to be very effective. Aim your communications with great precision and you will hit the desired spot.

Contracts and Agreements
You must be prepared to state exactly what you think your project is worth and be prepared to stick by that valuation. Look around until you find the right people to back you. Valuation is the only area where you are likely to be taken for a ride. Terms and agreements will not be much of a problem, providing you take a personal interest, read every aspect of the agreement with care and are careful to understand its import and the nature of the rights and duties involved.

Principal Attitude
You must carry the work through to completion.

Sources of Misfortune
Do not let a gentle and mild disposition get the better of you so that you lose sight of where you are going. Do not let others interpret gentleness as weakness and exploit it accordingly.

Sources of Good Fortune
Unravel the mystery; expose the difficulties; be clear and decisive.

——————— **THE LINES (CHANGES)** ———————
the Future-Links

Six at the beginning
When exploring the pros and cons of a dilemma, or when circling an idea in an exploratory way in order to understand it better, it is possible to grow dizzy. The act of consideration can itself be so obsessive an occupation that

you start to lose sight of the wood for the trees. Take your bearings. Which way are you going? Stop weighing things up now. Go towards your objectives as if wearing a pair of horse's blinkers, i.e., without being side-tracked by the terrain.

Nine in the second place
Trace influences back to source. Somebody has done something wrong in the past. Use your intuition. Employ the help of people with highly developed intuitive powers. Make careful notes. The answers are not readily to be had, they are floating about in intangible shadows, but the cause of what is wrong can be found and highlighted. Throwing light on the matter dispels confusion immediately. This is what is required. Exorcize the ghosts.

Nine in the third place
You can be said to understand the position in sufficient depth now. What you are required to do is act upon what you know, and vigorously at that. Be careful not to acquire a reputation among colleagues and fellow professionals as something of a mad genius – brilliant but ineffective. Be effective also.

Six in the fourth place
The three key elements come together and form a strong unity. Great success. You can certainly build upon this. The work has been done well. You have the reputation of being a careful and modest person and that is all to the good for winning the cooperation of others in important projects to come.

Nine in the fifth place
You have to change direction. The organization and the individual both undergo a redirection. Because such a change is radical, take time to prepare your mind and to consider what is involved. Think it all through with care. Revise it. It should take you about a week. Then make the change and review your first steps constantly until the new pattern has been established satisfactorily. Good fortune.

Nine in the last place
You see the evil in the system. Seeing it is enough: don't get too close to it, however, as you cannot change it at present. Absolutely no attempt should be made to challenge such a force. See it, recognize it for what it is, make a mental note and leave it well alone.

HEXAGRAM 58

The Joyous, Lake

JUDGEMENT

Success. You have more fun and enjoy learning when you do it in the company of friends. The ascetic and solitary life makes progress very difficult and arduous. You can make good times last longer if they are shared.

SPECIFIC MODALITY

Jovial and charming social behaviour. It is to be based upon shared values of truth and not on pretence and weakness. Learning with others in a relaxed atmosphere. Confidence in people you can call friends.

AMBIENCE

Warm and pleasant.

CONCEPT MODEL

(See also Hexagram 55: Abundance.) Here there is a real feeling of companionship; work rides along on top. Even difficult matters are more easily accessible when one is with one's friends. There is a specific focus upon education, training and the learning process in general. If people are expected to work alone through difficult material, and in an uncongenial social and physical environment, their achievement will leave much to be desired. Here, however, the picture is of a warm and congenial setting where friends are able to relax and enjoy the discoveries of their learning. Progress becomes a by-product of this fun. This is perhaps the most pleasant of all situations, where things have to be achieved and are achieved with no force of effort or will, yet without any loss of quality.

DECISION-BASE ASSUMPTIONS

The following values are given subject to the information given in the Changes. Remember, the Changes take precedence.

Management
Concentrate energies on making the atmosphere for learning, and for people to get to know themselves and each other, as pleasant and as stimulating as possible. This is where your energies will be best repaid.

Planning
Environmental and training changes need to be made if they do not fall into alignment with an atmosphere of natural ease. Arrange for people to work in pairs or in groups on individual projects. Organizational infrastructures should be based upon friendly–consultative lines. Other infrastructural changes will fall under another line of consideration. Changes in decor may be in order.

Communications
Throw a party.

Investment and Finance
Invest in ambience, people, education within your own organization at first. Beyond the imperatives of your own people consider which companies feel the same way about organizational values and investigate them. It is possible that they will be interested in you also. It is largely a matter of intuition rather than science. Ask your friends for their view.

Feedback
Excellent and encouraging. Difficult things become easy.

Growth and Productivity
The situation is favourable overall. Expect further enhancement.

Start-Up
Auspicious if you are starting with friends rather than 'colleagues'; people you like, know, trust and who are willing to back the project with hard work.

Backing
If the home front is strong in feeling, confidently approach backers – perhaps through mutual friends who have an insight into the management backbone of the new company. This can be the best reference of all: 'Those people will work together because they are such good friends.'

Advertising
Social images – images of people working together and enjoying themselves. Auspicious, but in an everyday way.

Marketing
Personable behaviour, but there is clearly a positive resonance, a sense of excitement. This can open up new opportunities.

International Trade
More dialogue.

Creative Judgement
Share your views. This will enhance your own understanding and lead to fresh insights. Learning is a connecting event, is fed by interaction, and creates a refreshing and changeful environment. See Hexagram 17: Following which discusses the values of adaptation through the symbiosis and interfusion of ideas.

Sources of Misfortune
If people are not allowed to work together or, for some reason, enjoying themselves is frowned upon, productivity and general spiritual vitality will fall – and profits with them. To begin with, generate dialogue and interaction to counteract such a tendency and develop the environment by brightening it up, literally (more colour, music etc.).

Sources of Good Fortune
(See Hexagram 16: Enthusiasm.) A positive feeling communicates very powerfully when people are working together on a project. This should be encouraged not dampened. Laughter is contagious.

——————————— **THE LINES (CHANGES)** ———————————
the Future-Links

Nine at the beginning
You are happily self-contained and also right on course without making any sudden moves. Good fortune.

Nine in the second place
This is not really your scene and you know it. Even they know it, so the temptation is not put in front of you. Good fortune.

Six in the third place
You are probably deluding yourself in thinking that this would be fun, but the imagining is more potent than the reality. If you really want to go that way, there is nothing preventing you, but is it worth the bother?

Nine in the fourth place
Choose your pleasures well; the higher and more cultivated, the better. There is an art to real pleasure. Finding a good use for one's spare time – as it's called – is indeed important, and the time must be spent in a way which you feel is worthwhile. There is no point in doing dubious things if you are only going to waste even more time regretting it later.

Nine in the fifth place
Some practices are corrupt. Avoid them.

Six in the last place
You have taken the wrong direction; you have given way to the wrong temptations and influences. You should now try to correct the position.

HEXAGRAM 59

Dispersion of Wealth and Dissolution

─────────── JUDGEMENT ───────────

Success if you forgive and forget. Tension can build up through holding grudges, jealousies and envy; if a wrong has been done to you, forgive it. Clear the blockage. The give and take of feelings works in a smooth cycle.

─────────── SPECIFIC MODALITY ───────────

Reaffirm beliefs and working assumptions. Communicate around the world; unify your people and your intentions through going out to them. Send messages and give things which have been long accumulated.

─────────── AMBIENCE ───────────

The process of clearing the air. A stifled atmosphere is refreshed by cool winds. A change of heart is taking place.

─────────── CONCEPT MODEL ───────────

The main idea is that of clearing away the things which are blocking up the tubes. To take breathing as a metaphor, the process is to clear congestion in the chest, blowing the nose, stretching up to give the lungs room to fill with fresh air. They have to be cleared if the organism is to work properly. It is the same with spiritual matters; harbouring secret resentments, jealousies, thinking envious thoughts all block up the works and prevent the 'spiritual organism' from breathing freely and from fulfilling its potential.

In business terms, the picture concerns, on the one hand, a management team too obsessed with the *status quo* to communicate effectively with each other or with anyone else (ego problems) and, on the other, with the dispersion of resources. Hoarding is the chief cause of this kind of blockage. Money and resources which are not circulated freely tend to congest the whole system. Organizational structures for the dissemination and distribution of capital and goods have to be set up so that circulation takes place easily and without restriction, not only within a company's own set-up (which is where it starts) but also in the world at large. If blockages take place, suffering and wastage builds up to such a degree that the whole organism begins to overheat and will eventually run down and die. Elsewhere this idea has been described in more detail.

This hexagram does not so much give a warning to clear the tubes and refresh the system, as describe a process which has already begun. Dispersion and dissolution of the blockage is taking place and the result will be that the system can run more efficiently and smoothly. It will begin to feel more healthy and functional. In real terms this means less wastage and so less cost in running. Energy and raw materials go further, the natural economy of the organism begins to find its own balance. In management and staff this tendency is reflected in a clearing of the air. Less lies are being told, a higher degree of honesty begins to open up frank and friendly lines of communication. In the case of a multinational company, its various offices begin to communicate as part of one large organism. Symbiosis begins to take place and assumes a natural rhythm. (Aspects of this process have been discussed elsewhere: see Hexagram 45: Gathering Together, in which a leader consolidates his resources and his team in the service of a higher idea, a venture or a project – this is, dynamically, the opposite of what is taking place here. See also Hexagram 40: Deliverance.)

The overall process represents a general increase in efficiency, a raising of attitudes and the expression of the power of forgiveness – a very potent source of energy in itself, for it releases spirit and intellect in a positive direction.

DECISION-BASE ASSUMPTIONS

The following values are given subject to the information given in the Changes. Remember, the Changes take precedence.

Management

It is good business to give as well as to create situations in which taking is desired. It is, as they say, more divine to give than to receive. This means letting things pass which, ordinarily, would be made into an issue. Forgiveness is also divine. The means to clear the air is yours, make excellent use of the facility. The general benefit will be felt by all. The whole company will be better able to do what it is supposed to be doing, though it seems patently obvious to point it out. First raise up your mind and then your heart will follow. The other way round works just as effectively. Others will follow suit and impediments will be cleared away.

Planning
The fulfilment of plans can be expedited with greater efficiency if the whole system is given an overhaul and a clear-out. It is not only a question of not being able to see the wood for the trees – which does not help when you are trying to plan the future (see the lines and the new hexagram if pertinent) but of being able to communicate effectively. Concentrate, for the time being, on present functions rather than future projections – they are the priority.

Risks
Inauspicious.

Growth and Productivity
By no means up to optimum. Room for considerable improvement with the minimum of extra cost and investment. You can make much better use of existing resources than you are doing at the moment.

Investment and Finance
Polish up your own operation before looking at the wider possibilities in the field of action. Is every part of it well nourished and running smoothly? What is preventing smooth running?

Marketing
You could have greater reach if you tidied up the home front. Do not push out further without first creating more open space at home.

Advertising
The images are too hard. People may get the wrong idea.

Feedback
You must clear the air. The present situation leaves a lot to be desired. There is room for much greater real understanding.

Communications
They will go far afield and have great effect if the ideas touch upon universals.

Creative Judgement
Improving.

Intuition
There will be a noticeable improvement after the clear-out.

Start-Up
You are not ready yet (see Hexagram 52: Keeping Still).

Backing
When you are ready, the master will appear.

Contracts and Agreements
You are not in a frame of mind to agree with very much; you may have a cantankerous attitude and be nit-picking and fault-finding. Better to leave the whole matter alone until a more auspicious time evolves.

Sources of Misfortune
An attitude of superiority which is not conterminous with your spiritual condition; such an attitude is an illusion created by the ego to protect you from confronting your own weakness. This is a block to progress. (See Hexagrams 6: Conflict and 26: The Taming Power of the Great.)

Sources of Good Fortune
Organize your spiritual orientations first of all. The rest flows from that and you will see the source of difficulties and how they can best be systematically overcome.

——————— **THE LINES (CHANGES)** ———————
the Future-Links

Six at the beginning
Make up quickly before it becomes a solidified issue.

Nine in the second place
A feeling of very heavy negative resentment, even hatred, towards others or a class of people. Check that feeling before your personality begins to coagulate around it – a very nasty state of affairs indeed. Aim to be clear again. It's a matter for an eyebath, figuratively speaking.

Six in the third place
Now your work has become so all-consuming that all other considerations come second. Normally this is not a good situation for it upsets the balance of energies between work and leisure but, in this place, it is applauded and well augmented. The work is important and very demanding, and you should give yourself to it wholeheartedly.

Six in the fourth place
Your work is of general value and benefit to others. This can be the occasion of a resignation from the company on matters of principle. It can even mean separation from family. But, as in the Six in the Third Place, the position is augmented and favourable here and the effects are auspicious. It takes a great resolve to make such a decision and it is very hard to carry it through, but there is corresponding value in the work and the wider benefit wins in the equation between personal and private interests. The dissolution of

social ties may be temporary but that is not a consideration here. What you see is the symbiosis of things (as described in Hexagram 20: Contemplation).

Nine in the fifth place
When your back is up against the wall, when things have come to a head, when a very tight spot traps the situation, what is the source of relief, of escape, of dissolution? An idea. The idea releases the tension and creates a new focus of energies. The idea is described as 'great' because of its effect in getting you out of the depths of the trap.

Nine in the last place
This is the line of the saviour. The person places himself in jeopardy deliberately in order to rescue others and save them from their plight. He enters into a situation which means a high degree of self-sacrifice. This may not mean, in every case, the sacrifice of life, but the sacrifice is nevertheless serious and real. He shows the way out by his light, by his example, by his good offices.

HEXAGRAM 60

Limitation (Boundaries to the Field of Action)

─────────────── JUDGEMENT ───────────────

Set the field of action; produce a cash flow but do not impose limitations upon yourself or the organization which will stifle potential and creativity; organize the terms of reference in appropriate structures. Good fortune if the benefit is not too limited.

─────────────── SPECIFIC MODALITY ───────────────

Expenditure must be planned carefully. The thrust of the idea is to organize and structure the field of action so that it can work effectively. Boundaries have to be drawn which are appropriate to the potential of the situation. Nothing can work without setting limits, but over-specialization is to be avoided.

─────────────── AMBIENCE ───────────────

The limits of a situation define the freedom which is possible. Without 'a boundary', freedom and action can have no quality, purpose or direction. The idea of *the limitless* (without definition) can have no meaningful residence in the human mind – regardless of its relative size.

─────────────── CONCEPT MODEL ───────────────

There are two key ideas: the first is expenditure – and the flow of capital and resources. The advice is simply to appraise the extent of funds and organize their direction and magnitude of flow so that you know exactly what can be achieved over a period of time. This specific idea involves cash-flow projection and the need to clarify the limits of available resources so that they are not wasted and can last through periods of decline (see Hexagrams 41: Decrease and 42: Increase, for a discussion of natural conditions which govern the magnitude of the flow of resources).

The second meaning of the hexagram is related to personal matters – self-organization. If you try to do too much you end up achieving little or nothing. If you set yourself too little to do, you tend to end up unfulfilled. The frame of action has to be defined in accordance with energy and aptitudes, but there must be enough to provide room to grow, function and be stimulated. If you dabble in this and that, nothing is finished or done well and so, once again, there is need for limitation – a need for definition of the field of action.

Since the hexagram is pertinent to the time, these considerations are germane to the present and require revision in these terms.

The setting of objectives has everything to do with limitation, for the process involves foresight and projection (see Hexagram 20: Contemplation, for a discussion of what is involved in the planning of resources and action). The primary purpose behind self-organization, the setting of personal limits (this does not mean self-denigration or the setting of heavy restrictions which people tend to associate with the idea of 'knowing your limitations' – see Hexagram 15: Modesty) is to be effective, efficient and to complete to a high standard of quality. The wider idea is, of course, self-fulfilment. This must involve creativity – which itself requires a boundary of action and rules. It is not possible to fill yourself unless you have a pretty shrewd idea of how big you are. You need a sense of your capabilities. You can develop this wisdom by setting limits upon goals, aspirations and projects, and then cautiously expanding them so that you take up your possibilities gently without overburdening yourself (see Hexagram 47: Oppression) and without destroying your enthusiasm. (See Hexagrams 16: Enthusiasm and 58: The Joyous.)

─────────── DECISION-BASE ASSUMPTIONS ───────────

The following values are given subject to the information given in the Changes. Remember, the Changes take precedence.

Management
Attention paid to the scope of staff and workforce, not only as a turnover machine but as a creative body, will pay dividends. The questions which must be asked about everyday running conditions are as follows: is our system too restrictive and, if so, is it having a counterproductive effect on productivity? What provision is there for creative expression? How much extra support does the company structure provide outside its working mandate and responsibilities

for developing the always latent potential of individuals? How much do our policies reflect a more all-embracing concern for the general welfare of our people – not only their financial welfare? What is the company's attitude towards leisure and how is it defined as distinct from work? Is the space between the two so great that they are both 'pressured' and potentially unfulfilling? How much real flexibility is there in communications? How rigid is the *status quo* and whose egos are being inflated through the corporate machinery? What specific system of feedback has been incorporated into the organizational framework? How human are we? Is there a clear and articulate relationship between the individual's personal sense of wellbeing and his productivity? Is there a specific set of working policies based upon that articulated relationship? Is the organizational structure too vague and flexible – to the extent that the work is not directed and focused efficiently?

Planning
Avoid sticking to rigidly constructed plans. There is a need to stretch out schedules or to tighten them. The balance is not quite right and, therefore, not realistic in practice. Look again at the volume and pace of work and set a trial period.

Growth and Productivity
There may be a tendency to be erratic. This can be corrected. The pendulum may be swinging too much between over-production and under-production.

Investment and Finance
Further details are required. Explore the matter before making a final commitment – is there enough scope for change? This is not an 'all your eggs in one basket' situation. Avoid that at all costs.

Risks
Only calculated risks and, even then, proceed extremely cautiously.

Creative Judgement
There is good discernment in general, but give time to sharpen up. If you are evaluating your own possibilities do not be so quick to jump to conclusions. You should not set schedules which are patently unachievable, but neither should you be so timid or self-limiting that you deny yourself a challenge. During such considerations avoid being weighed down heavily by pragmatics.

Start-Up
This is a matter of looking at available resources. Are there enough and do you have control over them? Cash flow?

Backing
The success or failure of the venture is not a matter for judgement here, but there is a requirement to see that you have given thought to needs plus unseen contingencies. How are your margin forecasts? They are either far too wide or far too narrow. Expand your range of considerations and organize a priority list. Spatial diagrams are best for this as they can provide a better idea of the relationship between forces of action *et al.*

Advertising
Either too ambitious or not ambitious enough.

Marketing
The question you should ask at present is this: what is the actual equation between supply and demand? Check the latest figures. It may be that an adjustment is in order.

Feedback
If it is a matter of planning, then discussion is crucial. Do your own thinking first.

Communications
You could be clearer.

Contracts and Agreements
If they are the dominant issues they need to be looked at again. Are the rights and obligations 'practical' as well as fair?

International Trade
Very careful planning required. Judgements have to be right here.

Sources of Misfortune
It is a matter of personal pitch as much as anything else. If you do not know your capabilities you could damage relations and possibilities. You might over-commit funds and gain no benefit, or you might under-commit funds and energy and lose out on a great opportunity. You have to know yourself well to make the most of times like these, otherwise there could be a marked decline.

Sources of Good Fortune
A strong marshalling of all the salient facts of all the issues at hand; strong creative judgement in their interpretation, and the ability to see the extent of things, their value and duration. The balance between rational understanding and creative intuition, not only in external matters but in respect of all aspects of your life, requires an equal measure of each. Your feeling has to be backed up by objective facts. If you are sure, you can act with confidence.

————————— THE LINES (CHANGES) —————————
the Future-Links

Nine at the beginning
There is no judgement on the value of your idea. Certainly, the effect of not being able to make progress can be severely irritating and you might want to push ahead even when this is impossible. The limits described here are both external (indicating forces beyond your control and upon which you can make no impression) and internal (lack of energy to make progress sufficiently meaningful). The right thing to do, therefore, is not to make any effort now, but to use the time to store up energy so that, when the opportunity comes to act, you can do so effectively and achieve a great deal with a major drive forward.

Another dimension of this line is this: keep your ideas and thoughts to yourself. Do not try to generate interest in your ideas. The people who are listening for new ideas are not honourable and should not be encouraged. Keep quiet and avoid exploitation. The other reason for keeping matters closely guarded is that new ideas or projects need time to form and become developed before they can be applied. This is such a 'gestation' time. Talking to others spoils that process and may set in motion forces over which you have no control and which may be of a destructive and unnecessarily inhibiting nature.

Nine in the second place
The import of the line is not that you should 'act now', but that you must be prepared to act after a period of watching and waiting for the right moment. The accent is on an attitude of readiness so that you are able to take advantage of a natural release of energies in the outside world. When the forces which determine good fortune or misfortune behave like dammed-up water, you have to be ready when the valve opens as the intensity of the situation is short-lived and bears great possibility of progress. In order to capture the momentum of such moments you must be in place. Timing is of the essence. But the accent in this specific case is on not being too late, rather than jumping the gun. The suggestion is that the time to act will come soon, so watch for your chance.

Six in the third place
You could have avoided mistakes if only you had recognized your limitations within the specific situation. It is all very well to counsel that one may learn from such misjudgements (lack of self-knowledge) but the important point is not to allow yourself to get into situations in which you over-spend for no good reason, i.e., pleasure and not business.

Six in the fourth place
Struggling against impossible odds entails a waste of resources. This is taking on too much in a situation which is hopeless (rather than challenging). Here, however, the forces of nature are working with you and the limitation is a directing and focusing force with which you can ride as, for

example, the force of gravity. Thus the achievement is made relatively easy and the outcome creates benefit.

There is also the suggestion that the laws of motion and the systems of energy which are used may be incomplete in conception and that there are untapped resources in the dynamic of nature which will enable objects to be lifted off with far less energy wastage than current methods. The implications of an energy system which harnesses the natural dynamics of motion more efficiently are far reaching and the possibility of such a device is suggested by the *I Ching*.

Nine in the fifth place

An individual, by his ingenuity and effort, sets an example to others by achieving something proportionately greater than the means would ordinarily allow. Where there are severe limitations such a person does not expect of others what he is unable to accomplish himself. The wider meaning is that, when there is little to go round, a leader shares with his followers. See Hexagram 41: Decrease, for an elaboration of this point. Here, a leader is prepared to impose upon himself the same limitations as that imposed upon others. This invites respect and loyalty because the matter is clearly visible to all.

Six in the last place

Beware of over-specialization. That is the first point. The second is as follows: too much self-discipline is as bad as too little. In Mencius, the rule of the Golden Mean is postulated as the best possible state for it describes the striving for balance. This state is specifically emphasized in this Change. Avoid imposing oppressive limitations upon people. They feel an unnecessary pressure and, after a while, react to it. In political affairs this can mean riots, revolution, strikes and other rebellious behaviour. Such events are symptoms of over-restriction and oppression, and point to wrong-headed policies of government which do violence to human dignity and self-esteem. They portray the lack of real contact (over-institutionalization and alienation) between people and their government.

The same principles apply to self-regulation, self-motivation and self-government. One must not oppress oneself with the acceptance of bad working conditions and stifling work loads. The effect will be counterproductive; spiritual distress and emotional imbalance will result. One must not drive oneself forward by negative emotional charges, such as fear or greed, as these motivations destroy one's capabilities in general and severely diminish creative abilities and happiness. Do not take pragmatism and competition to extremes. Negative emotion leads to spiritual instability.

HEXAGRAM 61

Inner Truth
(The Power of Truth)

―――――――――― JUDGEMENT ――――――――――

Business relationships are sound. The right people are in the right places and so the work goes well. Even people who are ordinarily unreceptive to new ideas and to change are influenced in a positive way. Good fortune.

―――――――――― SPECIFIC MODALITY ――――――――――

Communication with intractable and difficult people becomes successful through superior, yet compassionate, understanding. Unusual success is attainable; this is based upon truthful ideas as opposed to the cooperation one might expect among criminals.

―――――――――― AMBIENCE ――――――――――

An atmosphere of cooperation makes even the most ambitious project successful.

―――――――――― CONCEPT MODEL ――――――――――

Among the more important elements of business and interaction is cooperation, not only with people in one's own organization but also with colleagues here and abroad. Problems can become intractable if ideas cannot be effectively communicated. Here, even difficult ideas can be communicated to even the most narrowminded or prejudiced of individuals, through a penetrating understanding of the limitations of that individual's awareness. In Hexagram 57: Penetration, understanding is achieved by virtue of the individual's own power of mind, his ability to concentrate and to penetrate. Here, that process is, as it were, reversed. Communication and understanding are achieved by receptivity to another's awareness. Let the other talk, you listen.

--------------- DECISION-BASE ASSUMPTIONS ---------------

The following values are given subject to the information given in the Changes. Remember, the Changes take precedence.

Management
Even the best of friends and the staunchest of colleagues may become an embittered enemy if the relationship is not based upon upright principles and real honour. Such a relationship between honourable men cannot easily be shaken by outside events. True influence arising from such a force can win cooperation where otherwise it would be denied. In the case of an organization, this applies to colleagues and staff. Difficult undertakings are made possible because there is a deeper understanding.

Planning
It is difficult to make plans at present. You have to take each situation as you find it. Although circumstances might be outwardly difficult (see Hexagram 29: The Deep Waters) you have the necessary qualities to meet the challenges well and with every chance of a resounding success. Proceed with confidence and believe in the direction chosen.

Risks
Yes, circumstances will appear risky because the future is hard to discern. This is not because it is difficult to discern of itself, but because your current perspective makes it appear so. But that is no reason to feel that you cannot move forward without undue caution. In a sense, this is a risk situation, but one which ought to turn out well.

Feedback
You are in the controlling position. It is up to you to evoke responses, get people talking and make sense of reactions. Your power to influence and guide even the most prejudiced individual is strong and you can change the tone and tenor of negotiations by the power of your own 'charisma'.

Communications
Auspicious. Make known important points to those who would benefit from such information. The effect could be miraculous.

Start-Up
Auspicious, but do more listening than proposing once meetings have been arranged.

Backing
Auspicious. You could win more far-reaching support than you anticipated.

Advertising
Normally this would not be the means of influence. It lacks a certain personal touch. If a personal element can be introduced, so that communication is more direct, the response will be excellent.

Marketing
Too much effort is unnecessary. If ideas, products and services are made available, people will seek them out spontaneously. The situation is very auspicious. The dawning of a new force in the world would come under this sign.

Investment and Finance
Even the most unlikely ideas win support and do well. Be prepared to look beyond the orthodox and the traditional. If the ideas are 'truthful' let them stand on their own without softening them. The strength of the truth needs no temperance. Let it do its work 'as if it had a will all of its own'. There will be unquestioned success in this.

Creative Judgement
Superb and first class.

Growth and Productivity
The matter is wider than a mere expansion of empire or profit. It is the development of ideas which themselves fertilize the ground for general growth. Auspicious, but be open minded.

Contracts and Agreements
You will find that people are willing to see things your way without too much prompting. Trust the situation.

Sources of Misfortune
Do not be quick to judge or cut off heads. Mercy is the power of the wise. When it is clear that you understand, this will transmit and be lesson enough. What is the effect of your action on the minds of others?

Sources of Good Fortune
Be wise, be receptive, trust in your own honesty – these count for everything and shine brightly and visibly in this place.

THE LINES (CHANGES)
the Future-Links

Nine at the beginning
It will not help you to have secret alliances which you can activate 'should your personal need arise'. Subterfuge and conspiracy undermine strength and effective action. Be self-reliant. If honesty cannot achieve the ends you contemplate they are probably not worth achieving. Be watchful of allurements and temptations in this regard – they always create nervousness.

Nine in the second place
Here the power of truth makes itself felt. Beyond all marketing strategy and advertising techniques, the truth spreads on its own. People are moved by the real thing and it needs no promotion. If the ideas are well founded in truth they go round the world. The cause and effect seems mysterious, but people who seek favourable public reaction should sell the right ideas. Everything moves as a quality of resonance. If it is good, it will need no badge; it will be known. There is no need to plan for it. It seems to happen by itself.

Six in the third place
You do not know your own mind. You are too impressionable, too wayward, too easily distracted. You are not centred, you are out of tune with yourself. What this means in practice is that your moods swing easily from joy to sorrow. It is better to find your own centre and obey only that. This will help you find your way through life – naturally.

Six in the fourth place
Self-honesty and guidance can be fortified by associating with people stronger and more solidly centred than yourself. This does not mean blind loyalty to a guru, religion or system of belief of any kind, but rather means building up your soul energy. In this way you can keep a direction in life. This is particularly important for people who seek their answers in another person or another group. In itself there is nothing wrong in this; it can mean the difference between living in the light or in the darkness. The purpose, however, is not to 'follow the leader' but rather to strengthen your own understanding of yourself so that you can live your own life freely and with strength. In this way you can keep both independence of spirit and the fires of creativity alive in your heart. But the appropriate willingness to learn must be accompanied by the seeking of a guide. Don't go over the top, however.

Nine in the fifth place
You are the centre. People follow your example because you are strong in spirit and have immense personal charisma. The whole process works without conscious design or intention. This power is an expression of your natural self when you are completely yourself. The benefit to others is great and good and your influence goes beyond your reckoning and into unusual places.

Nine in the last place

Know when to be silent. You can exhaust your own energy in showing others the way to the best solution. Enough is enough; you must seize your own chance when it comes. Commune with others only as much as you commune with yourself. Run your own business also and do not lose opportunities by telling others how to grasp theirs. This is only a warning.

HEXAGRAM 62

The Preponderance of the Small

JUDGEMENT

Your power and influence are not strong enough to bring off a resounding success. Do not even try. But success in less ambitious projects is in order at present. Focus on those matters of which you are sure.

SPECIFIC MODALITY

Accept your limitations as they are at present. If you can work within them, even though this engenders some discomfort, you can make early success the basis for future ideas and projects. (Unlike the picture given in Hexagram 60: Limitation, this is the true meaning of 'knowing your limitations'.) Keep your feet on *terra firma*.

AMBIENCE

Discomfort. Do not bite off more than you can chew – you will have to spit it out.

CONCEPT MODEL

The essence of this hexagram is illustrated by the legend of Icarus who flew so close to the sun that his waxen wings melted and he fell to earth. It is a warning against vaulting ambition and lofty aspirations which are beyond the individual's (or the company's strength). The power to win a resounding victory is insufficient. But not only that; the attempt should not even be made because the failed effort means personal harm, either physical or to one's fortunes – or both. The meaning is plain: it is a question of knowing your capabilities. The best thing to do is to work on what is at hand and not let the mind wander into the realms of potential achievement.

─────────── DECISION-BASE ASSUMPTIONS ───────────

The following values are given subject to the information given in the Changes. Remember, the Changes take precedence.

Management
If it is outside your everyday routine classify it as 'a rash mood likely to cause complications and irreparable damage'. At another time your considerations might be very successful. At the moment they are out of order. Keep everything simple, straightforward, rational and strictly accountable. Boring, but imperative.

Planning
No rash moves. Do nothing out of the ordinary. Make no changes. You are either wearing your rose-tinted spectacles or your gloomy ones. Neither affords real 20/20 vision.

Creative Judgement
Certainly do not act upon it. In the field of everyday business your creative judgement is out of focus and misaligned. In the realm of imagination it is best kept quiet. Better still, shelve the whole lot and get on with something safe and relevant to the here and now. Define 'here and now' as narrowly and as boringly as possible.

Feedback
The mirror is telling you lies, but others might not be.

Communications
Keep them to a minimum.

Contracts and Agreements
No, not now.

Growth and Productivity
Look at the track record. Be guided by that and see the Concept Model.

Advertising and Marketing
Keep expenditures to a minimum or cut them completely for the time being.

Investment and Finance
Inauspicious.

Start-Up
Inauspicious.

Backing
Inauspicious.

Risks
Definitely not.

Sources of Misfortune
If you do anything which is out of the ordinary or unscheduled, or if you commit funds, make agreements or plans which have arisen suddenly or in the recent past there will be failure and misfortune. It may take more than two years to rectify mistakes made now.

Sources of Good Fortune
Stay on the ground and confine yourself to the limits of current work. Do not think about the future at the moment.

─────────── **THE LINES (CHANGES)** ───────────
the Future-Links

Six at the beginning
Your wings are not strong enough to undertake that kind of flight. Do not attempt it. Stay with convention for the time being.

Six in the second place
You are placed under the restraint of the parent company or the senior person in management. You cannot rise through the ranks, make decisions and change events. But you are able to bring influence to bear in another quarter, even though this is not felt to be as auspicious as the first option. Your attitude should be one of philosophical acceptance because there is little you can do. You should help and do your best wherever you are placed.

Nine in the third place
Your predicament is definitely misleading. You think you can hold your ground in this field of action. Your mistake is in the attitude you project. Even the challenge is a red herring because it is the catalyst for a potential conflict of personalities neither of which can really contain the objective situation (can you?). The only thing to do is to forget about standing upon ceremony and take a close look at the specifics. That is an effective aid to improving the overall situation and a suitable anaesthetic for the wily old ego.

Nine in the fourth place
You must try very hard but actually do nothing. This is an ambiguous state of affairs because the meaning is spiritual. Action of any kind will bring misfortune; this is the meaning of 'do nothing'. Being receptive and yet discriminating is the meaning of 'try very hard'. Such a combination of attitudes represents a stance, a perspective that you can adopt, without coming to harm, in relation to a dangerous situation.

Six in the fifth place
You are called to a great and important challenge which involves bringing

confusion to order, but there is little or no hope of succeeding without the right kind of help. But who is available and what kind of help can they give? You need people who have shining track records, people who have proven themselves time and time again to be especially competent, but who may otherwise be completely unknown (do not see fame as a criterion for the selection of assistance – use quality of real achievement). Your helpers, however, may not feel disposed to go to all that trouble. Convince them of the worth of the cause by your sincere, well-meaning appreciation of the problem – this in itself requires some depth of understanding (see Hexagram 15: Modesty).

Six in the last place
You need the wisdom to know when to stop. Enough must be enough, or everything will be undone or rendered less effective. This is a general statement for people who are developing projects which otherwise would bring a general benefit to others. It also entreats the individual to keep in mind his human limitations.

HEXAGRAM 63

Completion

────────── JUDGEMENT ──────────

The work is completed. You have understood the connections. A state of balance has been realized. (See also Hexagram 32: Duration.) Everything is in order. Reason prevails. Good fortune, though equipoise is naturally a transient idea.

────────── SPECIFIC MODALITY ──────────

In order to preserve the position of perfect balance *through movement* see the dynamics described in Hexagram 12: Standstill. The position here represents an evolved state of understanding – a level of realization, order, vision; the main integers of change have been established. Difficulties have been overcome.

────────── AMBIENCE ──────────

The tone and quality of events has now changed. A new time has dawned and with it a new *modus operandi*; a new set of possibilities. The main guidelines are in place. The code for a new cycle of evolution is now set.

────────── CONCEPT MODEL ──────────

The cycle of change, whether it is expressed in daily life or in personal enlightenment has a beginning and an end, a sequence; a system of reason, a moment of completion. The wheel of life seems interminable but there are moments when the end of an old cycle has come and, with it, the beginning of a new one.

Thus the notion of 'completion' is as much part of the transience of nature as any other specific dynamic. Its moment, though a landmark in itself, passes. It is for this reason that the personal awareness of good fortune arising from the completion of a cycle gives rise also to the idea of preparedness (see Hexagram 64: Before Completion) and the onset of flux and disorder. The times of

Completion are finite and impermanent. One cannot rest in these times, one must recognize the new demands.

In principle, the main elements of a new time are in order and in exactly the right place. The past now makes sense and the future is unknown once again. Everything undertaken now will have the quality of maintaining a new balance in new circumstances. The position is therefore ambiguous for, while there is a certain relief in having succeeded in bringing things to ripeness, even the ripeness turns to decay unless one keeps moving. Maintain an 'everyday' view. Everything can be achieved by continuing to allow events to carry you forward.

This is not the time to review extensively or to rest on your laurels. Events will not take care of themselves without further effort from you. Still further work is necessary, closer, more detailed work. All the fine tuning has yet to be undertaken. To make the work truly complete in every respect is a matter of adding what has been left out. These are the edges, the corners, the paintwork, the punctuation, the refinement of substance.

Thus Completion means also 'the need for further completing work' as well as 'completed as to principle and shape'.

DECISION-BASE ASSUMPTIONS

The following values are given subject to the information given in the Changes. Remember, the Changes take precedence.

Management

Great elation may be felt. A job is completed, an accomplishment realized; a deadline has been met, an order fulfilled, a deal agreed; a state of balance has been reached. See Hexagram 24: Return; in Completion, the response to a natural cycle is exactly the same, but in a higher manifestation. There are also added stipulations here – namely, attention to detail and finishing the work; but the same imperative not to run before the wind applies with even greater force.

Do not pre-empt, anticipate or precipitate change. The pace of change is fixed, cannot be speeded up and one must go with it. The cycle is becoming complete and so the most apposite attitude is that of elation with preparedness.

Planning

Prepare for new challenges, but not with over-eagerness or worry. Prudent caution in the light of achievement is appropriate.

Growth and Productivity

You have reached a high point and a new time has been born through the work of the past. But the demands of the new time arise out of the precedents of the past. The excellence of the next cycle depends upon the refinement achieved now. Do not leave important elements unattended if a higher level is to be attained in the next cycle.

Feedback

Accurate. What else is it telling you?

Communications

Do not expect too much, but otherwise auspicious. Understanding between people can lead to new possibilities which, when worked on, may blossom into tangible achievements. The position is one in which 'excellence for the sake of excellence' should be the maxim rather than 'excellence for more profit'. The two ideas are not necessarily incompatible as to effects, but they are worlds apart in 'excellence of motivation'. The former indicates a more 'complete' spiritual state.

Marketing

Success, but how long can it last? What has to be done to make sure of the past?

Advertising

So far so good, but the demands of the future have to be considered afresh, as if starting again. Do not count on good fortune coming automatically. Keep the position under control by staying in touch with it.

Investment and Finance

Investments have paid off so far. What you do now depends upon continued application of skill and care. Do not regard the situation as guaranteed even though the present is reasonably favourable.

Start-Up

Do not make a special issue out of it. It is far better to regard the situation as a continuation even though it is a new start. This is an artifice of attitude which has to be maintained in order to keep you on your toes.

Backing

You deserve it and there is no reason not to feel confident about future achievement.

Contracts and Agreements

Certainly, binding agreements and commitments can be sought with confidence but be careful of taking on too much or of expecting too much of others too soon. Let the time evolve.

Creative Judgement

Good intuition; excellent creative judgement. These qualities are augmented and heightened by the time. Indeed, you may even ask: How is it that I seem to understand even difficult ideas with relative ease? This is part of the meaning of completion. One tends to see things whole.

Risks

Ill advised if they are truly blind. What may be described as 'calculated risks' may be contemplated for the future, but this is certainly not the time to execute them. This is a time of caution and close attention; do not generalize. The name of the game is *specifics*.

Sources of Misfortune

Do not be so blasé and self-assured that you hit the wall with the back of your head. Neither should you try too hard to squeeze every last drop of benefit out of the situation; the effect could be catastrophic.

Sources of Good Fortune

Bring the matter to fruition with care and attention. Maintain some caution and preserve the pace of work but without resorting to artificial means. Let the new time arrive without impediment but do not increase the heat. Use your intuition to appreciate the meaning of the time of completion so that you can recognize it later in a still higher manifestation. There is a special value in this as all the other dynamics of change can make a great deal of sense in the light of the experience of this time.

——————— THE LINES (CHANGES) ———————
the Future-Links

Nine at the beginning
A major change has occurred. Significant events mark this in the general environment (national and global, as well as one's immediate environment). You know what is happening and you have a shrewd idea that new events are in the offing. But do not jump to conclusions or become overcome with the intensity of the situation. Do not fix plans as a result of current ideas; rather, come to cool and rational conclusions – conclusions which will enable you to make more sense of the present in the advantageous perspective of hindsight. Learning how to pitch your perceptions at this time is a significant achievement and highly preservational against precipitate and unwise action. Remains self-contained even when there is upset around you.

Six in the second place

The ignorance of others is not a judgement on your own worthiness. The position is that you have a great deal to offer but those who could use your competence and great heartedness have become corrupt and hold onto their power covetously and jealously. The effect of all this in someone who has 'come of age' may be to propel him into taking the initiative. There are times when this is indeed the correct thing to do, but this is not such a time. Wait. The time for you to show what you can do will come and cannot be hastened by force of will, frustration or a sense of urgency. These feelings are not 'ripe' and must not be acted upon. Do not feverishly apply for jobs, promotion and the like. What part you play in the future is best viewed right now as a matter of fate.

Nine in the third place

You have worked hard and won a place which offers security of future attainment. A certain expansion has taken place and there are increased possibilities. Everything is in order and you can survey the past with some satisfaction and the future with some confidence. The value of the achievement is clear. Do not be intoxicated by the ambience of present achievement and relative comfort (mental and spiritual as well as physical) and, as a result, award rank, position, authority and jobs to everybody who comes knocking at your door. You must look for able people who are competent so that future roses can come to bloom. In such matters you have to be crystal clear.

Six in the fourth place

Sudden uprisings which die down again into a semblance of order generate a false sense of security. The questions raised by such times are serious even though people prefer not to think about them and, instead, foolishly hope for the best. Such events are symptoms of deeper corruption and are portents of other things to come which will not be so easily passed over. But, bear in mind that there is nothing you can do about this at present, though you have done well to take careful note of the signs offered by the times.

Nine in the fifth place

The expense and luxury of the celebration is no index of the depth of the divine worship. Indeed, it is probably fake. Real feeling has no need of all this pomp and ceremony. All the sumptuous glitter merely conceals the spiritual barrenness at the heart.

Six in the last place

Keep your eyes on the road ahead. Imperative. Do not bother to look behind and luxuriate in the all too pleasant sensation of . . . 'phew! that was close!' You are not far enough out of the woods yet. Keep going.

HEXAGRAM 64

Before Completion

JUDGEMENT

Things are about to change; the transition is coming and misunder-
standings, confusion and distorted perspectives are about to be
overcome. Order is arising out of chaos. Success.

SPECIFIC MODALITY

This is an important time and a serious attitude is appropriate. Tread
carefully, be sensitive, intuitive, perceptive, test the ground ahead
before committing your weight to it. Be careful. Think strategically.

AMBIENCE

Tension in a dangerous manoeuvre. Banish any tendency to panic.
Be strategic and composed and above all do not worry or fret. Do not
be self-important.

CONCEPT MODEL

In a very real sense your position represents a challenge. There is a
tendency towards completion. Everything is changing and the effect
of the transition is the arrival of a balanced and ordered perspective.
Certain manoeuvres are necessary. You must adjust your position
and be prepared to distinguish the quality of the terrain, ascertain
what is reliable and dependable and what is chimera, quicksand, thin
ice. You are in the act of stalking the safety of the dry bank. It would
not be an overstatement to say that the position is quite precarious
yet, for all that, you have set your bearings, you have more than an
idea of what you are doing and why. This alone gives you better odds.
Had you been in the position of a fool aimlessly wandering into a
perilous situation with no awareness of the danger, as described in
Hexagram 4: Youthful Folly, you would be in a hopeless
predicament.

———————— DECISION-BASE ASSUMPTIONS ————————

The following values are given subject to the information given in the Changes. Remember, the Changes take precedence.

Management
The test of competence has begun but promises to conclude well. Consider the matter a challenge, but one which you have to overcome alone. Do not count on support from others. Even the presence of friends or helpers cannot do much to help though they may offer moral support. This is a matter of personal powers of judgement and discrimination.

Planning
You know what you are about. You have the objective in mind. You cannot rush to it and, in point of fact, there is no real plan or definite route. There is a procedure which is described in the Concept Model. Follow the procedure which speaks more about a preparatory and watchful attitude rather than describing specific markers. You have to discern the markers, as it were, but they lead to the shore.

Feedback
Largely intuitive.

Communications
It is better to keep to lighter areas of thought if others are present. This is more a tactic than a spontaneous gesture.

Start-Up
Inauspicious. Certainly do not even think about it yet. Concentrate only upon the matter in hand. New projects are for the future and they cannot be decided at present.

Backing
A matter for the future.

Growth and Productivity
The past record will have given you enough strength and experience to cope with the present challenge. Call up what you know from any field of action in which you have learned matters of value. The position is auspicious.

Risks
The situation is risky, certainly, but not beyond the power of reason to control.

Creative Judgement
Use it to the full to shine light on the landscape.

Intuition
Maximum alertness of all faculties. Be crafty, be brave, but be calculating and observant.

Sources of Misfortune
This is not the time to be self-critical or critical of others. It is time to make the most of your understanding in order to achieve the objective. The weakness is your lack of confidence. If you can overcome this, you can overcome misfortune as, in all other things, you can cope with the challenge.

Sources of Good Fortune
Proceed with your eyes open and maximize the light so that you can make the right distinctions and right judgements. The matter is one of observing appropriate values which fit the situation and the time. This ability to tune and resonate with the time is the secret of knowing what changes mean and how to adapt and flow with them, so that you can act without regret or blame and without bringing harm to your fortunes. Every completed undertaking gives rise to another perceptual challenge and is part of the progression in the kaleidoscope of change in the field of action, upward through the spirals of awareness. There is no need to force matters with aggression; it is a matter of tuning with people and events – and this is what the *I Ching* provides: a means to do just that.

─────── **THE LINES (CHANGES)** ───────
the Future-Links

Six at the beginning
The matter is a challenge for you. If you try to rush it you will certainly fail and this will be personally embarrassing. You cannot force events to submit to your will and you cannot make nature bend to your liking in order to satisfy your hankering for completion or achievement. This is a lesson you will learn well. In a sense all failure is a problem of tuning – discordant behaviour can spoil the journey as a whole.

Nine in the second place
A stay of action is called for. You have the ability to make a success of the situation but you need to come at it from another angle. It may well be that the means will be shown to you or hinted at by events. Do something to carry the feeling more easily. You cannot achieve this by a direct onslaught of energy. A means of raising the spirit through some other activity is suggested. Thus, you keep the goal in mind and can make the breakthrough

via another route which you patiently set up. Use a catalyst for change – music, sport, a game, some activity which focuses your feelings another way.

Six in the third place

To make the change you need to introduce others who are stronger than you, whose confidence you have and in whom you feel a certain emotional comfort. Such people can be relied upon to make up for your deficiency of strength. Call upon such help. There is a suggestion that this may at times refer to the calling-up of images or ideas of such people who have an invigorating and helpful influence – in the absence of their tangible presence. With their help you succeed, and so you may proceed now with confidence.

Nine in the fourth place

You achieve your goal by an attitude of determination. Forget the past. Forget guilt. You are in control and you take complete command of the situation. This is very fortunate and highly auspicious for the future.

Six in the fifth place

Absolutely radiant success. You have arrived and your success is so strong that people can see it, feel it and you win cooperation, congratulation and accord with others. The influence you bring to bear now is so salubrious and excellent that the benefit extends a long way. The future is bright and full of promise and completion has been attained. The feeling of the time is heightened because of the difficulties you had to overcome to reach the clear light of day. The position is one of good fortune.

Nine in the last place

The new era waits in the wings. It will make its appearance very soon. You wait for it to make its appearance, that is all you have to do. The situation is very pleasant and certain. This is not the time, however, to lose your good sense, even in joy.

Note: The achievement of a good order in the affairs of mankind is the business of the *I Ching*; the specific requirements of each situation, each dynamic, are pictured throughout – a natural symmetry of order within which economic and political, social and cultural organization can be made to prosper in the service not only of mankind's highest moral and spiritual aspirations, but of all life.